MEN AND GODS
IN MONGOLIA

WHAT AMERICAN CRITICS SAY
ABOUT HASLUND'S: TENTS IN MONGOLIA

This book has been reviewed from coast to coast and without exception every review has not only been favorable but the reviewer has been enthusiastic in his recommendation of the book. A high tribute to an exceptionally good book.

"The best book of travel and adventure in Mongolia since Gilmour of the Mongols died. Haslund writes as if the saga-makers of old had risen from their graves to endow him."
—*Owen Lattimore, Saturday Review of Literature*

"Mysterious. Exotic. It combines the dramatic glamour of straight adventure with the earthy, solid virtue of a story."—*William Soskin, N. Y. American*

"A book of thrilling adventures which offers so much and in such a wide variety that it is difficult to know just which of its appealing points needs to be stressed in order to establish its claim as a book of exceptional interest."—*Herschel Brickell*

"There is a thrill on almost every page of this narrative. A book into which dullness never enters. The narrative glows and coruscates to the end. It has the same dramatic quality as Sven Hedin."—*N. Y. Times*

"The best book of travel in Asia since Abbé Huc's in 1846. His accounts of Mongol and Soyote sorcery and his story of his imprisonment are models of story telling."
—*Rodney Gilbert, N. Y. Herald Tribune Books*

"Sven Hedin must watch his laurels. A beautifully written and richly felt autobiographical narrative which rings with truth in every sentence."—*Chicago Daily News*

"What a pleasant surprise. You feel that this handsome book is different the moment you glance down the first page. Exceptionally well written. A romantic tale of fact with a captivating element of suspense running throughout. Enchanting."—*World Telegram*

His Holiness Seng Chen Gegen, fifth reincarnation of the Tiger god
and ruler of all the Torguts. Commander of the Royal Vasa Order,
second class. 1884-1932

[*front*

MEN AND GODS
IN MONGOLIA
(ZAYAGAN)

By

HENNING HASLUND

AUTHOR OF "TENTS IN MONGOLIA"

Translated from the Swedish by
ELIZABETH SPRIGGE
and
CLAUDE NAPIER

WITH 57 ILLUSTRATIONS
AND A MAP

NEW YORK
E. P. DUTTON & CO., INC.

FIRST EDITION

PRINTED IN THE UNITED STATES OF AMERICA
BY THE POLYGRAPHIC COMPANY OF AMERICA, N.Y

FOR more than three years (1927–30) I was on active service with Sven Hedin's Central Asiatic Expedition.

In his already published books our Chief has described the main features of the great journey, but he has further exhorted the various members of the expedition themselves to describe their personal experiences.

This book is my attempt to do so.

To be engaged in such an expedition implies, first and foremost, work, but work that possesses all the attractions of adventure.

We who took part in the great adventure cannot but be glad of the opportunity thus afforded us of seeing, experiencing and accomplishing something beyond the life of every day. And in this our gladness we must above all proffer our thanks to the man who brought us there, our renowned leader and ever youthful comrade, Doctor Sven Hedin.

HENNING HASLUND-CHRISTENSEN.

CONTENTS

CONTENTS
BOOK II

LIST OF ILLUSTRATIONS

xi

LIST OF ILLUSTRATIONS

IT was in the little town of Chugochak on the borders of Sinkiang that I met Henning Haslund and enjoyed the pleasure, seldom vouchsafed to us Mongols, of talking freely and unconstrainedly about our country.

There was nothing for me to tell him or explain to him, for he was one of us.

Is it on account of the life we live, so unlike any other in the world, or because of the remote position of our country that mankind are disposed to regard us as strange beings, enigmatic survivals of a vanished world?

Or else they look upon us as complete children and say with a smile : " They are so primitive." Although there is a certain measure of truth in this conception, it is far from being all that can be said of the Mongols. Nevertheless, it is generally accepted.

The only way to learn to know and understand a people is to become one of them, to feel oneself one of them, to share their joys and sorrows. Haslund has done this ever since he first came in contact with the Mongols in 1923. He has lived among the Khalka Mongols on the boundless steppes of Outer Mongolia, the land of endless nomad wanderings, adventures and dreams. He has travelled with camel caravans through sun-scorched and wind-tormented deserts. He has lived among the Torguts, my own people, in Khara Shar, in Tsoltus.

And everywhere the Mongols have greeted him with " the inestimable gift of the happy smile," for with the fine intuition of the child of nature they felt the strong sympathy he had for them.

For him they have laid aside their reserve and became his friends, his trustful, loyal friends. They have confided in him their dreams and aspirations. They have related their legends and marvellous narratives from the history of their forefathers. They have sung the songs that are dear to their hearts. To him they have revealed the Faith they uphold, for they have known that he would understand. Even if their conceptions might at times appear childish, he would not laugh at them, because they were human.

What most strongly impressed him and delighted him most seems to have been the discovery of how close the Mongols stood to him. For a man who has lived in China, Japan and India and has felt as Westerners feel in the East it must have been a pleasant experience to find a part of Central Asia so much in harmony with his European temper.

I wish to emphasize that the European's way of thinking and attitude to life lies closer to ours than that of the other races. We have the same conception of beauty and of honour, the same sense of humour and, I would say, similar ideals. And I am grateful to Haslund that he has understood all this.

He has not only learnt to love the mountains and the steppes, the vast expanses, the clouds and the brilliant stars of Central Asia, but—which is far more important —he has understood what guiding stars they are that the artless, freedom-loving sons of the wilderness follow, eager to learn, ready to listen to tidings from the outer world.

Nirgidma of Torhut.

Princess of Torgut.

EREN KHABIRGA.

xiv

Was der grosse GOtt kan machen/
Seynd nur lauter WunderSachen.
Die er in der weiten Welt
Uns für Augen hat gestelt.
Wil man durch die wilde Seen/
Und durch frembde Länder gehen/
Trifft man solche Wunder an/
Die man kaum erzehlen kan.
Solche grosse Gottes Wercke
Zeigen seine Macht/ und Stärcke/
Güte/ weißlich Regiment/
Das der zehnte kaum erkent.
Denen das Glück nicht wil gönnen/
Daß sie diß selbst sehen können/
Nehmen dieses Buch zur Hand/
Es wird ihnen auch bekand.
Man kan in der Stuben stehen/
Und gleich als durchs Fenster sehen
Wie es in den Ländern steht/
Und es in dem Meer zugeht.
Gott wil dieses darumb weisen/
Daß man sol den Schöpffer preisen/
Der die grosse Wunder Welt
Hat erschaffen/ und erhält.

From *Orientalische Reisebeschreibung*, von Jürgen
Andersen—Schleswig, 1669.

MEN AND GODS IN MONGOLIA

BOOK I

CHAPTER I

RUMOURS OF A KHAN IN THE WEST

THE Mongols' twelfth month is bitterly cold. The snowstorms sweep across the Grass Country, and man and beast grow dispirited and full of longing for the spring.

But spring was far away, and I accordingly left for the nearest outpost of civilization, Ta-t'ung Fu, the ancient city of the Shansi Chinese.

From the top of the pass the smoke of those thousands of Chinese chimneys curling heavenwards was a promise of warmth, food, and much else that I was pining for, and before sunset I was jostling among the swarms of people riding and walking towards the massive walls of Ta-t'ung Fu. We slipped through the northern gate of the city just as it was bolted for the night to keep out the perils of the darkness.

Scarcely five hundred yards down the street lies Chiang Lan Chiao's tobacco shop. Here I received a most warm welcome. Old Chiang himself scuttled about, clapping his hands and shouting an endless stream of orders, and soon both the house and the yard teemed with the shop boys who darted hither and thither in their light velvet slippers to carry out their master's innumerable commands.

Chiang's junior shop-assistant took charge of my two lean and exhausted horses, which were only too willing to let themselves be led into a warm stall where asses and mules were their neighbours. Twenty-one months earlier exactly the same horses had at Chiang's earnest

I

request been left out in the yard tied to a solitary tree, and I myself had had to feed and groom them, because Chiang and his twelve assistants had considered the horses altogether too uncivilized and wild to associate either with Chinese errand boys or with refined asses and mules.

We went now into the warmth of the banqueting-room, and Chiang and the eight eldest boys smilingly speculated whether the four youngest servant boys would succeed in producing fresh bowls of the smoking Chinese food in unbroken succession, each before I finished the last. For a long time I held my own with them, but at last I had to give in, and the cook behind the scenes was called in, sweating but smiling, to receive his silver dollar.

And then came tea and those pipes which, when one is full fed, induce such pleasant companionship and intimate conversation.

CHIANG LAN CHIAO was one of those delightful old Chinamen whom one meets on one's travels in out-of-the-way corners of the Middle Kingdom. He was capable, honest and obliging, hospitable to guests, deferential to the Mandarins, and a strict but just dictator in his own kingdom.

Chiang's kingdom was the celebrated shop on the west side of Ta-t'ung Fu's northerly street, scarcely five hundred yards from the northern gate of the city, and he kept this shop of his well stocked with Chinese tea and tobacco, with English cigarettes and American petroleum. The business had been in the family for generations, and it was only seventeen years since Chiang had in the course of nature become the head of the family and of the old tea and tobacco firm. Before this, from his earliest youth until seventeen years before, when he attained dignity and splendour in Ta-t'ung Fu's northern main street, Chiang had lived for thirty long and strenuous years out on the steppes of the North. And it was his memories of these years among the Mongols that formed a tie between Chiang and me.

Evening after evening we sat on the warm *kang* by

the low Chinese lacquer table and talked of Mongolia
and the Mongols, while the boys kept on replenishing
our pipes and seeing that our cups were filled with the
most fragrantly aromatic tea of the house, while at the
same time they listened breathlessly to our conversation.

Chiang loved to tell stories of his years in Mongolia,
but he never failed to end up by impressing upon his
apprentices how frightful the time that he had spent
in that barbarian land had been. He had, however,
acquired vast quantities of silver and with it enhanced
the power and glory of his house. There were a great
many long tales about how the fortunes of various gay
but improvident Mongol princes had found their way
into Chiang's coffers by perfectly legitimate methods.

But these fantastically wealthy Mongol princes who
lived only for the chase, adventure and love, were no
more. They had been exterminated or banished by
the Red Soviet, and what was there for an able and industrious Chinaman to do in Mongolia among a lot of penni-
less shepherds ? Chiang's greatest achievement was that
he had succeeded, at the right moment, when the crisis
came, in transferring his capital from Mongolian horses,
skins and furs to the cigarettes and petroleum of the
West.

Chiang's façade on the main street was richly carved
and decorated as befitted a house of such ancient worth
and dignity. The site could not have been better, since
more than half the traffic of the town passed along the
main street from north to south. In the middle of the
town this street was crossed by another running east
and west, and at their junction rose the old watchtower.

Travellers from afar nearly always passed along this
main street from north to south, and in it were to be
found the shop fronts of the oldest and best-known busi-
nesses and the entrances to the largest *sarais*. Through
the south gate the main street ran straight out into the
old road to Tai-Yuan Fu, which is the capital of Shansi
and the residence of its governors.

Along this road goes a steady stream of travellers.
There are officials and traders, carriers of mails and
merchandise, and along the same way pass the countless

hordes of Buddhist pilgrims who are drawn from all the corners of Asia to the holy Wu-t'ai Shan, " the mountain of the five pinnacles ". Wu-t'ai Shan, which lies in the heart of the blue mountains of Central Asia, is one of the most ancient and holy places of Buddhism. It is the abode of Manyusri, the all-knowing god of Wisdom and protector of scholars who with his sword lays open the way through spiritual darkness.

Through the northern gate, on the other hand, one leaves civilization and enters the land of the barbarians. But on the way thither stands a mighty monument proudly bearing witness that, in the time of their greatness, the barbarians too had thought for something beside war and deeds of violence. Hidden behind the mountain which forms the present boundary between Mongolia and China lie the fantastically sculptured caves of Yün Kang—one of the earliest indications of the coming of Buddhism to China.

At the time when these grottoes were hewn out and embellished with innumerable images of Buddhas, Bodhisats and other minor celebrities of the Buddhist pantheon, the whole of this part of Northern China was occupied by tribes from the steppes whose chief proclaimed himself the founder of a new dynasty, the northern Wei. During the sixth century the Wei dynasty moved its headquarters to Ping Cheng, near to what is now Ta-t'ung Fu, and from there carried on a victorious campaign against the evicted Chinese and their adversaries. From their wars in distant parts the Wei people brought many prisoners home to Ping Cheng, and the story goes that over a million of these captives worked for more than a hundred years to transform the rugged side of the mountain into those strange caves and sculptured galleries which are now known as Yün Kang.

Now these hidden caves are almost forgotten. The chisels and hammers of those countless slaves have been quiet for fifteen hundred years, but Amitabha Buddha and his celestial kin still gaze out from the sandstone cliffs. Prisoners of war were brought thither from far-off lands of Western civilization, new generations of slaves were born in captivity, and all of them died in

4

The grottoes of Yün Kang

[face p. 4

The grottoes of Yün Kang

that foreign land. But their creations remain, and the stone figures stare unceasingly in the direction whence the prisoners came. The winds and weather of the centuries have completed the work of those by-gone sculptors and have shed a redeeming veil of mildness over the stern faces of the stone effigies.

The style of those sculptures at Yün Kang is completely un-Chinese and calls to mind the Buddhist art of the ancient Græco-Bactrian kingdom north and north-west of the Hindu Kush and the Gandhara art of Northern India.

As time went on the original strength of the northern Wei diminished and in the course of centuries the boundary rolled back and forth between the inhabitants and the nomads until at last it lay along the mountains south of what was then Kuko Khoto (Kwei-hwa Ch'eng). That Mongol city, too, and the whole of disputed Shansi fell to the Chinese, and the legend of how that came to pass is an illustration of the Chinese conviction that subtlety and cunning are better weapons than strength and courage.

Erh Lang, the most cunning of eight wise Chinese brothers, succeeded in enticing the chiefs of the nomads into a Treaty by which it was agreed that the eternal strife should cease and that the position of the boundary should be determined by Erh Lang's skill with the bow and arrows. As far as he could shoot an arrow north-wards the land was to belong to the Chinese, but all the land north of the point where the arrow fell was to belong to the nomads.

Erh Lang took his great bow and loosed an arrow which disappeared from view and which no one could find. But before this he had sent a rider out in secret to plant a faithful copy of the arrow he had shot at the foot of the mountains which formed the frontier of the Mongolian high plateau. The nomads took the incredibly long flight of the arrow for an omen and retreated to the steppes and deserts beyond the mountains.

To this day the nomads come down from the highlands, though no longer as galloping warriors on the track of plunder, but as humble pilgrims plodding towards that sacred goal, Wu-t'ai Shan, "the mountain of the five pinnacles" where the god of wisdom dwells. In small parties and large they trail past Chiang Lan Chiao's store, and all his twelve shop boys had strict orders to let Chiang and me know whenever any pilgrims from distant lands passed by. These were then called in, and this occasioned many a banquet in Chiang's innermost room; and if the guests proved interesting, they would sometimes be induced to stay for several days.

Such pilgrims as came from remote Tibet were invited to tea, food, and tobacco, because they looked so lost and miserable in that strange land among all those alien people. There could be no conversation between us because neither party understood the other's speech, but the Tibetans were most friendly and smiling and bowed their gratitude so that their long earrings glittered, and at parting they stretched their well-bred tongues far out in pure civility.

Sometimes there came lamas, ragged and famished yet secure and happy in the steadfastness of their faith, as they went their way to "the mountain of the five pinnacles" where they expected to be blessed with the gift of eloquence so that afterwards they might proclaim the true doctrine.

But most often came the guests we loved best, the bronze-brown nomads in gaily coloured clothing, who, in spite of troubles and hardships and although on penitential pilgrimage, still kept their carefree looks and the bearing of conquerors. And then the cook put meat, much meat, into his pan, and there was lively talk around the table.

CHIANG'S shop was an ideal place in which to hear news of fresh developments in the four Khanates of Outer Mongolia and in all the rest of Mongolia, for the passing pilgrims belonged to many different tribes, and all of them had gathered much news on their long journeys.

We heard that in Outer Mongolia the Red Soviet was more and more extending its power, that the lamas had been called up to the army, that high taxes had been laid on the people and that everywhere a " new free-dom " prevailed which the Mongols failed to under-stand. The ancient dress was no longer worn or was at least ill-made, and the proud times were past when chiefs and other free men galloped over the steppes with silver trappings jingling and peacock feathers flut-tering in the breeze. The four Khanates had been abolished and the whole of the Grass Country was ruled by a pack of ignorant young fellows who just danced to the *Oros'* (Russians') pipes.

But what was Mongolia and what were the Mongols without Khans and without chiefs of ancient lineage ?

The highest representatives of the land and the people had been driven out, and so had many of their religious leaders. Some had been killed or thrown into prison, others put in irons and sent away to degrading forced labour in Urga. Others, again, had succeeded in escap-ing to the territory beyond the boundaries of Outer Mongolia, where now they sought to maintain them-selves in exile among the poor shepherds of the country.

From time to time, however, rumours reached us of one Mongolian Khan who yet remained. He was said to be mighty and strong and to have kept full possession of all his power and dignity. He ruled over a land away in the west, far from all the pilgrim routes of the Mongols. Not one of the many Mongols I met at Chiang's shop had ever seen this great Khan or had visited his country.

We heard that many of the fugitives who left Outer Mongolia made their way westwards in the hope of finding a country where the true Mongol traditions were still maintained. Lamas who had been on pilgrimage to holy Lhassa in Southern Tibet related that they had there come into contact with pilgrims of that remote Mongol tribe. They called themselves Torguts and their ruler was the mighty Torgut Khan, and they dwelt so far away that the pilgrimage from their home steppes to the holy city and back again took a whole year. The Torguts dwelt to the north of Lhassa, and their rich

7

pasture lands were encircled by people of alien races and religions.

OLD Chiang did not at all understand my lively interest in these far-off Torguts and their Khan, and he obstinately maintained that since on his many and long journeys he had never come across any Torguts or so much as heard of a fifth Khan out in the west, the whole thing must be pure imagination.

But the unproven is often attractive, and nothing is so gorgeously romantic as the search for the unknown. So one day I resolved that as soon as my horses were in condition again I would set my course for the west, the far, far west, until I came to the mighty Torgut Khan. And I dreamed of a Mongol tribe whose traditions were still alive and which even to-day preserved its ancient way of living.

I would live among them as a nomad among nomads. By their camp fires I would sit and listen. And the Khan himself—he should be my friend.

And then the 13th January, 1927, arrived.

CHAPTER II

I BECOME A MEMBER OF THE SVEN HEDIN EXPEDITION

" MEET *train to Kwei-hwa at Ta-t'ung Fu Thurs-day 13th Stop Buy new toothbrush and be ready for the long trail stop Great news.* Larson."

So ran Larson's laconic message, which I received one brilliant, frosty Wednesday, and immediately felt cramped in Chiang's house, and the crenellated double walls of Ta-t'ung Fu seemed to become the walls of a prison. It was by no means unusual for me to receive similar messages from the " Duke ", but as this one contained the words " long trail ", and it was old Larson who used it, some very long journey must be in prospect.

One could not, however, travel very far to the north-ward without coming into Soviet territory, and that Larson was pretty sure to avoid. So perhaps this was the assent of the gods to my ardent wish to travel west-ward, far, far westward.

" Great news "—that sounded like the whisper of " a new orange on the way to my turban ".

The Ching-Chang railway, which starts from Peking, turns westward at Kalgan and continues by Ta-t'ung Fu and Kwei-hwa Ch'eng to Hsi-Pao t'ou, the terminus of the first railway built by the Chinese. After passing Nankow the line runs outside the Chinese wall through the territory that once belonged to the Mongols.

The railway station at Ta-t'ung Fu lies a little to the north of the town itself, and since the train indicated by Duke Larson might be expected to pass at any time between two in the morning and eleven, it was necessary for me to be outside the town wall before the gates were shut that same Wednesday evening.

That night I slept in an empty cattle truck in the station of Ta-t'ung Fu, and when at eight next morning the train rolled in I had already spent four profitable hours with the Chinese stationmaster, who treated me to fragrant tea and capital stories of the time when this frontier railway was constructed.

A shout of "Hey, Scandihuvia!" indicated which end of the train was Larson's, and soon I was hearing the great news.

Sven Hedin was to set out on an expedition to Sinkiang. The expedition was to be the biggest that ever penetrated into the vast unexplored regions of that part of the world. Three hundred camels would be needed to convey the expedition's baggage. Larson was to be caravan leader and camp manager, and I was to be his right-hand man. The expedition would travel through districts which neither Larson nor I had visited. Besides the three hundred camels the expedition was to consist of a staff of twenty-eight Swedes, Germans and learned Chinese, and forty Chinese and Mongols were to accompany it as servants and caravan men.

Larson had with him a dignified and kindly gentleman in a fox-skin coat, who had a sprained ankle. This was Sven Hedin's adjutant, come to look me over. "*Ausgezeichnet*," he said, and so I was immediately given my first job in the new expedition.

Larson was going on at once to Hsi-Pao t'ou with the adjutant to select headquarters there for the expedition, and I was to travel down to Peking to report to my new chief and at the same time to buy provisions and equipment for seventy persons for a period of two years.

Then we shook hands, clapped one another on the shoulder, and laughed with delight.

The engine whistled and puffed off in smoke and steam on its journey to the west, carrying Larson and the adjutant with it. It was then twenty-one minutes past eight.

IT was something of a responsibility to take upon oneself. Provisions and equipment for a desert journey for seventy men and three hundred camels. Of the three hundred camels, the forty camel-drivers and Larson himself I had a certain knowledge, but the thirty scientists were less in my line. Perhaps they were testy old professors and book-worms who were going to behave like babies in the desert. But the great thing for me was that the expedition was going westward. Its journey would follow the path of my longing—and so I turned my horse and galloped home to old Chiang.

He told me to my face that I was a fool. But for all that he made a little farewell feast for me and came with me to the train when I started that same afternoon for Peking.

In passing I looked up my house in Kalgan, where I roused my "boys" out of their winter lair. And when I went on to Peking I was fully and unusually smartly rigged out, and my "boys" were busy closing up my old headquarters.

The Hotel Wagon-Lits lies in the International Settlement of Peking, which is a town in itself and is surrounded and protected from the Chinese city by a fortified wall from the top of which the forces of the Great Powers keep watch in their respective uniforms round the quarter's Legations and banks and the Hotel Wagon-Lits.

The great hotel's magnificent vestibule is an admirable observation point for anyone interested in unusual people and unusual destinies. At that time the Hotel Wagon-Lits was, to put it shortly, the Far East's concentration camp for people of a kind one reads about in books but seldom encounters in reality. Of the kind which for want of a better word are called "types".

They crowd in front of the hotel's notice board to study the news from China's disturbed political horizons. In Hankau a hundred and fifty Europeans had been murdered, and the whole Western colony in that province was in danger. The American Legation had ordered its nationals in the country into protected zones, and the fleets of the Great Powers were cleared for action. The ruler of Manchuria, Marshal Chang Tso-lin, who with his victorious armies had occupied the whole of

Northern China, had now been defeated by the advancing army of the South, and it was feared that the Northern troops would plunder Peking in their retreat. All the rest of the superfluity of Chinese generals were fighting one another in hopeless contests, and large troops of bandits and robbers completed the disquiet and lawlessness.

In these troubled waters fished a crowd of international figures, greedy of adventure and sensation, from every corner of the world. One saw among them the young English Captain who had become a Chinese General and capitalist, thanks to his courage and his ability in the construction of artillery, and there were ammunition makers and arms smugglers, financiers and concession seekers, and vociferous journalists insisting that they were hundred-per-cent Americans and thinking themselves very smart.

" Hello, Kiddie," came a sudden cry from the depths of an arm-chair, and there in a corner sat the Australian, " Old But ", blowing vast clouds of smoke from his inevitable pipe. With his clear-cut and handsome features and the touch of silver on his temples he looked like an archbishop. But he was not. He was just an old Australian stockman, and still, though for many years he had been head of one of the biggest firms in China, wore riding-boots under his long trousers however he was otherwise attired.

But that day I had no time to listen to " Old But's " philosophical disquisitions. I was conducted to a pair of big glazed doors leading into the dining-room, at this time long emptied of guests. In the middle of the large room, surrounded by stripped tables, two men were sitting close together, discussing weighty plans. These were Dr. Sven Hedin and Professor J. G. Andersson, who, undisturbed by the babel around them, were cudgelling their brains to determine the route of a great scientific expedition. An expedition that was to go forth from Peking and its malignant gossip and political intrigues, across China with its Generals and robber bands, away from civilization, out to the barbaric kingdoms of the north-west, where independent thoughts could be thought unrestrained and where there was scope for individual achievement.

It was a relief to meet with Scandinavians again, and I was most cordially received by my new chief and his adviser. The rest of the day was devoted to eager discussion, and I obtained answers to almost all the questions that had arisen in my mind after my twenty minutes' conversation with Duke Larson on the platform at Ta-t'ung Fu the day before.

The German and Swedish members of the expedition were expected in Peking very soon, and everything was to be ready for a start when they arrived. I had to go on to Tientsin the same evening to complete the purchase, which Larson had begun, of equipment and provisions.

TIENTSIN lies five hours' journey by rail from Peking. In the time it takes to eat one's dinner and study the disquieting and reassuring news in the *North China Star* one covers the distance between these two cities which are the centres of two entirely different atmospheres.

Within Peking's ancient walls there is a perpetual simmering of political complications and intrigues of all sorts under the ever-courteous mask of diplomacy. The old city has for centuries been the centre of the philosophy and other profound learning of the Far East. For the hundred millions of Chinese, the representatives of the dynasties upon the Dragon Throne have been the incarnate Sons of Heaven, and from the mysterious Forbidden City have issued orders that a fourth part of mankind have heard and obeyed. The traditions and memories of the old imperial city surround it with a romance that has allured and still allures the soldiers of fortune of all the world from Marco Polo to our own day.

Tientsin seethes with active work. In its docks innumerable steamships of all nations load and discharge cargoes, and there the machinery of the West is exchanged for the natural products of Northern China and the Central Asiatic regions beyond.

In this mighty centre of trade our great expedition

was now to be equipped and provisioned. Before his departure from Tientsin Larson had begun to compile a list of what it was necessary to carry, and he had even started buying in accordance with it. I had now to complete this work in such a manner as to satisfy the many requirements of the various members of the expedition over a period of two years. I had not so much as seen any of them, and I could certainly only surmise a small part of what they would suppose themselves to need.

It was the devil of a job and one for which I had no qualifications whatever. My years in the wilderness had been spent on the lightest possible footing, and from my first day in Mongolia I had realized that the more the baggage the greater the trouble. Experience had also taught me that the greatest charm of the wilderness lies in the very fact that one lives like the people one is living among. On this subject the chief had the same view as I, but then there were the other twenty-seven gentlemen to consider.

Later on I got excellent help from two newly arrived German members of the expedition, and also from Mrs. Larson, and on the twentieth of March our train actually started for the north, carrying twenty thousand dollars' worth of food. Every dollar spent was going to increase the load of the caravan by four and a half pounds.

In Peking the slow goods train made a whole twenty-four hours' halt, and I employed the time in paying a round of farewell visits to my friends. This, as we know, is a very arduous labour, and when, after some hours, on my way through Morrison Street, I passed a music shop, I halted the sweating rickshaw coolie, so that we might both have a moment's relaxation. He got himself a watermelon, and I went into the music shop to see whether the new gramophone records were worthy to be included in the expedition's programme. But they were not. Shrieking jazz music would only have produced discord in the desert.

I expressed my dissatisfaction to the little lady of the shop and enjoined her to put her whole soul into the task of procuring me a melody for men who for years were going to tread unknown ways in the great deserts, far from home and friends, wives and sweethearts ; men who were going to fight with hunger and thirst and dangers of all kinds. It should be a melody that would give them strength upon their way, enhance their longing for that which awaited them at the goal and which could also harmonize with the beauties of the great nature into whose bosom they were soon to throw themselves. If she could procure me such a melody, the gratitude of a score of white men would often seek her out here where she lived her lonely life in the dark little shop among the silent instruments.

The little lady grew hot with zeal and helpfulness. The desired melody proved, however, impossible to obtain, but while I waited I discovered that the girl was sweet, and by the time I left the shop a quarter of an hour later I had heard her story.

Poor little thing, she was a half-caste, and everyone who has lived in the East knows how grudgingly the sun shines upon these beings. Her father had been a blond soldier in the German Legation-Guard in Peking, and her mother was Chinese. For a time there had been real domestic happiness in the little home, but it had not lasted long. The fair-haired soldier had been ordered home to his distant fatherland, and the parting, though melancholy, had been lightened by the promise of early reunion. But the reunion never came, nor was anything heard of the soldier, and when the family applied to the Legation for information, all they got for answer was that the distant Fatherland was at war and that its soldiers had other things to think of than Chinese " wives " and half-caste children.

That evening I dined at the Danish Legation, and on that occasion the Minister, his Excellency H. Kauffman, and his charming lady surprised me by presenting me with one of the Legation's big Danish flags to take with me on my journey.

Next morning I was early at the station, and at last the train moved off. " Take care of yourself, boy ! " This was George Olsen, the Danish artilleryman, who had once emigrated to the United States, where he

15

became a palæontologist, and had afterwards been a member of the Central Asiatic Expedition—in the service of which he acquired the honourable title of the champion egg-hunter of the world, after he had dug out the first dinosaurus egg ever seen by human eyes.

The train had just begun to move, and I was standing by the window to wave to my friends on the platform. Suddenly I became aware of a female form hurrying towards me.

" I have found it, I have found it, the—melody that you and your white men are to have with you."

Both the train and the little shopkeeper increased their speed, and I hung out of the window to reach the flat parcel. And we succeeded.

Though by no means convinced that it would be the right melody that she had handed me, I was both pleased and amused by the incident, and I carefully packed the record in my suitcase.

BUT that same melody was to become the expedition's favourite tune ; its stimulating notes were often to cheer tired wanderers on laborious desert journeys and diffuse happiness round the nightly camp-fire.

CHAPTER III

THE WORK BEGINS

THE expedition's long caravan journey was to set out from Hsi-Pao t'ou which is the terminus of the Ching-Chang railway and the last outpost of mechanical civilization in that part of the world, and it was in this Chinese town that the whole staff of the Sven Hedin expedition and its numerous rank and file foregathered for the first time. We represented three European and two Asiatic nations, but it was not long before our common labours in the multitudinous preparations for the start welded us into one big family.

By the end of a fortnight our expedition's baggage had been stowed in the camel-packs, and we were ready to set out. But we were still held up for a long time at Hsi-Pao t'ou waiting for suitable travelling weather. It was then decided that the expedition's film-photographer, Lieberenz, and I should undertake a journey through Inner Mongolia by way of Kalgan with a view to taking film pictures and collecting on our way a number of camels which the expedition had bought. We were then to join up with the main expedition at its first assembly camp on the steppes to the northward of Hsi-Pao t'ou.

ON the twenty-second day of our march Lieberenz and I reached a long ridge in the undulating steppe landscape, and from its crown a magnificent panorama met our gaze.

In front of us a rolling steppe plateau extended, whose soft carpet was shot with golden brown and green—for last year's dry grass was already mingled with the vivid green of the spring growth. Across the steppe we could

17

see a dark watercourse, and close beside this, scarcely four hundred yards away, the Sven Hedin Expedition lay encamped.

The bright blue tents lay in neat rows on the steppe, and two slender radio masts and the Swedish flag stood out against the clear blue sky and the scudding white clouds. Pillars of smoke rose from numerous fire-places, and human industry lent movement, life and activity to the scene.

We were strongly drawn to all we saw down there and would have liked to set off at a gallop, the sooner to meet our travelling companions, but the scene was so fair that we must first record it on the celluloid ribbon of the film camera. While we were getting ready to do this Larson's eagle eye perceived us, and from the moment he announced our arrival to the camp the picture was destroyed—and we went down to the city of tents.

Not until we had exchanged greetings innumerable and consumed colossal quantities of civilized tinned food could we make our report and swap news.

Lieberenz and I had brought from Baying Bulak the sixty-five camels which our expedition had taken over from the completed one of Andrews, and all the animals had accomplished the fourteen severe marches to this place. We ourselves had done twenty-two marches from the time we left the railway at Kalgan to the meeting camp here. During the journey we had taken several thousand yards of film of Mongolian life.

The main expedition had only arrived at the meeting camp a few hours ahead of us, so the time of conjunction had been correctly calculated. From the railway terminus at Hsi-Pao t'ou, where the loads were taken over, to this place had occupied eight marching days, for which reason the camp here was called No. 8. And in future the main caravan's camping places were to receive numbers indicating the number of marches accomplished between the starting-point and the respective camps. Thus we provided exact appellations for the camping-places in a nameless no man's land and were able to avoid the misunderstanding which might easily have arisen if we had adopted the native place names, often difficult to understand.

The transport of the main expedition's two hundred and seventy-five tons of baggage had up to now been performed by camels hired at Hsi-Pao t'ou. But as the owners of these would not allow their caravan to cross the western deserts in the summer, the expedition was now obliged to purchase its own animals. So far we had only the sixty-five brought by Lieberenz and myself. The rest had still to be acquired.

Our most experienced Mongols were accordingly sent out as buyers to the steppes in the north, and soon there came into camp flocks large and small of camels purchased for heavy silver dollars.

Prices ran between eighty and a hundred Mexican dollars per animal. The Mongols of the district were, however, poor folk with small herds and to get hold of powerful and well-nourished animals our men had to seek further and further to the northward, out on the more fertile steppes. Thus it was two whole months before the number was complete and we were able to leave Camp No. 8.

During the time of waiting numerous minor expeditions were undertaken with the camels from Baying Bulak to range over and explore the neighbouring tracts. Under Bergman's leadership the archæologists now made the finds which lifted the extreme edge of one of the veils that conceal the prehistoric secrets of Central Asia. Norin was perpetually wandering over steppes and mountains with a view to investigating their geological properties. The topographers filled in several of the last blank sheets of the atlas, and at home in the camp Haude and his staff of meteorologists began the systematic work, which afterwards continued for years, of determining the laws governing the mighty continent's climatic conditions.

Every time such an expedition returned to camp it brought new observations with it, and each new observation produced new riddles to be solved.

In the Chief's tent all the young investigators were

received by ripe and tried experience, but also by the kindling spark of eternal youth.

A passion of work prevailed in Camp No. 8. There were days when the young and newly formed company of nomads was fired with the enthusiasm of research which for many of us came to mean a life's task. And there were moments when unspoiled nature and unknown surroundings touched unsuspected strings which generations of evolution in other directions had robbed of their resonance. But we were not so far removed from more primitive ages but that our new nomad existence soon lured forth a deep reverberation in our souls which produced in a present-day investigator an inward understanding of the primeval phenomena for which he sought.

LATE May passed into early June, and we experienced the swiftly advancing summer that is the spring of the steppes.

The camp's little watercourse, Hojertai-gol, rushed along in spate with greetings from the snow fields of its source. The lovely cups of irises threw a shining blue veil over the green luxuriance along the banks of the stream. The Mongols call the iris " little daughter-in-law ", for it is the fairest flower of the steppe and as longed for and as welcome as the little daughter-in-law in the camp. · And just as the iris is the ornament of the steppe, so is the son's young wife the delight of the tent, since the tent's own young daughters must early leave home to adorn the tents of others.

The jerboas crept forth from the ground and leapt about in the grass like elegant miniature kangaroos. *Tarbagan* (the marmot) sunned its sallow winter coat in cautious proximity to its hole. And far out on the waterless expanses of the steppe antelopes and gazelles gathered in vast herds, for it was time for the does to drop their fawns.

In the Mongol camps richly coloured festal garments and heavy silver ornaments were taken out of the chests, for the feast of Maidari drew near. Of all the great festivals of Mongolia this is the most important and is kept in honour of Maidari, the Messiah of Buddhism, who shall one day come to reform the world and save mankind, and we were anxious to seize this chance to get a rare pageant recorded on the film.

Early one July morning Lieberenz and I started on our new filming expedition to the Maidari festivities at the monastery of Bater Halak Sume, and as there was not the least suspicion of illness in camp, Hummel too came with us to take anthropological measurements of the Mongols taking part in the festival. We took with us six camels, two Mongols, a Chinese boy and several thousand yards of film.

On the evening of the first day's march we encamped in the steppe territory of Prince Darkhan Beil. The Chinese call this district Pai-ling Ti, the Land of Larks, and the name well describes it. Everywhere larks rose in front of us, pouring out ecstatic notes as they soared vertically heavenwards. The lark is the song-bird of the steppes ; its glad unchanging song is in profound accord with the loneliness of those boundless spaces. Everywhere on our Mongolian journeys we encountered larks, and a lark's voice was the last music to reach us before the dead silence of the stony desert of Khara Gobi enfolded us.

The Chinese, who delight in bird song, prize especially the Mongolian lark, and the larks from Pai-ling Ti command a high price in the bird markets of China. In the early summer, when the young are big enough to look after themselves but are yet unable to fly, Chinese bird catchers in hundreds betake themselves to the Land of Larks. All the captured fledglings are reared until they are old enough for their sex to be determined, and then the hen birds are released. As soon as the cocks begin to sing they are classified according to their capacity as songsters—for not even the larks from this famous Lark Land are invariably superb songsters. But a mediocre voice can sometimes be developed if the bird be kept with an experienced master singer. And it is worth the trouble. An untried lark may be bought for a few cents, while the most richly endowed fetch a higher price than a horse.

21

Next morning, in sight of our camp, we found a hollow of the steppe full of yellow antelopes. Through glasses we could distinguish, among the swarming hundreds of animals, numbers of new-born fawns taking their first tottering steps beside their mothers.

The antelopes had calved.

Cautiously we tried to move towards the enchanting spectacle. The sun threw upon the white-flecked coats of the one-night-old baby antelopes and on the tender dew-wet grass a gleam which completed the beauty of this picture of young unsullied morning on the steppe.

The herd was made up of mothers with their young and the childless dowagers of the antelope community, but no bucks were to be seen. The nearer we approached the more disquiet arose in the assembly, and the dowagers advanced towards us and stamped angrily on the ground with their forefeet. The uneasy antelope mammas gave their offspring the first warning of their lives of the perils of existence and slowly retired followed by the bigger fawns. In the end, when we were only twenty yards away from the herd, the peril of our presence was so imminent that mammas, matrons and young vanished like lightning behind the nearest hillock.

But the most helpless of the young were left behind in the grass, and lay there regarding us with bright astonished eyes. We were strongly tempted to go and stroke the enchanting creatures. But on the crest of the hill behind which the herd was hiding we could descry the mothers of those left behind, could see them calling and stamping in an agony of solicitude, and this led us quickly to withdraw.

Only on two days in the whole year is it possible for human beings to come so close as we had just been to the swift-footed antelope of the steppes. This was the only time I have enjoyed the experience.

At their calving-time the antelope herds of Mongolia are very severely decimated, for in these days they form an easy prey for wolves and rapacious birds. The Mongol hunters, however, do no great harm to the herds, because, as they say, some animal in so great a herd must be the incarnation of a saint, since it is able to gather so many followers around it. And the risk of slaying a saintly being is one no true-believing Mongol will take. If the Mongol is ravenous for flesh, he tries to drive some solitary animal out of the herd. Such a one he can then shoot without anxiety, for the incarnation of the saint must still be in the great herd, because this constantly remains with him.

WE went on rapidly southward across hillocky grassland. The sun ran its happy course over our heads, and its warm rays brought out a glory of bright flowers. Far out in the wide expanse we saw great herds of cattle grazing contentedly. Suddenly a herd of several hundred horses, white and brown, tore past us at a thundering gallop, led by a couple of loudly singing herdsmen. Some of the leading stallions carried amulets sewn up in felt on their broad chests, showing that they were sacred beasts and that the herd belonged to a monastery.

The narrow track we were following was joined every now and then by other narrow tracks, and by the time the sun was at its zenith we were travelling along a wide steppe road made by the trampling of innumerable hooves towards the same goal. All the narrow tracks were lines of communication between the widely scattered Mongol camps on the steppe and the monastery, and at this time all the nomads of the surrounding district were on their way to the same destination as we, the Maidari festival at Bater Halak Sume.

From time to time we passed large parties of slowly riding nomad families. Their dusty exterior showed that several days' journey lay between them and their home tents, now guarded only by their fierce dogs and a few young married women. As many as possibly can join in this journey of penitence and festival. The elders from yearning to have their sins of the past year forgiven and blotted out, the young for an occasion to show themselves in full pomp and state to as many observers as possible.

In the van of such a family group ride the active men of the camp arrayed in vividly coloured silk robes and

23

with heavy silver ornaments jingling from their belts
and round their wrists. The expressions on their
weatherbeaten faces change swiftly between haughty
sternness, frank enjoyment, and admiring curiosity about
everything they see. In front of them on the saddles
the babies of the camp are perilously perched, and the
radiant, childish enjoyment of these small people is a
delightful sight.

In the middle of the group rides the principal woman,
wife of the headman of the camp. She is decked in
the family jewels proper to her position and makes a
picture of proud dignity as she rides along surrounded
by the younger wives of the camp and the bigger children.

Last in the troop ride the aged widows of the camp,
the chief paternal grandmother, and the other grand-
mothers on both sides. They wear neither jewellery nor
other festive display, for they have for ever renounced
worldly splendour at the time when their black hair
fell under the razor after they had lost their lords and
consorts and the tent-wife's place by the fire. The
hundred and eight beads of the rosary pass diligently
through the old women's fingers, and they mutter
prayers which are only interrupted by friendly words,
and greetings to passers by. " *Amergan sain* " (peace,
blessing), " *Mendu sain* " (good health to you).

The old women's eyes often look with pride over the
troop in front of them, their vigorous offspring who
bear witness that they have fulfilled their destiny on
earth. The humility they display is but submissiveness
to Fate. For as the arrow pursues its path unchecked
from the moment it is loosed by the strong arm of
conscious purpose till it is stopped by its mark, so is
the life of mankind an unchecked flight towards a goal,
from birth to death. Every year, every hour, every
second brings the goal nearer. No one, nothing can
lengthen the course to death, for such is the Creator's
will.

A galloping youngster stormed past us like a wave of
youthful vigour and joy in living. The home camp's
most splendid horse had been put at his disposal, for
to-day he was a free hawk in quest of prey. The sun

glittered on his silver-mounted knives, and the wind
tore at the long ends of his fluttering yellow sash and at
the silken tuft of his jauntily set cap.

He rode up to a nomad family proceeding at a foot
pace and then made his horse show its best paces. The
hoof-beats sounded like a roll of drums and he himself
swung out of the saddle with swaggering audacity and
elegance. In the centre of the group rode a marriageable
and desirable young girl, and to her he made his fiery
declaration of love.

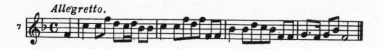

" Look at my horse. Its head and ears vie with one another.
Look at my saddle. It is heavy with silver mounting.
Hey, you flower of the steppe ! In the camp they are making my
first tent.
Are you willing to light the fire in it ? "

Everyone laughed good-humouredly ; only the chosen
one turned her eyes upon the ground before the horseman's bold glances.

From time to time we passed red-robed and yellow-
robed lamas and wandering pilgrims carrying their
worldly goods in a little wicker-work frame on their
backs. Many of these pilgrims were emaciated wanderers who spent years of their lives in penitential
journeys from one Buddhist holy place to another. Now
they were hurrying towards Bater Halak Sume so as
not to miss the Maidari festival there.

This holy cloister, to which were all bound, was
widely famous in the lamaistic world, for there it was
that Yolros Lama meditated, the one of lamaisms
hutuktus who, next to Bogdo Gegen at Urga, was regarded by many as representing the highest divine
incarnation in the land of the Mongols. Moreover,
this monastery was renowned because it bred lamas
who could be transformed into *gurtums*.

The holiness of a *hutuktu* is the result of many earlier
existences, and he is therefore a being of superior nature,

highly exalted above the multitude. To show this
veneration to a *hutuktu* confers upon pilgrims renewed
strength to endure their troubles and confirms their hope
of one day reaching the right goal.

. Great crowds of pilgrims come to the monastery to
obtain the blessing of the Reborn ; some desire to gain
a supernatural insight into future events, many seek
healing for a tormented soul or an afflicted body.

I questioned several of the pilgrims about the mysterious Yolros lama, and all spoke with like enthusiasm
of his purity, loftiness and great supernatural gifts.
But of the actual person of the Reborn and of the strange
power that he incarnated they knew nothing or would
not tell.

Towards evening the temple city came in sight. It
grew out of the earth before our eyes in the same moment
that we topped the ridge, radiant with its white façades,
its boldly curved roofs and gilded minarets glittering in
the sunlight. The chiming bells rose up to us, and a
dull rumble as of kettledrums.

The holy cloister city was awaiting us.

CHAPTER IV

YOLROS LAMA

OUT on the steppe innumerable saddled horses were tethered in small groups, and in every direction as far as the eye could reach one could see swarms of nomads and pilgrims streaming along every track.

In the immediate vicinity of the monastery the many paths ran together into one broad road encircling the cloister city. We mingled with the arriving participants to the eastward of the monastery so that we might approach the holy place from east to west, in the direction of the sun's course, following the rotation proper to the Wheel of Life and the way of fortune.

On the side next the monastery this broad road was divided by a row of stones from another narrower road. Along this latter at a slow pace passed an unbroken stream of remorseful, penitent, devout worshippers demonstrating the sincerity of their faith by making these wearying circuits of the cloister city. Many of them had been doing it for days, others for weeks. Some carried on their backs heavy burdens of holy books, others " measured the distance with their own bodies ".

This laborious form of progress involves that the whole of the route covered shall have been in contact with the suppliant's body. The pilgrim casts himself at full length on the ground, and mutters his prayers with his forehead pressed against the ground. After this he makes a mark in the ground with his outstretched hands, rises and walks forward to this mark whereupon he casts himself down again once more and lays his forehead to the earth while he prays. This penance is repeated without a break until the distant goal is reached.

Everywhere in the lamaistic world one comes upon these fanatics who measure the pilgrim way with their own bodies. From all the corners of Central Asia they work their way to the holy places of pilgrimage and the goal may be as remote as Wu-t'ai Shan of the many legends, or Dzarung Khashor, the domed pagoda in still more remote Nepal.

Alone or in small groups they crawled along across steppes and deserts, over mountains and rivers, overcoming all obstacles that met them on their way. When the route lay through unpopulated and barren country its length was doubled, for food and water had to be carried with them, and every time the pilgrim had measured out a few hundred yards he had to return over the same stretch to fetch the indispensable provisions.

Such pilgrimages often take years and frequently the frail body does not reach its goal. The thought that Death may meet them on the way has no terror for the faithful, for the soul that is set free on such a journey rises to a higher plane than that on which he lived during his time on earth and the ultimate goal draws nearer.

Many times in dismal and Godforsaken regions I have come upon such dying pilgrims. And I have tried to still the hungry conscience of the well fed by filling them up with my superfluity of material goods. They have accepted them with friendly but impersonal gratitude. They have sat by my fireside, covered in rags but with a soul made whole. I have listened to their words and understood that these expressed what was for them a deep and sincere truth. And I have sat there and watched them resume their agonizing course towards that enticing distant goal, followed their tardy disappearance. And into my mind has come what a wise man once said to the modern youth of a new civilization : " For God's sake *believe in something*, even if it be the Devil ! "

THE blue and white travelling tents of the nomads shot up like mushrooms out of the ground on the steppe around the monastery. Horses, turned loose, spread themselves over the Grass Lands. They rolled on their backs to rub off the smarting sweat-irritation after their

28

gallop, they nuzzled acquaintances and played in the tall grass of the river bank.

Nightfall was announced by a red-and-gold-clad lama who from the highest platform of a tall tower rising from the monastery wall blew several deep, long-drawn notes on a great conch. The last rays of the sun made the temple roof gleam with all the colours of a dying fire, until the glowing sky became the background to a jumble of dark fantastic silhouettes.

We pitched our tent down by the river at a discreet distance from the monastery and from the most out-lying of the pilgrim's camps. Over us and about us was a hemisphere of night sky spangled with stars, and the flickering glow of innumerable little fires quested like mysterious search-lights about the tent sides in the Mongol encampment. The silhouettes of the grazing horses moved ghostlike out upon the steppe, and the air was full of sounds.

The Mongolian monastery of Bater Halak Sume is called by the Chinese Pai-ling Miao, which means the Temple of the Larks, and " Belimiao " is in its turn a Scandinavian simplification of the Chinese name. The Mongols' name for the monastery Bater Halak Sume, means " the monastery of the strong gate ", and they explained the name to me by telling me that this mon-astery constituted the Mongols' firmest stronghold on this part of the front for religious and moral opposition to the Chinese encroachment from the south.

The monastery was once burned and plundered by Chinese fugitives from the garrison in Urga which had been driven out by Khalka Mongols. This happened in 1911, immediately after the revolution which trans-formed the Chinese empire into a new republic without traditions, impossible for the Mongols to respect. Yuan Shih-K'ai, the first president of China, was, however, particularly anxious that the tribes of Inner Mongolia should continue loyal to China, and in order to atone for the crime which his soldiers had committed in burn-ing the holy place of the Mongols and to pacify the out-raged nomads on the border, he defrayed the cost of rebuilding the monastery in its present splendid form.

By means of this wise move Yuan Shih-K'ai averted the alliance of the inhabitants of Inner Mongolia with the Khalka Mongols who had broken away and were now independent of China.

But in spite of this the Mongols of these regions regarded the Chinese with suspicion and contempt. *Irgen* is a Mongolian word for anything coarse and plebeian ; in this district it also denotes a Chinaman.

The prince of this country is known as Darkhan Beile Wang. *Beile* means a prince of the Third rank. The added *Wang* implies that he has been further promoted to one of the two highest classes of princes, and this distinction was conferred on him by Yuan Shih-K'ai as a reward for not having allied himself after the revolution with the rebellious tribes in Outer Mongolia.

Darkhan is a purely Mongolian word for a craftsman, usually one who works in metal. Mongolian craftsmen are scarce and the profession generally goes by family inheritance. The works produced by Mongols are more individual and often more complete in form and execution than the imitative Chinese productions, and a Mongolian *darkhan* family is very highly thought of among the nomads. The presence of the word *darkhan* in the title of this prince implies that the princely rank is hereditary in the family just as the craft is in the craftsman's family.

The Chinese who visit the country call this prince Pai-ling Wang, which means "The Prince of the Larks". These terms, "Monastery of the Larks" and "Prince of the Larks", are, however, not of such poetic origin as one might believe. It is only the bird-catcher's technical name for the monastery that dominates and the man who governs the steppes where the Chinese snare their best larks.

THE mournful and mysterious notes of exotic instruments announced the awakening of the cloister city.

Out on the open steppe round about our tent, in the fresh beauty of the morning, a happy buzz of activity prevailed. From the small tents Mongols crept in astonishing numbers, morning greetings were exchanged between the camps and the night's new arrivals were welcomed warmly and according to all the rules of ceremony. Soon the place swarmed with boisterous youths vying with one another in the collecting of horse and cattle droppings, and among the tents rose ever more columns of smoke from ever more fires.

The view to the north was entirely dominated by the monastery with its dazzling white walls and glittering roof, a fairy palace conjured up upon the steppe. The monastery itself consisted of nine *duguns* (temple buildings) each of which constituted a place for its own special deity and his following. This block of sacred edifices was surrounded by a mass of low white buildings, all alike, gathered into groups within high walls, and between these walls ran the narrow alleys which formed the means of communication of the cloister city. From these narrow lanes double doors of beautifully decorated red lacquer led through the walls into the enclosed quarters, and in the small houses within these the monastery's fifteen hundred lamas had their cells.

The monastery was terraced within a hollow in the southern slope of the ridge that bounds the outlook to northward and was so constructed that all the temples and all the holy images inside the sanctuary faced southwest towards Lhassa, the holy city of Lamaism. Every temple was surrounded by a spacious walled courtyard and all the lesser temples lay gathered round the main temple whose double roof overtopped the pinnacles of even those temples lying highest on the slope.

The view across the cloister city was enchanting. Its background was the vast green ridge which carried seven pagoda-formed *soboroks* [1] on its crest. And underneath, the shining golden roofs of the temple buildings hung like flounces one beneath the other. The sinuous line of each roof stood out against the upper third part of the white walls of the temple next behind it. Everywhere the eye was captivated by minarets and pinnacles, sym-

---

[1] *Soborok* (Tibetan *chorten*)—a pagoda-like building in which the relics of a deceased *hutuktu* or high lama are preserved. The form of the *soborok* symbolizes the five elements into which the body is dissolved after death.

31

bolic figures and the gilded images of fantastic beasts. And all this splendour looked out towards the sun and towards the holy city of Lhassa and towards us three white men as we bathed in the blue brook.

WITHIN the monastery all was feverish bustle, for the morrow was the first day of the festival. Armed with cameras we made a tour through the lanes and round the walls that hid the temples. Wherever we showed ourselves we were surrounded by curious young people who seemed to grow out of the earth and finally pressed so closely round us that any photography of interest was rendered impossible. From time to time we tried to make our way through the doors to the temple courtyards but were always met by police lamas with stern countenances.

I made repeated efforts to get into conversation with the more friendly looking monks, but they immediately discovered that they were in a hurry. And if I tried to photograph some passing dignitary in full canonicals, he instantly turned his back. These Mongols were in the highest degree discouraging, and we were in despair at perpetually coming up against an impenetrable wall of animosity.

A Chinese trader told us that a few weeks before a couple of the Chinese students attached to our expedition had tried to photograph the interior of a temple which was for the moment unguarded. But they had been caught in the act by a pair of lamas and driven out by the infuriated inhabitants of the monastery. We also heard that a Chinaman who had been present at a temple service had afterwards mocked the officiating lamas and asked them how all their worship of the gods had helped them the time when the Chinese burned and plundered the monastery in 1911.

How could we strangers make the monks realize that our minds were free from scorn and irony and our designs entirely peaceful? And they absolutely must realize it before the next sunrise!

AFTER a pretty fruitless conference back in the tent, we set to work on our other task, that of taking anthropo-

Photo Lieberenz

Yolros Lama

Photo Lieberenz

Shirup Geling with Yolros Lama's dog

metric measurements of the Mongols collected for the festival. A couple of young men visiting our tent consented after minute explanations to go through the ordeal. But when Hummel opened his case and displayed the many shining instruments which were necessary for calculating the shape of the head and taking other measurements they slunk quickly away, leaving behind them the promised silver dollars.

We had better luck with one proud soldier, for after I had egged him on by comparing him with the dauntless warriors of some imaginary race in the north, he wanted to demonstrate both his build and his courage. Sweating with concern he underwent a twenty minutes' examination before a large and admiring audience. Finally Hummel was to take a specimen of his blood with a hypodermic needle. The fellow got his little prick, but we did not succeed in getting his blood, for this innocent operation gave rise to a hysterical yell and caused great commotion among the onlookers.

Before noon the news of our mysterious designs had spread over the whole monastery and the needle prick had become a bath of blood. For a long time Hummel and I sat outside our tent demonstrating needle pricks in our own fingers to show how innocuous they were, but we only got them ripped to bits without convincing a single Mongol.

We were further from the goal than ever.

It was clear that the anthropometric venture had not improved our chances of getting inside the temple walls. So Hummel packed up his fine instruments again and instead went out to collect riverside plants, insects and steppe-mosses. This gave rise to an animated discussion among the Mongols, but the calm conclusion of it was that the white men must be some sort of colleagues of the Chinese lark-catchers.

ONE thing was clear to us : the only way for us to overcome the distrust we had already roused among the masses was to win the favour of the Highest.

I had known our Mongols Tsereat and Gombo for several years. We explained our predicament clearly to them, and they understood the situation. With all the photographs of brilliant princes, princesses and high lamas that Lieberenz and I had taken during our journey through Inner Mongolia stuck into their blouses, our servants mingled with the crowds of brethren of their race and faith who were streaming towards the monastery.

Some hours later they came back beaming with satisfaction. They had gone on a mission of supplication from temple to temple and at length had come before Yolros Lama himself. He had been interested by their Chahar clothing and had asked them the object of their journey and enquired for news from the east. They had told him of their white travelling companions and of the many dignitaries they had visited in their company, and finally they had pulled out the photographs. The sight of pictures of the chiefs and high lamas whom Yolros Lama knew so well by name and reputation but had never seen had aroused the holy man's deep interest.

The Mongols had reported how we foreigners were everywhere made welcome and had even become fast friends with the Prince of Sunit himself. We had the best of intentions, and it would be a shame if on our westward journey we were to meet new chiefs and high lamas and not be able to show them pictures of this famous monastery, its saint and high lama.

Yolros Lama had asked to keep the photographs until the next day, and at the end each man had received his blessing.

Just after sunset a friendly and dignified lama came on a visit to our tent. From the reverent demeanour of our Mongols we realized that they knew the guest and that he was a personage of rank. For a while the conversation flitted courteously backwards and forwards as is the custom in Mongolia, and only when he had drunk tea and declined tobacco did the visitor mention his errand, which was to convey Yolros Lama's desire that I should pay him a visit.

This communication threw us into such rapture that it was hard to conceal under a mask of seriousness.

Accompanied by Tsereat carrying our gifts for the Holy One I followed the envoy into the presence of the

34

man who was worshipped as a saint by millions of his fellow-creatures, a supernatural being in possession of omniscient and divine powers.

Tsereat prostrated himself with his forehead pressed to the ground, and I showed the same marks of respect as to a great chieftain.

From the opposite side of an elliptical room a pair of eyes, full of penetrating intensity and mysterious attractive power, gazed upon me. I had a strong impression that the moment was an experience.

The man I saw before me, whose body had been chosen as the earthly integument of high divine powers, had reached the autumn of life.[1] His clear-cut intelligent face moved imperceptibly as he murmured a welcoming blessing. His complexion was sallow from want of sunlight and fresh air. His forehead was wrinkled and his cheeks intersected by deep furrows. The face was that of a recluse, marked by a long life's profound meditation over exalted problems and by the constant calls of those around him upon the divine powers that had his poor frail human body for their dwelling.

His earliest memories were of being assured that he was not as others. He had never known parental love, and his upbringers had been high lamas full of nothing but dogma and the mysticism of cloistral life. Never had he been regarded as a human being, never had the humanity in him experienced human love or friendship. Throughout a long life he had been sought out by innumerable pilgrims from near and far, he had been worshipped, honoured, deified, questioned about problems and things demanding a divine omniscience. But none had sought him as a human being; all had come for the superhuman powers that he incarnated.

It was the product of all this that I saw before me,

[1] When three years later, in 1930, I revisited the monastery of Bater Halak Sume, *Yolros lama hutuktu* had " changed bedding ", that is to say the divine soul had migrated to a new body. The cloister city mourned, for the rebirth had taken place in another and a distant monastery, in the body of a child born at the moment when the man whom I now saw before me ceased to live.

a poor human being who had lived through the desolation of loneliness and the agony of doubt, but who in the end had attained a supermundane peace.

Yolros was a divinity, both in the belief of his coreligionists and of himself.

A LONG silence followed. Yolros Lama prayed softly while his thin, aristocratic hands turned over again and again the rustling oblong sheets of manuscript in the thick pile in front of him. He had assumed the posture of a sitting Buddha, and his crossed legs were hidden by a wide red skirt. The upper part of his body was covered with a jerkin of gold-embroidered silver brocade and his bare arms were thrust out from its wide armholes. Over his shoulders and round his waist lay the ample draperies of a toga of red silk.

The five layers of cushions in the sacred colours on which he sat were among his privileges as *hutuktu*. The cushions rested upon a wide throne which was a masterpiece of carving and tastefully blended gilding and barbarically vivid colour. The high back of the chair was draped with brocade. Above the sitter's head floated a baldequin of gold brocade from which three silken flounces of different colours hung down. On his right stood a carved table on which lay sacred books and religious objects worn and patinated with many years of diligent use.

The walls of the room were decorated with temple flags and pictures of Buddhist places of pilgrimage. A set of coloured oleographs of the emperors and princes of the late Manchu dynasty bore witness to a conservatism unaffected by republican ideas.

The longer sides of the room were bordered with benches, and at the upper end of the bench to the right of Yolros Lama was a seat of honour upon which an attendant lama invited me with a mute gesture to be seated. I presented the offering I had brought, and this was carried away by the lama, but the heavy silence in the room was not lightened. Soundlessly I was served with tea and nuts. Then Shirup Geling, the lama who had brought me here, withdrew, and I was alone with the Holy One. I tried to give a little nod and a friendly smile, but he was far away in his prayers.

As I sat wondering what was going to happen, I suddenly dropped my tea-cup on the floor, and this at once brought about a change in the situation. A ferocious barking sounded from the *hutuktu's* ample skirt, the folds bulged and swayed and out popped the flat-nosed head of a miniature pekingese. Another shrill yelp, and in a couple of jumps the dog scuttled down from the throne and on to my knee.

We immediately became good friends. I petted him, but stole a glance at Yolros Lama to see if by doing so I was committing a breach of etiquette or hurting his feelings. Instead I saw for the first time some human kindliness in his eyes and a faint smile about his mouth.

After visiting me the little dog wanted to go back under the protecting skirt, and while I lifted him up on to the high seat I came in contact with both the throne and its occupant. We both fondled the animal and it licked both the Holy One's hand and mine. And when the dog presently drew back again under his master's skirts Yolros Lama and I were engaged in human and friendly conversation.

In my eagerness I sat down in none too respectful proximity to the edge of the very throne to show my photographs, and I allowed my imagination to gallop along Mongolian paths so as to conjure up the picture which should make clear to the Holy One our sincere friendliness and our desire that our sentiments in this respect should be reciprocated.

We talked of dogs and horses, which indeed may house the wandering souls of dead humanity, and we talked of this little dog that was so fond of Yolros Lama, and I understood that he found in the animal comfort for the lifelong void that lay between him and his fellowmen.

OUR *tête-à-tête* was interrupted by the return of the attendant lama. Again I sat in my remote place of honour, and again the *hutuktu* relapsed into profound meditation. The attendant looked sourly at the broken tea-cup, and I got a disapproving glance on account of the long duration of the audience. I wished the man where the pepper grows.

Suddenly Yolros Lama gave an order to the disturber of the peace who disappeared, and the next moment Shirup Geling came in. To him the *hutuktu* now announced that I and my companions were to be his guests while the festivities at the monastery were in progress. The southern pavilion would be at our disposal, and the lama was to assist us in all ways. Such was the *hutuktu's* wish, for such was wise and right.

The forbidden cloister had thrown its doors wide open to us, for what Mongol sets himself up against those who are the actual guests of the living Buddha?

Reverentially I walked backwards towards the door, trying all the time to maintain the human contact of our eyes in my desire to show my boundless gratitude. But his gaze was once more vacant, infinitely far away. At the threshold of the entrance hall and in view of the assembled lamas I paid to Yolros Lama all the homage due to a *hutuktu* of the Mongols.

The same night Hummel, Lieberenz and I slept in the most holy part of the holy monastery.

CHAPTER V

THE DANCE OF THE GODS

EARLY next morning both ourselves and the monastery were awakened by the notes of the white conch. From the topmost platform of the high tower the lamas were sending out the notes of the instrument symbolic of good fortune to the ten regions of the world. Our bedroom, which occupied the entire width of the pavilion, had Chinese windows facing both the inner and the outer courts. Yet another guest had been received during the night at Yolros Lama's, and he had been given the room above ours. This was Barun Kung, the western Duke, chieftain of the westernmost of the Darkhan Beile " banners ".

Both courtyards were beginning to fill with people, for to-day the otherwise so unapproachable Yolros Lama threw open his gates to the stream of pilgrims of both sexes. The crowd was immense. Distinguished men of wealth and poor herdsmen, monks and soldiers, men and women, old and young, and children of all ages jostled one another in the struggle to reach the place from which the *hutuktu* would sprinkle his holy water.

From our window we had the best possible view of this picturesque spectacle and, ourselves unseen, were able to use our film apparatus and cameras through the window.

Every one of the arrivals brought his tribute to the *hutuktu* in the form of *hadaks*,[1] and these were supplemented by gifts, varying with the means of the giver from horses and cattle, silver and silk, to brick tea and

[1] *Hadak*—a long piece of silk, usually blue or white, which is presented to the gods or to exalted personages as a mark of veneration. A *hadak* is holy and pleasing to the gods ; it possesses secret virtues and symbolizes the rainbow.

39

bladders of butter. Slowly the closely packed multitude moved forward to the inner court, and at every step of the stairway leading to the *hutuktu's* pavilion each one knelt for a brief prayer. Some counted the beads of their rosaries, others turned praying mills and all muttered prayers. Within the sacred room they were blessed in droves.

Suddenly all pricked up their ears, for loud clamour and shouting penetrated from the outer court. The perspiring Lieberenz made haste to swing his film camera over to the window facing in that direction. An imposing procession was filing through the gate in the outer wall. Two young warriors rode in front and cleared a way through the throng with heavy long-lashed whips. The whips whistled and cracked, the people shrieked with terror, and as if by magic a path several yards wide opened through the court which just before had seemed filled to capacity. No one was hit, for the whips had only whistled in the air, and I learned afterwards that the stern horsemen with their terrible whips were no more than a ceremonial announcement that the ruler of the country was approaching.

And then came Darkhan Beili Wang.

The King was surrounded by richly garbed princes and chieftains, and in his company rode proud women in sumptuously embroidered dresses gleaming with savage colour, clattering silver, coral and amber. The horses' hooves pranced on the stone pavement of the court, and the long plumes of peacocks' feathers on the men's caps swung and swayed in the sunshine as the cavalcade dismounted.

It was the ruler of the country and the people, come to make humble obeisance before his overlord, the tired old Yolros Lama.

LONG-DRAWN muted notes from gigantic Tibetan bassoons followed by the booming of gongs announced that the festival was about to begin in the court of the chief temple. The participants hurriedly turned away from Yolros Lama's domain and slowly followed the pilgrim throng.

" The festival place lay bathed in sunlight . . ."

A solitary, meagrely clad little old woman pattered to and fro several times between the two courtyards. In her outstretched hands she carried a small faded *hadak* and a shabby leather bag. I asked her through the window if she, too, was not going to the place of the festival. Yes, indeed, that she was, but the crowd and all the noise had made her giddy in the head. She had come from far out on the steppe where she lived alone with her seven goats, and she was so poor that she had only been able to bring this little bag of goat's milk cheese. Now she did not know whether to offer it on the altar of Maidari or to lay it at Yolros Lama's feet. It was a terrible problem.

I escorted her to Yolros Lama's door and observed with what trembling supplication she approached the Great Miracle. Her old knees creaked as she tried with the help of her stick to get down into a kneeling posture to present her offering.

When she came out again into the courtyard she had jingling silver money in her hand and two bricks of tea under her arm, and her face was lighted up with happiness. She had been the recipient of the most personal and kindly consolation and blessing of any on that day.

When, soon afterwards, we three strangers were escorted to the place of festival by Shirup Geling, we left behind one solitary man. Yolros Lama, himself a deity, could not take part in a festival in honour of the gods.

The way to the chief temple lay deserted and silent, and only a few masterless dogs prowled about the sun-baked precincts.

THE vast, overcrowded festival place lay bathed in sunshine. When we arrived the throng made way for the festally attired Shirup Geling, and gazed with wondering curiosity at us and our servants who toiled after us with the instruments, boxes and stands. For all knew by now that the three white men were quartered in the Holy One's territory and were his honoured guests.

After some hesitation Shirup Geling agreed to our placing the film camera on the six-foot pedestal of one

41

of the two masts that had been set up in the middle of the ground. From this elevation we had a splendid view of all we wanted to see—all that so few white men had ever seen.

The centre of the immense space was paved with large flat stones, unhewn but worn smooth by countless dragging steps. And this clear space in the middle was surrounded by thousands of spectators who thronged along the temple walls. The area was skirted on all four sides by temple buildings. To the north lay the lofty and dominant main temple whose façade was half darkened by the shadow of its projecting double roof. In front of this was stretched a huge banner, thirty-two feet by twenty, with the image of Maidari the Messiah of Lamaism executed on silk in gorgeous colours and gold thread. At the foot of this stood a long altar laden with offerings and all the splendid, glittering accessories of lamaistic worship. Behind the temple banner stood a richly carved sedan chair beneath the baldequin of which a shining statue of Maidari had been placed. The chair was flanked by two sixteen-foot statues representing Maidari's servants and assistants, Tsamba and Jobting. Opposite the main temple lay a building intersected by a wide porched portal, and this formed the entrance to the temple court. The archway was guarded by two statues representing warriors of grotesque appearance.

To east and west the temple court was bounded by two low buildings which contained the monastery's colossal library. In front of these buildings places of honour had been arranged with mats gleaming with the ancient authentic colours of the East, with embroidered silken cushions and back-rests hung with tinselled brocades that glittered in the sunlight.

And round the courtyard a whole nation of nomads was drawn up. High lamas, whose brocaded breasts glimmered between the folds of their red togas, sat in a half-circle in front of the main temple to the north. To the west sat the men and on the opposite side of the huge arena sat or stood their women, a compact mass of brilliant colour. Straight in front of the entrance building on the south side the monastery's orchestra was stationed with all its queer instruments. The sun shone upon the gilded roofs and enhanced the colour of the fantastic picture before us.

Again we heard the brutal sound of whip-lashes announcing the arrival of the earthly ruler, and through a forest of kneeling people who all touched the ground with their right hands the chieftains and their women advanced to their seats of honour, the men on the eastern side and the women on the western.

A shrill trumpet-call cut through the air, and thousands of faces were turned towards the temple entrance. A wave of religious fanaticism and excited anticipation stirred the multitude.

The *Tsam* dance was about to begin.

SLOWLY the central doors of the main temple opened. Instrument after instrument took up the long-drawn wail of the bassoons. The notes grew louder, the dull sound of the drums struck in, bells pealed their treble, until the air was filled with an unbelievable clamour which culminated in an appalling clash of cymbals. Then for a little while the orchestra was silent, and the din died away in waves. We felt as if our ear-drums had burst and clearly perceived the sense of the uncanny that had taken possession of the multitude.

Once more the clarionets struck up with melodiously plaintive notes. Six apparitions ran quickly out of the temple, slender white-clad figures with great grinning skulls upon their heads. Black lines painted on their tight-fitting costumes indicated the bones of the skeleton. These beings walked with shuffling, lingering steps, and their movements were slow and uncanny. These were the " rulers of the steppes of the dead ", " masters of the burial grounds ". Slowly they glided round the arena, swinging in circles ; each step they took was accompanied by a clash of cymbals from the orchestra. They bowed to the ground and stretched up towards the heavens, till at last they withdrew to one corner of the arena, where they remained throughout the whole ceremony, now sitting on their haunches, now perform-

43

ing little circular dances. All the time they were present and keeping a look out—like Death.

The music fell silent, and a new figure was carried in and placed in the middle of the arena. The figure rubbed its eyes, stretched its limbs and rose slowly with the help of a staff. It was an old, old man with long white hair and beard. Its big head, admirably carried out in papier mâché, had the features of a sly but kindly humourist. This was Tsagan Oborgon, "The White Old Man", the earth-spirit who is the protector of pastures and flocks and bestower of the fruits of labour. He is the most popular figure in the show, on his appearance a sigh of relief goes up from the multitude, and he is greeted with hearty cries of delight. He is conspicuous throughout the festival, now out in the arena, now among the populace. He is the only one who performs no ceremonial dance and the only one who speaks. Sometimes he jests with the spectators, and plays clownish pranks, sometimes he is the venerable old earth-spirit welcoming the dancing divinities from within the sanctuary among the people in the arena.

DRUMS and cymbals awakened eerie anticipations in the audience. The whole orchestra joined in with its mysterious and alien notes that rose and fell in intervals strange to our ears and threw us into amazement. But as the motif recurred and the ear learned to follow, it conveyed an impression of ritual sublimity.

A trumpet-call announced that new dancers were approaching. Out of the temple rushed the forerunners of the god of death, a flock of fantastic, terrifying figures. Half of them represent *Buga* (in Tibetan *Saba*), and the rest *Bukha*. The former wear big stags' heads between whose antlers *Cintamani*, the mystic jewel that grows in the depths of the universe, shines forth. Their long, wide cloaks are richly ornamented with brown, yellow and wine-red. The *Bukha* wear blue yak masks, and their wide cloaks are shot with blue, rose and yellow.

The dancers moved in small circles round the outer edges of the stage, swinging gleaming swords and clanking rings in their hands. The dance was wild but rhythmical ; the gay coloured cloaks, reaching to the feet, shimmered in the sunlight and whirled round their legs with a rustle of silk. The tempo was accelerated in time with the music, and the dance rose to a wild ecstasy under the influence of the furious rolling of drums and the crash of cymbals.

Group after group of fresh dancers streamed out from the temple on to the arena. All were clad in long, wide, many-coloured robes. Some wore masks representing terrifying fanciful beasts, others huge human heads of papier mâché with prominent bloodshot eyes and distorted features. In their hands they carried bloody human hearts. On their heads they wore crowns whose spikes were skulls.

These monstrous beings inspired the musicians to diabolical uproar. The tempo increased more and more, but the time was never missed ; simultaneously the step changed, simultaneously the motley maze of figures carried out its plastic arm movements. In a wide circle they followed one another's footsteps, swung round on one leg, and then took another long step forward in the gyrating movement. Weapons and symbolic emblems flashed in the air, and floating, swinging silken cloaks flamed in the sunshine.

The faces of the spectators were imprinted with terror. There was confusion on the women's side, and hysterical seizures spread like an epidemic. It was as though we were seeing hell's own devils, listening to the din of hell itself.

YET all know that the grisly masks do not represent evil spirits who are hostile to religion, but that in fact they are gods who have put on these terrifying appearances so as to be able more effectively to protect religion against its foes, the many powers of evil that bear malice against the faith and seek the perdition of mankind.

Now the dancers all stood motionless along the outer edge of the arena as though petrified by some magic formula. The music died away in a low lament. Only two shrill clarionets repeated a tragic motif, occasionally accompanied by a distant muttering of muffled drums. "The rulers of the steppe of death" glided out again from their corner to perform their thrilling, ghostly skeleton dance. A cloud passed over the sun like a menace, quenching all lustre in colour and metal and throwing the arena into heavy shadow. A deathlike silence prevailed. All eyes ranged over the circle of motionless terrifying figures and followed the swirling death masks in their midst.

And in brains aroused to ecstasy the image of Tsaghuradu, terrible and admonitory.

Tsaghuradu is "The Land of Confused Ideas", the region plunged in fog, in whose uncounted labyrinths the soul must wander after death unless in life it has assured itself of the right way. For seven times seven horror-haunted days and nights the soul released by death must seek until it find a new rebirth along some one of the innumerable paths leading to a higher or a lower plane, nearer to or farther from Nirvana.

In its wanderings the soul comes to glorious regions, but the paths of these lead to the land of the Passions, and wondrous and alluring beings draw it towards invisible abysses. But in Tsaghuradu the soul also encounters all the terrifying figures that are impersonated in the *Tsam* dance, the guardians of religion in their grisly guise. And he who flees at the sight of these monstrous beings falls into the abyss, but he who confidently draws near to them, remembering that behind the ferocious mask are concealed the gentle features of a god, is led on the right way.

"The guardians of religion" were once the demons of wild nature. But long ago they were converted by the higher gods to the true doctrine and are now its most active defenders against all the evil which they themselves once represented.

The *Tsam* dance and its symbolism has no place in the original Buddhism, which is the expression of the philosophy of a highly civilized country. It belongs to lamaism, the religion of the nomads and other peoples living close to nature, a product of primitive philosophy and of a still older mysticism.

At the time when the nomads of Central Asia were converted from Shamanism to Lamaism they evaded the greatest difficulties of such a change by announcing the simultaneous conversion of the demons of their fathers, and all the rest of the spirits of Shamanism. Thus they now live under the new religion, without disloyalty to the old. And faith and loyalty are qualities deeply rooted in the nomads.

Again the " rulers of the steppes of death " withdrew outside the circle of *dokshit*, who now turned towards the entrance gate of the temple from which a few lamas had just emerged. These carried a large brocade-covered wooden tray which they placed in the middle of the temple court. On the tray were a number of mysterious objects, and in the middle of it lay a fifteen-inch puppet of dough representing a human being. This was the human sacrifice *linga* surrounded by the mystical cult objects *sor*.

Again the full orchestra struck up, and its strains swelled to a deafening din which announced that the climax of the ceremony was at hand.

From the dim interior of the temple a colossal figure stepped suddenly into the sun, a devil of the pit whose appearance bore witness to the most ferocious savagery. A gasp of dread went up from the multitude at finding themselves face to face with Ikhe Khara himself, " The Great Black One ", lord of Sickness and Death and Prince of Hell. The enormous head represents an ox, and the long horns are surrounded by metal ornaments in the shape of gilded flames. A third eye of wisdom stares wildly out from the forehead, and long wild boars' teeth jut from the mouth. His garb is in gorgeous colours embroidered and decked with gems, for Ikhe Khara is the foremost of all *dokshit*, the strongest of the defenders of the faith.

He took up his position at the boundary between sun and shade. In his uplifted right hand he held an avenging sword, in his left the " magic club ", a staff gleaming with metal, at the end of which a skull was fixed.

With a majestically long-paced gait he strode across

47

the arena to throw himself at once into a maniacal dance. All the other *dokshit* followed his example and the scene became once more a picture of fantastic and ferocious savagery.

The spectators were seized by a hysterical ecstasy. Some wanted to rush forward and cast themselves down before the Mighty One, others tried to clutch at the passing dancers' swaying cloaks, and the police lamas had to keep on swinging their metal mounted staves in order to hold the crowd in check. The savagely threatening eyes of the dancers passed close under us where we stood on our pedestal, and a hysterical Mongol close beside us shrieked : " May the enemies of religion and all who hinder the spreading of the faith be turned to dust and ashes."

While the " Prince of Hell " was hewing the pseudo-human sacrifice asunder in the middle of the courtyard, all the *dokshit* were performing the wildest capers, slashing about them with their gleaming weapons and tossing their antlered heads as if they would hew in pieces all the demons of the world. The orchestra evoked a hellish din of discord, and those assembled in front of the temple chanted noisily :

" Trample upon and slay that enemy who has done evil to the threefold jewel ; separate him from the good that was his at birth. Tear him from his tutelary deity. Annihilate him and let the rain of sickness and poisoned wounds fall upon him, and let the sword dismember him."

The slaughter was ended, the foe vanquished. With long and solemn steps, the " Prince of Hell " strode back towards the temple entrance followed by all the *dokshit.* With plastic movements of their arms, gyrating like automata, they disappeared into the mysterious interior of the temple.

The orchestra was silent and the arena empty.

A couple of raven masks tried to approach the demolished sacrifice, but were at once chased off by hurrying " rulers of the steppes of the dead ".

The exorcizing ceremony of the *Tsam* dance was at an end.

"On the south side the monastery orchestra was stationed"

Photo Hummel

Tsagan Oborgon, "the white old man"

" One of the last to go up to Maidari was my little old
woman. . . ."

Photo Hummel

The twenty-four *Shanag*

[face p. 49

THE multitude breathed more freely.

They were still in the land of the living ; there was still time to mend their ways. The sunlight and the fresh wind from the steppe mitigated the horrors they had just lived through.

And from the great swaying cloth in front of the temple the image of the gentle Maidari, the Messiah of Lamaism who shall one day come to redeem the good among mankind, looked down. The wind gently stirred the heavy silken banner and breathed life into the embroidered features of the face. And the gospel of mercy came into their thoughts from Tushita, the heaven of happiness where dwells the Saviour, biding his time.

All now trooped up eagerly and thankfully to Maidari's altar to present their offerings. They threw themselves on the ground, turned their praying mills and told their beads. Gifts of all kinds lay heaped before the god, and the multitude stood packed, waiting to approach the altar.

Gradually the crowds of people dispersed over the huge area of the monastery, and the temple court itself was emptied. One of the last to go up to Maidari was my little old woman from Yolros Lama's courtyard. She doubted no longer but tripped along purposefully and full of confidence. She laid two bricks of tea and a handful of silver coins upon the altar, and as we left the place she still lay bowed in her painful attitude of prayer. Slowly she let herself down to touch the worn stones of the ground with her forehead, painfully she got up again. It tried her old limbs hard, but a strong faith gave her the power to do it.

After many years I still see her face before me. It is one of the memories on account of which I cannot endure the word " heathen " ; neither the word nor the import which some Christians attach to it.

THE rest of the day was fully occupied with work in our quarters. Lieberenz made test developments of a piece of each roll of film exposed, so as to be able to correct any errors of adjustment before the next day's new exposures. Hummel and I questioned Shirup

Geling about all the things, so puzzling to us, that we had seen that day. We had to try to understand the Mongolian view of it so as to reduce to order the jumble of new impressions while they were still fresh.

The *Tsam* dance is a magic ritual, and the dance of the masked lamas is, in the eyes of the faithful, a religious act and is accordingly viewed with reverence. During the continuance of the ceremony the dancing lamas are the gods whose appearance they have assumed. To be a spectator of the dance removes the burden of sin from the believer's heart.

The sinful and the negligent of religion realize at sight of the death masks their duties to the faith and its moral precepts. They are reminded of the transitoriness of life and the inevitable approach of death. Every life is hurrying towards death without the possibility of a moment's check, like water pouring from a steep cliff. With each departed day, with every vanished night we draw nearer to the end of this existence, and our life here is either the way downward towards a lower existence or upward towards a higher.

Superfluity of all kinds, of friends and fortune, power and riches in this existence does not help us in the next, for naked we must go hence, alone and with empty hands we must step into the next. Only the Doctrine can guide us, only the Faith is an enduring wealth.

BACK in our sleeping-bags that evening we were the victims of the most complete mental exhaustion. Our ear-drums re-echoed the clamour of unaccustomed sound. Confused images and overpowering impressions clung to our brains and made all idea of sleeping impossible.

So we went out on to the steppe. Sounds of laughter and song came from the town of tents. The old were singing of horses, and the young of horses and love. Grazing horses were scattered over the steppe ; we could hear the crunching sound of grass tufts being bitten off. Lusty young Mongols were roaming about on the love-hunt. They sang their declarations of love in soft tones, and now and then came the shy answer of a girlish voice to guide their steps.

The nomads were not brooding over the terrifying impressions of the day. For nature was undefiled, the steppe was fresh and they were living their life under the fiery stars of night.

CHAPTER VI

THE DANCE OF THE MAGICIANS

NEXT morning the sun was again shining over the temple city and its setting of far-flung steppe land.

But before the rising of the sun, before even the paling stars were quite wiped out in the changing colours of the dawn, one of the smallest temples of the cloister city had awoken to mysterious life. This building, which forms an easterly extension of the main temple, is built in purely Tibetan style. Its flat roof interrupts the gracefully sweeping curves of that of the main temple, and its massive rectilinear forms have the effect of a precautionary anchorage for the larger building's whimsical and airy lines.

Out of the dim interior of the side temple issued a hum of many sombre voices, sometimes accompanied by the hollow thud of drums. Now and then could be heard outbursts of snorts and groans, violent clattering of jingling metal and shrieks and turmoil as though from men fighting.

It sounded as if they were exorcizing an evil spirit, as if they were chaining a wild beast.

At the entrances to the temple lamas stood on guard to protect its intimate mysteries. Within, those versed in the scriptures and adept in magic formulas were busy incarnating the godhead itself in the *gurtums* for whom the monastery is widely renowned. It is by no means every monastery that can point to lamas with supernatural qualities, and the merit is not in the lamas but solely in the monastery that produces them.

EARLY that morning one of Darkhan Beile's whip-armed bodyguard came to our pavilion with a message that

his master desired a visit from us.   Taking with us our
finest *hadaks* of ceremony we accompanied the splendid-
looking guard to the prince's monastery residence which
lay outside the temple precincts.

Three spacious buildings bordered a large courtyard,
and the whole block was enclosed by a high wall.   In
the courtyard swarmed Mongols who had come to pay
their loyal respects to the ruler.   In the windows of
the side buildings we caught a glimpse of the curious
faces of the chieftain's wives and merry young princesses.

A single crack of our conductor's whip sufficed to
clear a way through the crowd.   Thus honoured we
stepped through the doorway in the middle building
and stood before Prince Darkhan Beile, administrator
of these steppes by appointment of the gods, earthly
protector of the monastery and the lamas and ruler over
all its women and pigtailed *harhungs*.

The slender, greying pigtail that the prince wore
indicated that he himself was of worldly condition.   The
showy peacocks' feathers in his cap proclaimed him one
of that condition's nobility, and the pale, red, carved
coral that fastened the plume to the top of his headgear announced that he was a chieftain of chieftains, a
prince of the first rank.   Over his long yellow silk
cloak he wore a short cobalt-blue jacket.

When we entered, the room was full of waiting Mongols, but at a sign from the ruler the bodyguard bellowed
a word of command that sent the crowd falling over
each other to the door, and we were left alone with the
prince and his grim guards.   With dignity he motioned
us to take the seats of honour on his right.   The guards
poured out tea into silver-mounted birchwood cups, and
we were treated with all the courtesy and friendliness
due to honoured guests.

Then we showed our own good breeding by enquiring
after the state of his grazing grounds, his own health,
the condition of his flocks and herds, and whether he
sat securely on the high seat of his illustrious position.

And all was well.

We presented our *hadaks* with the wish that the causes
of his prosperity might endure for ever.   He declared

his confidence that we were good men since we were the guests of Yolros Lama himself, and he had summoned us because of the responsibility he felt for our persons during the time we stayed in his domains.

He exhorted us to take thought for our safety that day and to keep out of the way when the *gurtums*, possessed by terrible gods, were let loose. We had nothing to fear from the lamas of the monastery or from his nomads, but a possessed *gurtum* was not a human being but was the god himself incarnate in a chosen human body. No man could be responsible for the actions of a possessed *gurtum*, since during his ecstasy he was a god. A *gurtum* carried the god's dangerous weapons, and it might happen that the god's will was to make away with an objectionable person.

We were strangers here and acknowledged gods who were unknown on the steppes, and the sight of us might call forth the infuriated *gurtum's* lust for vengeance. No Mongol could protect us against *gurtums*, for the people of the steppes could not set themselves against the gods of the steppes.

We reassured the kindly old prince by a diplomatic promise to be prudent, and he showed his relief by at once turning the conversation to gayer matters.

The lower halves of the windows had all the time been covered with faces belonging to the Mongols who had been driven out on our arrival. Their noses were tightly pressed against the panes and their eyes bulging with eagerness to miss nothing that was going on in the room. As soon as they saw the first smile upon the prince's lips they began to steal noiselessly back into the room. Soon it was once more packed with people who permitted themselves to join noisily in their ruler's gaiety and threw themselves eagerly into the conversation.

And it was quite the thing to do. The grim guards doubled up with laughter and were on the best of terms with them all. And the prince was a kindly old grandfather who knew each one of his dependents and shared their joys and sorrows.

After half an hour we too knew them. Namserai's

Ted

Steve Sheese

317-0659

4-24-04

called
4/6/04

call
2:35 p.m.

wife had had a baby after eight years of childless marriage. Bimba's camp had been enlarged by the addition
of a new tent, and Yetom's herd of cattle had been
attacked by wolves.

Lieberenz enticed one of the guards out to be photographed, and the man good-humouredly posed for him
against a sunlit wall with his whip, stern expression
and all. He got a silver dollar for his pains. First he
stared wonderingly at the bright coin in his hand, then
suddenly ran in to the chieftain and held out the coin
while he told how he had got it. The prince smiled
and nodded and returned the coin to the guard. And
in deep gratitude for this mark of favour, the man bent
his knee three times before his lord, each time uttering
his acknowledgements as he touched with his forehead
the hem of the prince's cloak.

Lieberenz got the photograph he wanted and many
more, but he got no other thanks. For the fact that
the silver coin became the Mongol's possession did not
depend on Lieberenz but on the prince's grace.

We wanted to photograph the prince himself, but he
suggested that we should rather make pictures of pretty
young women than of an ugly old man like him. So
he conducted us to the two side buildings inhabited
by the women of the family, and we found them all
busily engaged in repairing the dancing dresses which
had been torn in the wild ceremonies of the day before.
The making and keeping in repair of these sacred dresses
is a privilege belonging to the noblest women of the
land.

From the monastery came the booming of a gong
announcing that the new day's ceremonies were about
to begin, and we hastened to take our places in the
temple courtyard.

Again thousands of Mongols gathered to take part in
the spectacle for instruction in the Doctrine, again the
monastery resounded with the appalling din of the
lama orchestra, and the gods in frightful guise once
more trod out their dance upon the earth.

The climax of the day, however, was a new scene

55

whose yearly repetition is a reminder of the victory of Buddhism over the ancient magic.

The orchestra played subdued melodious music, and out of the temple glided pair after pair of decorative figures. They were clothed in long black silken capes embroidered with yellow symbolical designs. They wore no masks but had broad-brimmed hats on their heads from which long black silken fringes hung down and obscured their faces. These black hats were adorned on top with death's heads mounted in a shining aureole of gilded metal and this served at the same time for the fastening of a fan-shaped ornament of long pea-cocks' feathers which shimmered in the sunlight and swayed with every movement of the dancers.

These are the twenty-four *shanag*, magicians of the fellowship of the black hat, and the origin of the panto-mime they perform is explained by a historic legend.

In the ninth century Langdarma ruled over Tibet. He was a bad king, a fierce opponent of the new religion, and he did all he could to prevent the true doctrine from spreading among the people. He himself was a prominent magician and defender of " the black doctrine "

Langdarma had the Buddhist monastery burned, and his soldiers scoured the land to cut down the adherents of the true doctrine. However, a Buddhist ascetic, Pal-dorje, determined to free the land from this tyranny, and disguised in a magician's black robe he set out on the journey to Lhassa where Langdarma dwelt. He rode a white pony but just before his arrival at the city he poured black charcoal dust over the animal so that it became black.

Black magicians were always welcomed by Langdarma, and Pal-dorje received permission to perform a magic dance in front of the king. When, under the spell of the dance, he came near to the disguised dancer, Pal-dorje drew from his wide sleeves a bow and a poisoned arrow and shot the king dead.

During the tumult that arose the lama succeeded in escaping on his horse. He was followed by furious soldiers but as he crossed the river that ran past the city he pulled off his black cloak and the water cleaned the horse of charcoal dust. Up on to the other bank of the river stepped a yellow Buddhist lama riding on a white horse. Pal-dorje was never captured, for the soldiers were looking for a black-cloaked magician on a black horse. Thus Pal-dorje took vengeance on the black doctrine and in memory of this deed the greatest festival of the year in the whole lamaistic world is celebrated with a performance of the " dance of the black hats ".

SHANAG spread themselves over the whole arena and went through certain ceremonial plastic movements with their arms. Now they moved round in a ring dance, now grouped themselves about the leading dancer who was even more gorgeously arrayed than the rest. Then once more they formed themselves into a statuesque group preparatory to plunging into a wild whirling dance. The tempo of the dance followed that of the orchestra and the whole thing gave a fantastic impression of freakish rhythms, queer compositions of form and sombre harmonies of colour.

All at once the orchestra grew quiet and the dancers stiffened into statuesque attitudes. Shirup Geling whispered agitatedly that now was the time for us to disappear.

The piercing howl of a wild animal from the northeast corner of the temple courtyard made all the sitting Mongols start to their feet. The howl pierced through bone and marrow and lacerated our already overwrought nerves. Long afterwards the sound echoed among the temple buildings, and there were signs of panic in the densely packed courtyard.

We were pushed towards the narrow gateways at the southern side of the courtyard, we were hustled and jostled and we ourselves hustled and jostled to save our costly instruments from destruction.

At more frequent intervals those dreadful sounds kept breaking out behind us, and they came nearer and nearer like the horrible torments of a nightmare. An arrow whistled over our heads but disappeared into the dazzling rays of the sun. We were mauled and battered by the raging breakers of the human sea until at last we landed outside the gates in the great open place where the flood of humanity had more room to spread.

We ought now hastily to have sought our quarters, but how was that possible when the mystery was approaching and we had not yet seen it? We had lost Shirup Geling, who was so solicitous for our welfare, in the crowd. We dragged one another up on to the flat roof of a lama's dwelling and sought shelter behind its low chimney. A couple of hundred yards from us lay the gates of the temple yard continuously disgorging hysterical mobs of people. Thence too would the mystery come. The film apparatus was ready on top of the chimney.

The pressure at the gates abated. The place in front of us was packed with people, a motley, moving mass. The eyes of all were turned on the temple gates in intense expectation. No one had thoughts or eyes for us up on the roof.

Some police lamas appeared in the gateway carrying heavy metal mounted staves, and Lieberenz began to turn the handle of his apparatus.

And the Mystery came.

A pair of grotesque apparitions rushed out of the temple closely surrounded by red-robed lamas. On their heads were shining helmets and from their backs fluttered long, many-coloured streamers. In their hands they held bows, arrows, swords and other weapons. Their faces expressed complete madness. Their eyes bulged, bloodshot and staring, their cheeks were swollen and livid, and white froth foamed from their slack drooping mouths. The creatures reeled as if drunk. From time to time they crumpled up and would have fallen to the ground had not the attendant lamas held them upright.

The air was rent by a hideous roaring, and with the strength and agility of wild beasts the two possessed creatures rushed with drawn swords towards some imaginary prey in the fleeing panic-stricken crowd. Countless people were wounded and red blood flowed.

Everyone regarded the two *gurtums* with reverence,

for in their present condition they were not human lamas bearing the dress and symbolic weapons of Damchan. No, they were possessed by Damchan who had changed their appearance to his own and the deeds they performed and the words they uttered were those of the god himself. All true believers, therefore, were overcome by the greatness of the moment, filled with awe at the sight of the god who had come so close to them, and eager to catch the words that fell from his lips.

Damchan is one of Tabun Khan, " the five kings " who have given a sacred and eternal promise to protect religion and who are the lords of all magicians and the wisest of all soothsayers.

Lieberenz had had enough, but not so Hummel. He wanted to see the two *gurtums* at close range so as to be able to judge whether the inhuman expression of their bloodshot eyes could be due to the consumption of a colossal quantity of alcohol. We succeeded in slipping down among the crowd without being noticed and pushed our way forward into the proximity of the possessed. The doctor's opinion was that the swelling and alteration of their faces could not have been caused by alcohol but must be the extraordinary result of a peculiar kind of hysterical ecstasy.[1]

We wanted to come into contact with the possessed lamas when they returned to their senses, but it was explained to us that this was not possible for several days since the men lay in a lifeless trance after the terrific spiritual stress of the day.

THE same afternoon we received two notable visitors in our pavilion.

A middle-aged man presented himself as the com-

---

[1] In the year 1897 there came to St. Petersburg a lama who declared that when in a state of ecstasy he was possessed of Damchan, and through him able to answer questions about the future. During his ecstasy he was examined by doctors and other men of science. They witnessed how his face and expression were transformed. His head swelled to such a degree that his helmet, which in a normal state had been too large, could not be removed.

mander of the force combating the brigands of this district.

The man looked hearty and well-fed, and his decayed yellow teeth betrayed the fact that he had forsaken the simple meat diet of his forefathers for Chinese kickshaws. His dress consisted of some faded remnants of a Chinese officer's uniform completed by a green Mongol cap with a red tassel and a pair of embroidered Mongolian riding-boots.

Damding Surong was his name, and it was a name known and feared on the steppe along the long wall from Ta-t'ung Fu to Hsi-Pao t'ou, for Damding Surong had himself been a harrying robber chief before he changed over to become an avenging fighter against bandits. He had made wise dispositions for the practice of his new calling, for when he himself was converted into a guardian of society he took the boldest and most dreaded of his robber comrades into service in his new army.

No one knew whence Damding Surong had originally come, but he did not belong to the Mongols of these parts. Now he and his riffraff band bore an honourable and decent reputation along the caravan routes on which the caravans from Kwei-hua-chen and Hsi-Pao t'ou maintain connection with the Central Asiatic markets.

Damding Surong had received his appointment as chief of the robber fighters from the Chinese authorities who for many years had been trying to get the better of him, and he received a handsome allowance for himself and his band from a coalition of the caravan owners whose consignments he had earlier plundered. The ex-robbers now led the secure life of pensioners and enjoyed a well-earned ease after the hazardous exploits of their manhood's years.

Still it was constantly happening that Damding Surong and his men were obliged to take the field, for new bands of robbers often appeared along the boundary and tried to carry on his old trade. But none had yet been able to hold his own against him and to this day his name was a terror on the steppe to all dishonest folk, just as it had formerly been to honest ones.

Consorts of the Chief and curious Princesses

Photo Zimmerman

Gurtum

Leave taking from Lamas and Chiefs at Bater Halak Sume

[face p. 61

Damding Surong was an entertaining visitor, full of stories and sketches of both the honest and the dishonest periods of his career. And he was avid of all the new knowledge we could impart to him, for a wise leader of men must be better informed in every sphere than his people. And Damding Surong was a wise chief.

He soon perceived the importance of taking anthropometric measurements—and of the silver dollar we offered for every victim he procured for us. And before he left, after our enjoyable evening together, he swore by all his gods that his people should be placed at Hummel's disposal next day.

OUR other visitor, Barun Kung, was a very young and bashful chief who had not yet learnt to take his power and dignity as a matter of course. Only two months earlier he had succeeded his stern father, and the young chief's conduct and deportment were still under the supervision of one of the tutors appointed by the deceased.

Twenty-one burgeoning springs had Barun Kung lived through, for he was born in the auspicious year of the " Firehorse " (1907), but none like this one. For among the Mongols too the twenty-first spring is the spring of springs, and Barun Kung's chief interest in this festive gathering of relatives and friends was the choosing of her whom he would soon carry as his wife to his new chief-tent on the westward steppe.

A strict Mongolian upbringing had made of him a lithe and elegant cavalier. The hunter's life and the hardships of long journeys had braced his young muscles, and the steppe's Spartan diet of half-raw bloody meat had whitened his strong teeth. Fresh winds and bright sunshine had given to his young face a splendid colouring of bronze and red. He was a true son of the steppe, a part of its hard life, early innured to difficulties and reverses.

This was his first public appearance in a chieftain's garb, and he took a shy, uneasy pleasure in his own elegance. He had not yet acquired the arrogant assurance of air and movement which is so much admired and sought after among the Mongols. He was still only a chieftain's gallant son with all the qualities of chieftain-ship still untried.

A long cloak of sky-blue, lustreless silk was fastened round his powerful shoulders and slender figure. Gold and silver brocade edged and ornamented the blue. Over the cloak hung a short armless jacket the wine-red colour of which deepened and paled in sun and shadow like wine in a glass. The gay, clear colours of the silk were reflected in one another, and a lovely play of chang-ing colour followed the man's movements.

The slenderness of his waist was emphasized by a tightly drawn sash twelve inches wide, to which his many richly chased and heavy sword-slings were attached. The long silver-mounted knives were stuck through the sash at the back from left to right, so that he could draw their keen blades from the handsome silver sheaths with a sharp pull of the right hand.

His pigtail was full and glossy black and so long that it was necessary on practical grounds to thread it twice through the sash. The riding-boots that appeared under his cloak were of black velvet with thick white felt soles which accommodated themselves flexibly to the young man's lithe gliding gait.

In Mongolian eyes Barun Kung was a fairy-tale prince of wondrous beauty. I had myself noticed with what interest and admiration the eyes of the little princesses in Darkhan Beile Kung's suite followed him, when with shy dignity he advanced through the yielding crowds in the temple court to take for the first time a chieftain's seat on the right of his king.

The evening passed quickly, and we found much to talk about to one another, much to ask and much to tell. He displayed all the impetuosity of youth in a violent but short-lived interest in all the unaccustomed things we had to show and all the new things we had to tell him. We sat long by the fire in Mongol fashion with fragrant tea and smoking pipes. The firelight played in the gay colours of his dress, flashed on his coral and turquoise studded bracelets, and even threw shadows and faint suggestions of colour on my poor khaki.

We talked of hunting expeditions and long journeys, and of how strange it was that his eyes should be black and mine blue. Later we passed on to speaking of his birthplace and of my native land, of manners and customs there and here. Then he wanted to know how a man of my people greeted a kinsman and friend.

Over that evening's dying fire we clasped hands with a firm grip, for his fists had been trained in the same school as mine. It felt fine and confidence-inspiring, and we smiled at one another. The glow lit up his strong teeth, but was too faint to let me see the colour of his eyes.

CHAPTER VII

ZAYAGAN

EARLY in the forenoon of the third day of the festival Damding Surong came in to say that a party of his soldiers had come to be examined and measured by the doctor. They were now waiting by the brook a little beyond the monastery. Hummel and I at once packed up our instruments so as to seize the proffered opportunity, and Damding Surong pointed out that it would save trouble to bring along at the same time the silver dollars we had spoken of the night before.

It was a band of wild blades that awaited us by the brook, noisy hard-swearing fellows with scarred and weather-bitten faces. Most of them had some scrap of Chinese uniform, one a cap, another a pair of trousers. Others had tunics almost devoid of buttons. Only a few were in possession of all three items. What was missing was filled in with motley bits of Mongolian clothing, and every man of them was hung with heavy silver bracelets and rings set with coral and turquoise.

The band was composed of the most unsettled elements of various races, and the types of features were as anomalous as the costumes. Many were pronounced types of the man of mixed race attached to no community.

Damding Surong now announced in a loud voice that we were good men with no evil intentions, as was proved by the favour and protection which Yolros Lama himself had extended to us. He followed this up with a vernacular explanation of the examination which they were now to undergo, and the one-time brigands listened with childlike submissiveness to their commander. They stood round-eyed and open-mouthed, nodded and said: "*Tsa, tsa,*" not in token that they themselves under-

64

stood but in confidence in the understanding of their chief. What he said must be right.

But when we set up our instruments, a certain uneasiness nevertheless pervaded the group, and when Damding Surong called out the first, the fellow's eyes were full of panic.

It was a difficult and tedious job taking the required measurements. Damding Surong chattered and swore to encourage the man under operation at the moment. And those who had been through it helped us by scoffing at their timorous successors, saying that old hardened warriors ought not to be scared at a little thing like that.

In this manner the expedition made its first twenty-four anthropometric measurements. And Damding was the richer by twenty-four silver dollars. And twenty-four is a good number, at least so Damding Surong said when we finally wanted to measure his own interesting cranium.

The sound of the orchestra from the cloister city announced that the day's religious festival had begun.

Out from the enclosure round the main temple filed a festive procession preceded by an orchestra whose sixteen-foot bassoons rested on the shoulders of novices walking in front.

In the midst of the procession the richly decorated and canopied palanquin that concealed the gilt and jewelled bronze figure of Maidari was borne by lamas of high rank. From the palanquin blessing was conveyed to the multitude by means of long, red silken cords, and the ends of these were held by lamas who in a wide circle attended the god's progress through the thronging thousands of worshippers.

To right and left of Maidari were carried the colossal statues of the god's coadjutors Tsamba and Jobting. Between the orchestra in the van and the litters marched all the lamas who had taken part in the *Tsam* dance, wearing their grotesque, enormous masks and gorgeous dresses. They took slow dancing steps, swung round on their heels in swift pirouettes and whirled weapons and symbolic emblems in the air. The antlers crowning

65

the colossal masks and their tall metallic embellishments rose high above the forest of human heads.

The spectators crowded closely about the moving column. The women's heavy head-dresses, set with blue and red stones, framing their red-brown faces like Macedonian silver helmets, glittered in the sun. From the men's caps fluttered iridescent peacocks' feathers and long silk ribbons, red tassels or grey squirrels' tails.

Slowly pacing, the procession wound with its long train in a vast circle round the monastery from left to right, keeping the temple sanctuaries always on its right. At each of the cardinal points a halt was made, and the lamas read long prayers. Further benediction was dispensed from Maidari's palanquin by two high lamas who with long staves touched the heads of the eagerly approaching people.

After the thousand yards' progress round the monastery the gods and the officiating lamas disappeared into the temple. Meanwhile the mass of people was shepherded by the police lamas out into the large field in front, where they ranged themselves in two compact columns with their eyes all turned towards the temple. The queues of people grew so long as to extend southward far out on to the open steppe. It was a whole population drawn up here with its gaze unremittingly turned towards the sanctuary. All wished to partake in the final ceremony of the festival, the rite which should cleanse them from sin and deliver them from misery. Our own Mongols too had fought their way to places in the ranks.

The lamas now assembled in front of the temple round a large dragon-like object. Their chanting grew in strength and was accelerated in time till gradually it passed into wild fanatical howling.

At once the whole of the Mongols ranged in the queues sat down on the ground and began praying and beseeching. The dragon-like paper object was set alight, and two young lamas ran down one of the rows of people carrying the blazing thing between them high over the people's heads and then continued along the squatting people in the other long row. All who have had the burning dragon over their heads are cleansed, for all evil is consumed and annihilated by the flames.

Then the dragon's glowing skeleton was carried far out on to the steppe, and while the lamas shouted their incantations and the people joined in with frightful threats, the detested object was flung upon the ground where it was soon utterly destroyed by kicking, trampling feet.

The festival of Maidari was over.

The moment was one of triumphant joy, for all that had weighed upon the conscience had been lifted from it, and all were pure and good as newborn babes. Singing, hallooing and in rollicking spirits the nomads turned their backs upon the gloomy monastery and ran down to their airy tents. And soon they were busy breaking camp and loading the caravan animals, and by the time the sun next rose they would all be on the way to the isolated life of their scattered dwelling-places.

The lamas, exhausted after three days of intensive exertion, quickly dispersed across the vast precincts of the cloister city to disappear into the small white dwellings.

And the temple lay in blessed silence.

BARUN KUNG came to say good-bye and wish us a fortunate journey. He was radiant with happiness for he had found his princess. He confided in me who she was, and it was the very flower of the steppe whom I would have chosen had I been a Mongol prince.

The same evening he sat his horse proudly, directing the breaking of camp. It was as though the most important conquest of his life had at once transformed him into a full-fledged chieftain.

We went with him a part of the way, but scarcely had his heavily laden caravan began its march before, with a shout, he sent his horse flying towards the setting sun. And with its last ray his galloping silhouette vanished on the way to the white tent of happiness over which " the western banner " floated.

FOR us too it was time to break camp.

But before we left the monastery we wished in some

way to show our profound gratitude to the man whose
confidence and friendly understanding we had entirely
to thank for the success of our visit to the temple festival.
We consulted Shirup Geling as to how we might best
give pleasure to the lonely old *hutuktu*, and the lama
went to apprise him of our purpose.

On his return he declared gravely that we ought to
carry the feelings of gratitude which we entertained
towards Yolros Lama into the presence of the gods in
the main temple, for thus we should best please the
hutuktu.

SHIRUP GELING conducted us through the empty lanes
of the cloister city into the temple court lately so full
of turmoil, now so silent and deserted. And with a
feeling of devotion far stronger than our curiosity we
went up towards the great sanctuary.

The temple's mysterious interior lay in darkness.
Only at the furthest end warm lights burned in the
lamps of tall silver candelabra. From the invisible roof
deep-coloured temple banners hung.

With slow and lingering steps we went through a space
of unsuspected dimensions along aisles of lacquer-red
columns, forward to the distant gleam of light.

Then we stepped into the narrow circle of light
and found ourselves face to face with the cloister's
Holy of Holies, in the presence of great gods—images
that symbolize the noblest conceptions of an ancient
faith.

The undying flames from the candelabra swept hither
and thither at regular intervals as if following the breathing of the gods. They shone warmly over Gautama
Buddha's exalted features and the mild countenance of
the coming Messiah. They cast a transfigured light
upon the gilded limbs, and the multitude of encrusted
gems radiated life.

Shirup Geling lay at the feet of the gods sunk in
humble supplication, and all about us was unfathomable
darkness.

On the altar we laid two handfuls of silver coins and
covered them with a pale blue *hadak* of thanksgiving.

LATER we paid farewell visits to the principal lamas of
the monastery and gave them some small presents of
knives and photographs as parting gifts and tokens of
gratitude. Finally we were going to take leave of the
Holy One who had been our host, but we were informed
that Yolros Lama could not receive us, since he was
now sunk in profound meditation.

Everything was packed and ready for an early start
next morning, and the camels had been brought in from
the steppe. We ourselves were in splendid spirits.
Shirup Geling was sitting telling us about his youthful
student days in distant Lhasa, of his devotion to Yolros
Lama and of the happiness it had brought him to live
for so many years in the *hutuktu's* near neighbourhood.

A lama came to fetch our Mongolian attendant Tsereat.
Yolros Lama desired to speak to him.

Shirup Geling told of the country in the west, of the
monasteries we should pass on our way and of the
High Lamas and other noble men he himself had met
more than thirty years ago. And it grew late and time
to think of sleeping.

Suddenly Tsereat appeared in the doorway and signed
to me to come out. The young Mongol was beaming
with happiness, for he had spent long hours alone with
Yolros Lama who had questioned him about much and
informed him about more. And the *hutuktu* had blessed
him. Round Tsereat's neck hung a new amulet, and
in his hands he held two small objects which he regarded
with deep reverence. The two objects were a gift to
me, and Yolros Lama had said that it might be that
one day they might bring me help. But until such
need should arise they were to be entrusted to Tsereat's
keeping.

Now the *hutuktu* wished to see me before our departure,
and Tsereat brought me to his holy dwelling.

Silently we passed in at the door. It was almost dark
in the room ; only a little naked flame lit up the immediate surroundings of the " holy chair ". The flickering gleam deepened and blackened the furrows in the
hutuktu's ascetic face and shone on the thin, intelligent

hands that rested among some sheets of gilded rice-paper.

The air was thick with smoke that rose from the two wide bowls on the altar in front of the Holy One. This smoke was unfamiliar to me, not suffocating but stimulating, and clean as the scent of an unknown mountain flower. From time to time it rose like a veil of light mist over a meadow and set a space of unreality between the divinity and me. The outlines of the roof were lost in drifting clouds of smoke.

A faint voice that seemed to come from far away bade me come nearer.

Grave eyes regarded me ; a magnetic unfathomable gaze drew me to itself.

" You are here to bid me farewell. I see your path. Your course lies westward."

Yolros Lama drew from his sleeve a folded blue silk cloth and spread it out before him. In the cloth lay a silver box out of which he emptied three vertebræ. He sat with closed eyes muttering some formula. Then he took the three pieces of bone between the palms of his hands and carried them to his forehead while he continued to pray.

Suddenly he let the vertebræ fall on the cloth as one throws dice. This was thrice repeated. All the time he muttered prayers, and after each throw he narrowly observed the position, prone or erect, of the bones and their distance from each other.

" Zayagan," he said. " I see your road. You were born in the year of the sacred Fire Ape (1896). The Fire Hare (1927) the Earth Dragon (1928), and the Iron Snake (1929) are propitious to you. Desire arises through life like the eastern sun. If your desire be lively it shall attain its goal. And new desire shall arise like the rising of the sun.

" Your way lies to the west, like the sun of Life. I see your path. A great *hutuktu* awaits your coming, and it is the will of the gods that you shall meet." He nodded slowly. " Go. *Zayagan* lies before you."

Once more the *hutuktu* sank deep in meditation. He sat with unseeing eyes and relaxed lineaments, as in a trance.

Tsereat rose silently from his crouching position and touched my arm.

In the temple court the freshness of the dark summer night received us. The monastery slept. Only the little bells at the corners of the temple roof tinkled out the quiet melody of a steppe night, and above the roof we were aware of a pale gleam of stars. The air was full of a sense of good fortune, and Tsereat's young face was lit with joy.

"*Zayagan*," he whispered, "that is the great good fortune; that is the luck of the road."

CHAPTER VIII

SUIDOR DISAPPEARS FROM THE CAMP

SOON after our return from the Maidari festival at Bater Halak Sume the expedition left the assembly camp at Hojertai-gol where we had now spent two whole months in preparations of all kinds for the great start.

Our caravan consisted of two hundred and eighty-nine heavily laden camels when on Friday the twenty-second of July we were ready to set out. This country we were to traverse was unknown to the caravan people, and our camels were unused to carrying loads, all of which gave ground for anxiety.

And by the time we reached the monastery of Baying Shandai Sume we had been on the march thirty days and had spent the same number in resting.

Unfortunately our expedition had been obliged to start its long caravan journey in the month of July and moreover, on account of the work of the scientists, to travel by daylight and under the most merciless desert sun. To remedy this disadvantage the expedition's camels had as far as possible been recruited among young animals which had not before been used for caravan service and had not been severely tried during the previous winter. But these young untried animals were so untrained and unaccustomed to carrying heavy loads that they soon lost condition. Work under the grilling sun and in the heavy sand soon worked a melancholy change in the caravan which had looked so gallant at the start, and the camels were already in need of rest.

The Bactrian camel, which is used in the Gobi Desert, works only in winter and rests in summer, when it lays up new stores of strength to resist the hardships of the next winter. The conception one obtains from novels

[*face p.* 72

The Mongolian Monastery of Baying Shandai Sume

about deserts and tourist camels, that the " ship of the desert " belongs among palm trees in tropical heat, is particularly misleading in regard to the two-humped Bactrian camel, the animal upon which one depends for travelling in the Mongolian deserts. The difference between *Camelus dromedarius*, the single-humped camel, and *Camelus Bactrianus*, the two-humped camel, is so fundamental that, as regards their habit of life and performance, they are no more to be confused than a team of Arctic dogs and a pack of Australian dingos.

After a summer's rest the Bactrian camel works admirably throughout the whole winter. Its thick winter coat protects it against the severe Central Asiatic cold, and the beast can travel for weeks through completely sterile regions, utilizing the stored nutriment of its humps, and is satisfied with the moisture it can obtain from the snow on the ground.

Their capacity for work in the winter accordingly depends entirely upon the care taken of them in the summer. In summer they shed their coats and are susceptible to chills and other ailments. So as to hasten the shedding of the old coat and the growth of the new they are taken to places where certain chemicals are present in the soil. When the hot weather arrives the new coat should have been grown, for the camels are then taken up to the mountain slopes where the climate is temperate. Moreover, the animals are thus delivered from the swarms of gadflies and other even more dangerous insects which appear in such multitudes that they could kill the toughest of camels.

During the early months of summer the camels recover from the privations they have suffered in the winter, but it is only in the latter part of the summer, after the rainy season has coaxed forth a maximum of the scanty Mongolian vegetation, that the camels' humps stand up again, as they accumulate stores of nutriment for the coming winter.

As the great expedition could not lie idle, on account of the camels, waiting for the winter, it was arranged at Baying Shandai Sume that the caravan should be divided into four columns. The first and largest, the " advance column ", under Larson's guidance, consisted of all the camels carrying such of the provisions and equipment as would not be required during the next few months. This column, which contained a hundred and fifteen animals, was to proceed as directly and easily as possible to Etsin-gol unencumbered by the troublesome scientists. The " scientific column " started from Baying Shandai Sume eight days later than the advance column and consisted of sixty-seven camels, and of this I was caravan leader. In addition, two independent columns of twenty-six and fifteen camels respectively were to be formed under the leadership of Norin and Yüan.

Before the start there had been eager discussion of the relative merits of different methods of travel, but since the caravan men were as inexperienced as Larson and I in marching under these special conditions and since our respective views were widely different, we finally agreed that each caravan leader should pursue his own tactics.

On September 8th the " scientific " column arrived at Khara Jag Hutuk. The water in the well was strongly alkaline and almost unfit to drink, and our only consolation lay in finding abundant evidence that the place had once, before the great drying-up period, been a blessed oasis in the pitiless desert. In its clear waters man and beast had sought and found refreshment, and in the shade of its blossoming tamarisks travellers from afar had rested and gathered fresh courage to penetrate further into the dismal and sterile regions.

Khara Jag signifies " the dead ", literally " the black tamarisks ", and the name was indicative of the place. Around the camp stood a whole forest of dead and dying tamarisks which had long since lost their pristine vitality and were no longer capable of putting forth their wealth of violet blossoms. Round the salt well we found the crumbled ruins of buildings long ago abandoned.

At the camel inspection that evening it appeared that one of our camels was missing, and all the Mongols and Chinese were sent into the tamarisk thickets to search for it. I myself rode round the whole tamarisk area to ascertain whether any camel tracks led out into the

74

surrounding sea of sand. The tamarisk belt extended for a mile or so from east to west, but was only a few hundred yards in width. Round the whole area the surface of the sand lay undisturbed ; only the wind had fashioned it. No living creature during the last twenty-four hours had ventured forth from the tamarisk grove out into the desert.

When I got back to camp it was night, and the Chinese and Mongolian searchers had already returned without having found the vanished camel. It was hopeless to continue the search in the dense darkness, and since the animal must clearly be in the tamarisk thickets I turned in, after having first given the camel keepers a good dressing down for their lack of vigilance which had given us so much extra work during the sorely needed resting-time.

When at four o'clock next morning I appeared in the camel drivers' tent to give orders for renewed efforts, I found a great commotion there. Two of the Mongols had on the evening before been reviling the two Chinese boys who had been on watch on the disastrous day, for having, by their negligence, kept us all stuck in a place where there was neither grazing for the camels nor water for any of us. And the result had been that the younger of the two sinners, in his shame and despair, had gone out alone into the darkness to try to find the camel. He had not yet come back and had taken with him neither water nor food, and since he had gone out before the evening meal and had been out on guard duty all day he must by now have been without food for a whole twenty-four hours.

All available hands were immediately sent out in search for the runaway camel and the lost little Chinaman. It was now daylight, and the area was so limited that it should not take long to explore it. While we were searching, however, the sun rose, and with it came the merciless heat. And he who tried to refresh himself by drinking only grew yet thirstier from the alkaline water.

The Mongols came back at eight o'clock bringing in the runaway camel. They had not seen the little Chinaman. It was highly perilous for both man and

75

beast to be compelled to prolong our stay at this inhospitable place, but we must find the lost man before we could go on.

The returned caravan men declared positively that the boy could not be in the tamarisk thickets. They supposed that he had deserted from shame and fear of the consequences of his negligence. But I did not believe that Suidor was a deserter—where, after all, could he have deserted to ?—and Bato and I set out on the caravan's best camels.

We had picked up Suidor from a solitary Mongol tent at one of the caravan's earliest camping places. He had been employed for several years as herdsman by the austere inhabitants of the tent at an annual wage of five dollars, but having fallen in with our caravan people he had suddenly been seized with the lust to travel. He proved trustworthy and smart at his work, though slow in his mental processes, and we had engaged him on the ground that he knew both Chinese and Mongolian and because he always looked friendly and cheerful. He himself believed that he was twenty-five years old, but he was probably barely twenty.

After having searched the outer edges of the tamarisks for half an hour we found the track of a man who had passed the most northerly bush and then gone on among the sand hills. Hour after hour we followed that solitary trail that wandered at random in a north-westerly direction, perpetually choosing the highest sand hills. We had long left the last tamarisk behind us, the midday sun burned, and the everlasting white sand reflected its beams and tormented our eyes.

Suddenly the trail turned in a westerly direction and continued in aimless curves, always up towards the largest sand waves. Our camels were so exhausted by now that we had to drag them after us. We were often obliged to stop while I made the notes which were to guide us back to the camp.

At noon we halted for a consultation. We could not go on in this way any longer. Both the camels and ourselves were completely exhausted with struggling forward in the soft sand of the unending dunes, and one of our water flasks was already empty. It was well-nigh impossible to get the camels going again after the halt ; every step was accompanied by their plaintive scream—but we must go on.

The trail now took a southerly direction, and on the top of a turret-shaped dune we found the impression of a human being who had thrown himself down on the sand. A tired and despairing man had rested here not long since, here he had lashed the sand with his camel whip, and a few yards further on he had thrown away his boots.

Then we held another consultation. We persuaded one another that we were not at all tired, and since the trail was clearly that of an exhausted man, we must surely be able quickly to overtake him.

I was just collating my observations so as to work out the quickest way back to the camp when suddenly a gust of wind tore the paper with my notes out of my hand. Bato dashed off after the little scrap of paper which to us in that place and in that situation was a document of such importance, but he came back dejected with his errand unperformed. The puff of wind was followed by a persistent gale that set the light sand in motion. The air was soon full of flying grains of sand, and our range of vision was limited to a few yards. The midday sun was changed to a pallid spot upon a grey heaven and the trail in the sand was blotted out before our eyes.

In a few minutes the surrounding landscape was completely changed. The horizon had vanished, the storm whistled and howled around us and the sand rose like a grey mist several yards into the air. A tall sand-pillar whirled howling past—it sounded like a threat from the desert powers that were raging round us—it felt as though the wind were bringing unknown dangers ever nearer, and the consciousness of the presence of Death took hold of us with all the silent thoughts that this involves. But that consciousness also rouses the instinct of self-preservation and we soon found ourselves fighting for our own salvation.

If we kept on a southern course it was obvious that

77

we must hit upon the great caravan route somewhere to the westward of the camp, and we hoped to be able to intersect the road at some point where it was clearly marked. Once we found the caravan route, it would be easy to follow it to the eastward, and thus we should be certain of reaching the camp where there were friends and tents—all that constitutes a nomad's home.

The gods of nature were not altogether ungracious to us, for the wind and its sand clouds attacked us from the north and tended to accelerate our progress. And the gods continued to smile upon us, for after an exasperating march across the innumerable wave crests of a storm tossed sea of sand the gale subsided as suddenly as it had sprung up. And the sun broke through once more from a clear sky, the fuming sand lay down to rest, and from the high sand dunes we could again make out the distant horizon.

We allowed ourselves each a pull at the still unemptied water bottle, tried hard to gargle our mouths free from sand and then spat out the water into our cupped palms to wash the sand out of our eyes and noses. This procedure worked wonders, and soon we were again full of optimism and certain of success in the undertaking that had brought us from the camp.

But the search really seemed quite hopeless, for all tracks in the sand were now wiped out, and the wretched Suidor had been without food and drink for more than thirty-six hours, so that it was doubtful whether he was still alive. The only rational course, even from Suidor's point of view, was to go straight on to the southward and try to find the caravan route which provided a certain connection with the camp, from which one could then send out fresh search-parties.

The camels had resumed their weary trot when suddenly Bato pulled up with a joyful cry. In front of us lay a grinning skull and the bleached leg-bones of a camel. It was Death who gazed at us from the desert sands, but yet with the glad tidings that here the living had once gone their way. The bones sticking up out of the sand had been bleached by the sun and polished by the chafing of the sand for countless years until they had acquired the same colour as the grinning teeth of the skull.

We found no other trace of life there, but, riding on towards the east and following the contours of the desert landscape along which we ourselves would have led a caravan, we passed the remains of seven more animals and thus established that we were on the right track.

What we had to do now was to get back as soon as possible to the camp and thence to start an organized campaign with many search-parties on rested camels, carrying plenty of food and water. The patrols would also take fuel in order to light fires when darkness fell and would keep burning a ring of shining beacons on the tops of the highest sand hills to recall the little strayed Chinaman from the desert—if he were still alive.

SUDDENLY we pulled up our camels. In front of us in the deep sand were lines apparently drawn by dragging human feet.

We dismounted. Yes, they were the tracks of naked human feet, but the man must have been so tired out that he was dragging his legs after him. The trail crossed the caravan route at a place where the latter was quite plainly marked and continued in among the piled sand waves to the southward.

We gazed at one another. Could it have been Suidor who had passed this way? But if so, why had he not followed the caravan road, the one slender line in this infinitude of desert that pointed to deliverance?

But it must have been Suidor. Who else could it have been. And the tracks must have been made since the storm subsided, and the weary wanderer could be at most half an hour in advance of us.

The camels were very unwilling to turn aside from the direction which instinct bade them take, but with the aid of our whips we got them to plunge once more into the untrodden wastes to the southward.

Again we had to follow devious tracks, to the right, to the left, round and round and in zigzags, but always leading to the summits of the highest dunes. So as to spare the camels we proceeded by a new method which made our route shorter than that followed by the walking man. While I remained on the crest of a sand wave Bato followed the trail, singing at the top of his voice, over the tops of the dunes and down in the valleys between them, until I could hardly hear his song any longer. Then I gave a shout which resounded across the sands and which was the signal for Bato to go on to the top of the nearest wave and stop there till I came up to him. I rode towards him in a straight line from my starting-point, thus sparing my camel the erratic detours.

Then I rode forward and calculated the distance at which we could be expected to hear each other, and Bato followed me up and saved his camel the detours of that stretch. This procedure suited the camels, but the excessive singing and shouting made us men drier and drier in the throat and frightfully thirsty.

More and more frequently we came to places where the creature had thrown himself down, flogged the sand with his whip and rolled in despair. Over long stretches he had crawled forward, and we found the impression of his face in the yielding surface on the sand. He had torn off his clothes and thrown them away. The trail grew plainer, and he could not be far off now.

" We must be careful," said Bato. " Suidör has gone mad. Hydrophobia, obviously. Perhaps it would be better to leave him in the desert."

BUT Suidor had not gone mad. From the next ridge we could see him lying on the crest of a dune, half buried in sand, scarcely a hundred yards away. He was half naked and was pressing his face into the sand, his whole body shaken with weeping.

We shouted his name as we ran forward to him, but he did not stir. He only sobbed quietly and trembled all over his body. I lifted him up, and what I saw wrung my heart with the deepest compassion. Terror filled his eyes which seemed to be hunted by all the demons of the desert. Sweat and tears had ploughed deep furrows in his grimy face and had changed the physiognomy of the little Chinese boy beyond recognition. Eyes, nose and mouth were filled with sand, and his feet and hands and the naked upper part of his body were torn and bleeding.

With the little drop of water we had left we washed his face and his eyes and we gave him a soaked handkerchief to suck. Soon the terror in his eyes gave way to an expression of the deepest gratitude. One cannot but feel it as the richest reward to see the eyes of a child of nature beaming upon one with pure and genuine feelings of gratitude.

We calculated our position as being a bit to the eastward of the place at which we had left the caravan route. Suidor was put into a jacket and lifted on to one of the camels and then we set off again. And it was remarkable how much more easily our journey now went, and although the way was long we presently came in sight of the tamarisk wood and knew that we were saved.

By 4.15 p.m. we were in camp and were received with great rejoicing by its inhabitants who had spent the day in anxious suspense.

It was now necessary for the caravan to go on to seek a camping-place more inviting than the salt well by the dead tamarisks. The long stay there had upset the digestions of many members of the expedition.

Our chief started in advance at five-thirty on the same afternoon, so as to employ the last of the daylight in mapping the new line of march, and an hour later the caravan broke camp.

" Yabonah, Yabonah ! " sounded through the camp, and section after section filed off to disappear among the tamarisks.

Once more the course lay westward, out into the unknown, to encounter unimagined adventure, but we were conscious of the security of travelling with ninety two camels laden with tents, provisions, water and everything else that could defend us against the hostile immensity that surrounded us. After having made the customary inspection to make sure that nothing had been left behind at the abandoned camping-place Bato and I followed the long caravan.

We came through the tamarisk belt out into the open

81

desert, passing the eight dead camels and other dead caravan beasts—martyrs showing the way to the living. Dusk fell. The scene changed colour, and then the first stars of night were lighted. The long train of the camels moved forward like a row of fantastic silhouettes, and the great stillness was broken only by the creaking of the saddles.

Suidor lay upon the last camel.

" He who saves a man's life has responsibility for the saved, and the saved has obligations to his deliverer, obligations which are as great as the value of a human life." Bato quoted the ancient dictum of the East. " Our responsibility is as great as his obligation."

He said it a little dejectedly, as if he almost repented of that day's deed. But I took the responsibility upon myself, and from that day Suidor accompanied me as a devoted follower upon many journeys.

CHAPTER IX

BRIEF ENCOUNTER WITH THE ADVANCE COLUMN

IN the course of the first hours of the night the caravan found itself moving among high rocks between which light winds whispered and sighed. The stars of the night sky sent their steely light down between the black shadows, and the rock formations, bleached by time and worn by sandstorms, glided slowly by like a procession of fantastic ghosts.

Every word of command, every sound from our long column, came back to us in hollow echoes from the hanging walls of rock. The camels walked with groping step, lifting their feet high, their heads swaying forward from one side to the other and their unfathomable eyes staring anxiously out into the darkness as though they would unveil the secrets of the night.

We now came to a deep narrow gorge whose steep sides shut out the feeble starlight. All was silent, and in the stillness one only heard the creaking of the saddles. The trail ran in curves which hampered our progress. At abrupt turns the Mongols got ready to keep the camels to the course with their whips. I went forward with three Mongols to look for a way that would make further progress possible. We had to shift great rocks out of the way and call the attention of those who came after us to the difficulties and dangers of the crossings.

All the time the same silence prevailed. No one whistled, no one sang and no one spoke discourteously. For these black rocks through which we were now filing rose high above our heads in four proud pinnacles which by day glistened in the beams of the desert sun, but which now slept. A frightful punishment would fall upon the unfortunate who should disturb their night's rest. Many occasions were on record when the four brother peaks had set the surrounding desert and its confederate winds in tumult to visit with the scourge of the sandstorm him who had failed to show them due reverence.

The Mongols felt uneasy during this passage. The place and the darkness of night brought danger so menacingly close. Night is deceptive, for the colours of nature are obliterated and distances become incalculable. From what is quite close it is only a step out into the unknown.

Ever since the beginning of the journey the Mongols had seized every opportunity of questioning travellers from the opposite direction about the dangers that lay in wait on the unknown road to the west. Each of course knew that the greatest perils come from the Nature Spirits and that the most dangerous spirits are those that dwell in foreign lands and whom they do not know.

We had also heard tell that the rocks in these western tracts were inhabited by " hairy wild men ". And these " wild men " would be covered with long white hair which protected them against arrows and bullets, they would have the strength of giants and be epicures of human flesh. It might be that their dens lay just behind the rocks we were now passing.

Finally we emerged from the gorge and left the rocks with the stern brother-peaks, the " hairy wild men " and all the rest of the unknown dangers behind us.

We were once more out on the sand dunes. The camels resumed their wonted trot, the Mongols again struck up their tuneful songs, and from the crests of the dunes we saw the stars twinkling above us and around us right down to the low horizon.

A fire flared up somewhere far ahead of us, but proved in reality to be so near that we were soon pitching camp by the light of its flames. We had reached Odakroi where Sven Hedin and his company had found water, good sweet water.

NEXT morning we discovered that we were encamped in a picturesque landscape of yellow sand dunes and a brilliant green, weathered outcrop of rocks. A few dead or dying tamarisks stood around the well.

The tamarisk provides the desert's best fuel, and that thrifty shrub, which is so strikingly beautiful in bloom, has been found by the desert dwellers worthy of the name " *Modo'en Khan* ", " the king of trees ". It has not, however, acquired this name of honour for its beauty, but for the proud manner in which it meets annihilation. Tamarisk burns, that is to say, with a little blue flame that shines steadily and resists a gale. Without flickering or crackling like other woods, *Modo'en Khan* burns in silence till it falls into a white powdery ash—without complaining, " meets death worthily like a king ", the Mongols say.

Beside the well we saw clear traces of Larson's column having also camped here, and the droppings of his camels and the tracks in the sand indicated that he could be at the most a couple of days' march ahead of us.

What if we should succeed in catching up Larson, and his swift column ! The idea was discussed with enthusiasm in the Mongols' tent and brought about a hasty departure.

Now began an exacting day's march across immense sand dunes and among drifted-over sandstone rocks. Now and then we were cheered by the sight of a few tamarisks. The well of Shara Holos disappointed us with water so salt as to be undrinkable.

Suddenly the track of Larson's caravan turned off to the southward, away from the caravan route, and we came into a labyrinth of sand waves as high as houses. Over and over again we lost the trail, and the exhausted scouts had to spread out fanwise to pick it up again. We all went on foot to save the last powers of the animals —all except Oborgon, the aged Chinese who was the eldest of the camel drivers. He had complained so pitifully of fatigue that he got permission to sit between the empty water casks on a powerful camel.

THE sun went down behind the western horizon in a symphony of splendid colour, but after a moment the blood-red got the upper hand. It was indeed from

Hussein's blood shed into the sand that Allah created the evening flush. The shadows of the camels grew longer and moved across the sand like enormous and fantastic beasts, the inequalities in the ground were filled up by darkness, and the hour had come when one wished to sink into mute reflection, silent worship and deep awaiting of the thoughts which perhaps will now be wakened into life in some slumbering corner of the soul.

The sun's disk now rested upon the horizon. In less than four minutes it would be gone like the day we have just lived through. But during that short while, as brief as a few hundred palpitating heartbeats, the soul pulsates in harmony with nature; one is permeated with joy and gladness and filled with faith in what is real, pure and beautiful.

Then the sun disappeared and the day with it.

The Mongols walked crouching so as to be able to keep to the trail in the dusk. They ran through the sand like bloodhounds seeking to seize firmly on the signs that could lead us forward. Later the moon came to our aid, and at length we sighted the fire which showed us we had reached our goal.

It was almost midnight when we filed in among Larson's tents, and we were so tired that we only wanted to be allowed to sink down upon the sand.

But in Larson's camp there was great excitement at our arrival, and our rested friends received us with cordial demonstrations of delight. We soon felt splendidly refreshed and enjoyed a rest by the glow of the night fire, while Larson's rested Mongols took over the caravan and pitched our tents out in the surrounding darkness.

We did not know where we were, since in the last stage on Larson's trail we had turned a good piece off from the caravan route, and our brains were too dull to make calculations. But wherever we were it was good to be there. The water tasted as if it came from a medicinal spring, and the last hundred yards of our march had lain through the most splendid camel fodder of short, juicy reeds.

86

One of Larson's outriders had the day before found this hollow in the sea of sand in which fresh green reeds revealed a vein of water near the surface and by digging he had struck bubbling sweet water. The exhausted caravan had at once been brought there and had been refreshing itself in this splendid place for a day and a half. For the hundred and eighty miles the advance column had needed nineteen days, of which five had been rest days at places where it had found water. The result was eleven dead camels, and a further score that were too weak to keep up with the caravan.

My idea had been that, since the scanty water we met with was alkaline and had a laxative and exhausting effect upon both man and beast, and since the grazing in the desert was so scanty and so poor that it could not restore the strength of the animals, days of rest were only a prolonging of the agony. The paradise of Etsin-gol was indeed the goal which lured us on and urged us to renewed efforts, for there was to be found all that we lacked in the desert. But the glories of Etsin-gol would end with the coming of winter, and for this reason the thing was to get there as quickly as possible. Every day's delay in the desert meant a day less for recovery in the only place on the journey where the caravan could gather strength for the great effort of the winter, the advance through the desert lying to the west of Etsin-gol, " the black Gobi ".

For this reason the " scientific " column had marched at full speed, so as not to give the animals time to collapse at places where neither the water nor the feed was of a quality that could set them on their legs again. And we had covered the hundred and eighty miles in thirteen days, through heavy sand, mostly on foot and without any rest days. Dead tired we were, both man and beast, but after a brief rest we would still be fit both in body and soul to continue the persistent and mechanical rhythm of our march. We still had every one of the column's camels with us, and next day at dawn the whistling of whips in the morning air and harsh cries would once more get the beasts on to their legs to resume the march to the west.

We could not help crowing a little.

The fire burned down. Soon there was dead silence in the sleeping camp. Only the full moon sailed on past the brilliant stars of the desert sky.

NEXT morning at three o'clock the advance column was making ready for a start. Larson and I sat on the top of a sand dune and held a last conference before we once more parted. Everything was soon ready, and the stout fellow mounted his imposing camel and gave the sign for *Yabonah*. And the first rays of the sun gilded his long train of camels before they were swallowed up by the sand to northward.

It was a marvellous morning.

The newly risen sun still retained its crimson, nature its dewy freshness, and the pastel colours of the morning threw a veil of softness over the sand configurations that were so harsh in outline in the full light of day. I tramped round barefooted in the ice-cold sand, buried my head in the clear water and inhaled all that freshness with delight.

From the blue tents below me the sleep of the righteous could be plainly heard. The camels, in two long rows, were lying with outstretched necks and breathing deeply. All else was still.

Far away to the northward Khan Ula, " The Prince Mountain ", could be seen as a blue vision drawing the eye from the surrounding infinity of yellow sand. The sun mounted slowly over that dream landscape, but brought with it no awakening of nature. Only the caravan dogs, black Hoilok and yellow Hami, waved a morning greeting with their bushy tails as they passed trotting on tender paws on their way to the waterhole.

In the loneliness of the desert a man is conscious of nature's greatness, his own littleness. Everything seems at once so infinitely far and so infinitely near according to how you look at it. The written law does not suffice, for one must frame one's own commandments one by one if one is to live by them with the joy of conviction.

CHAPTER X

DESERT JUSTICE

IT was full day and high time for the sleeping camp to awake to fresh action. Oborgon should be roused first, for it was one of his duties to collect fuel and light the fire which was the signal for turning out the cooks. I went to do this, but the Chinaman was not in his sleeping-place, nor was he to be found in any of the other tents.

This was very odd. The day before the otherwise tough old man had been so ill and miserable that he had had special permission to ride. And on arrival in camp he had soon fallen asleep after having mourned and lamented for a little while. Had he now gone out of his mind from too much sun and sand and severe exertion? Such things happened.

I awoke his tent fellows and they took a quite different view of the matter. Oborgon was a scoundrel and had certainly deserted. And a hurried investigation showed that they were right. His tent fellows found that they were the poorer by several silver coins. In the cooks' tent a bag of rice was missing, a bag of flour, sugar and tea, and Batu's saddle was not in its place. An evil presentiment sent me at the gallop down to the camels, and sure enough two animals were missing, and they of course were the very two that had been most spared and were the fittest in the whole caravan. The old heathen's name became the target for a furious string of full flavoured oaths.

Oborgon had become a member of our wandering community at camping-place No. 21. At the time he had announced himself by some such euphonious name as Liu Jaw Jyä, but the Mongols had soon changed that to *Oborgon*, " the old man ", which was more descriptive.

89

During the thirteen days the man trudged at the head of one of our camel sections he had heard no other name. It was impossible to determine his age, and he himself neither knew nor cared about it. His face was furrowed, sunburnt and wind-bitten, but he was so well preserved that to everyone's surprise he appeared to be able to work at least as nimbly and effectively as the other caravan men.

He had come wandering into camp No. 21 straight out of the great desert to the northward, clothed in rags and shrivelled as an old mummy, but with a light-hearted grin on his yellow-toothed mug. His face was pock-marked, and sand and sun had transformed his eyes into a pair of inflamed but gleaming slits surrounded by innumerable roguish wrinkles. He had, he said, travelled near and far through steppes and deserts, and his battered appearance substantiated his assertion far more clearly than his flowing volubility. He was not exactly of a type that inspires confidence, but I often enjoyed the entertainment he provided in our monotonous life during fatiguing marches by his stories of journeys in still heavier sand under even more fiery sun.

It was often difficult to keep track of him in his narratives. One day he was a great merchant on the way with richly laden camels from imperial Peking to far Uliassutai. The following night he would have me believe that he had been one of the mandarins of Urga decked with gorgeous brocades and nodding peacocks' feathers and had galloped at the head of a roaring band of Manchu warriors out into the wilderness to shed the blood of desert robbers in the sand.

Had he met with the " mad baron " or the false lama Dambin Jansang ? Certainly, he had fought with them or against them ; and he immediately scooped out from his store recollections of those memorable days. He had heard, seen and experienced incredible things and he knew how to tell of them. Much of what he told was perhaps not in strict accordance with the naked truth, but the old fox had in any event experienced enough to be able to stage his dramas with magnificent imaginative effect. And one appreciates that when one is trudging in the heavy sand of a remote desert.

But in the drama which was enacted on the sand dunes round about the waterhole of Huron Dorgoi September, 1927, the robber Liu Jaw Jyä, the Oborgon of the Sven Hedin expedition, played in any case the leading part, and the heroes of the piece were our splendid Mongols Tsereat and Matai Lama.

A CAMEL thief in our caravan, a tent thief in our camp! The whole of the Mongols were wild with rage and righteous indignation.[1] On the camels depended the very existence of the caravan, and we, the Mongols and I, were responsible for them. The malefactor Oborgon was a deserter who had offended against the written and unwritten laws of the desert, a faithless wretch with all humanity's worst qualities.

I had to employ a stern tone of command to check the outburst of fury which followed the discovery, and then it was a question of getting the Mongols' savage lust for vengeance directed into a channel likely to produce results.

The sand round Huron Dorgoi had been trampled by Larson's camels, and we had to conduct a systematic

[1] The man who is taken with a stolen horse or camel shall return the stolen animal to its rightful owner and also pay a fine to him of nine animals of the same kind as that stolen. If he cannot pay this fine he shall give his children in place of the animals and if he have no children the criminal shall be slaughtered like a sheep, that is to say his legs shall be bound together and then his belly ripped open and his heart squeezed by the slaughterer's hand till the criminal dies.
Jenghiz Khan's Yassa.

He who steals a camel shall pay to its rightful owner nine times fifteen camels. *Tsachin Bichik of 1640.*

He who steals two camels is punished by transportation for hard labour in an unhealthy climate for life and a hundred and ninety stripes. *Penal code for Mongolia compiled by the Chinese Foreign Office, 1789.*

As these stipulations show, the laws in Mongolia have always been severe regarding the theft of horses and camels. For him who robs a traveller of his transport animals in a place where these cannot be replaced the punishment, says an unwritten law, cannot be severe enough, and in practice it often happens that in the event of the malefactor being caught he is killed in a rage by the man robbed. And I have heard of a recent case of such a horse or camel thief being "slaughtered like a sheep".

search to find the tracks of the two animals that had been carried off from the herd. From a look-out point I divided up the territory between the various Mongols, and these galloped off like a pack of bloodthirsty hounds. Bato and I stayed on the high sand dune anxiously awaiting the report which should determine a direction for the pursuit.

The accursed Oborgon, whither was he now fleeing with our two best camels ? A cunning fox he was, who had led us all by the nose. On the last day's march, which had tired out all the members of the caravan, he had shammed sick so as to be completely rested on the critical night. He had chosen for his flight a place the desolation of whose surroundings might deter us from pursuing him, and by taking the swiftest and strongest camels he had greatly increased his chances of escape. To let such a thing go unpunished would be to diminish one's prestige, and, in the East, to " lose face " is a serious matter.

But what at the moment worried us even more was the probability that Oborgon was a spy sent out by one of the many robber bands of the desert, which had chosen this out-of-the-way place for an attack on our caravan.

Suddenly Tsereat and Matai Lama turned up with the information we were so impatiently awaiting. The tracks of two camels which had left the camp during the night disappeared in the direction of the chain of mountainous sand dunes that limited our outlook to the southward. Since the chief was still resting in his tent after working late into the night, the alert Major Waltz was in charge of the situation. The Bavarian warrior's eyes sparkled with anticipation when I told him we must be on our guard against a possible attack.

And in the company of four Mongols, all of whom were skilful trackers, I myself rode in among the sand hills to the southward.

OUR little patrol was quite strong. There was the powerful and quick-witted Bator (" the Hero "), the lame but capable and high-spirited Tsereat (" Golden

Gleam "), the circumspect and reliable Mendo (" Serenity "), and the instructed and ever-smiling Matai Lama. All of us except the lama were armed with modern rifles. In consideration of his spiritual status Matai refused to be armed, but brought along instead long strings of Tibetan and Mongolian prayers.

Hour after hour the hunt went on. Three mighty chains of sand dunes now lay between us and the camp, the sun was getting high and the camels were tired. We found ourselves in a veritable ocean of surging sand waves. From the crests of the dunes we had a hopeless view over a lifeless immensity. And when we rode through the hollows between the dunes we saw only a limited ring of yellow sand, the upper edge of which met in every direction a circle of sun-baked sky and torrid, trembling air.

Anywhere within a few hundred yards an army might lie in wait. Everywhere one suspected invisible hiding-places—and at a nod from the desert powers the storm might be let loose and set the sand in motion and give new shapes to this oppressive superfluity of yellow, unfettered drift-sand.

But all lay silent and still, and the trail led us on. A new disappointment met us upon each laboriously ascended sand-wave, but hope beckoned always from behind the next. The tracks often changed direction, and in one place the trampled sand showed that the robber had made a halt and had afterwards ridden to and fro in uncertainty.

Then the tracks went on again towards the northwest, and after having followed this new line for a mile or so we suddenly encountered a surprise. Hidden in a ring of slopes overgrown with tamarisk stood a solitary poplar in the shade of which was a reed-built hut. No living thing was in sight, but there were many camel tracks round about.

Was it a trap ? An ambush ? That we would only ascertain by closer investigation. While two of the Mongols stood ready to shoot, with their eyes fixed on the hut, and a third kept a look out on the slopes behind, I approached the oasis.

All was silent, and the hut was empty. But a lot of rope and bits of felt and the smouldering embers of a fire showed that the house had been visited not long before. The waterhole which rendered the place habitable was surrounded by a sparse growth of reeds. A circular ride round the oasis showed that since the last storm it had been visited only by our robber with the two stolen camels and one other rider, in whose company Oborgon had left the place in a south-westerly direction.

Who was the unknown rider with whom Oborgon had fallen in ? Was it a prearranged meeting ? We gathered for a short rest and to make new plans in the shade of the poplar by the good cool water. It was clear that Oborgon knew his way quite well about these wild regions in one of the most uncharted regions on earth. And this mysterious oasis was probably one of the resorts of the robber band. During his thirteen days with our caravan Oborgon had had opportunity to assure himself that we were a stout-hearted party and well armed, and he had sought a means of escape so as to tell his associates so. Now he was on his way back to the band to wait with the rest of them for easier prey. This was the Mongols' explanation, and I could not hit upon a better.

Most of the tracks in the surrounding sand were those of our stolen camels, and this suggested that Oborgon had stayed here for some time, and the smouldering remains of the fire showed that the place had not long been abandoned. So as not to lose the time we had thus gained upon him we immediately resumed the chase after refreshing ourselves and the camels with a parting draught from the water-hole.

The trail now led us by a wide bend in a south-westerly direction. Suddenly Bator, who was riding in the lead, gave us a warning sign, which made us take cover at lightning speed. His finger on his lips indicated dead silence, and his thumb pointing to the ground that we should dismount. Softly Matai led the camels back while we got our rifles ready for action. Quivering like hounds of chase Bator and I stole warily forward to take a look.

Scarcely five hundred yards away six gesticulating men stood peering at the horizon. Were we now face to face with the robbers ? Had these six men confederates on the other side of the sand dune ? With two of my Mongols I approached them openly on foot while the other two Mongols kept guard on the camels and our line of retreat.

The men had the cross-bred, reckless look characteristic of the bandits of those tracks. We asked them who they were, whence they came, whither they were bound and what was their business in these uninhabited parts. They were peaceable folk on a journey. None of them had seen our robber. Though we showed them that his tracks disappeared in the direction whence their own led. They had no mounts, no weapons. They insisted that they possessed nothing, were only homeless men on the tramp.

These were manifest lies, but no other information could be got out of them, and after long hesitation we determined to take up the trail again, despite the risk of having these mysterious men in our rear.

But we had scarcely picked up Oborgon's tracks again before fate intervened to help him. An appalling, whistling noise sounded in our ears, and fine cascades of sand from the crests of the dunes gave warning that the desert was preparing for a new step in its eternal movement. The sand smoked, and millions of rising and falling grains crackled in emulation of the dull, long-drawn sighing of the desert wind. The dead desert took breath, sighed and lamented, hiding its outlines in a long haze of swirling sand that swept against the camels' legs. The tracks which were to lead us further were beginning to be smoothed out.

Soon all search became hopeless. We cursed our ill luck and decided upon a manœuvre which might perhaps give us one last chance. It was likely that by now Oborgon would suppose himself safe from further pursuit and fearing that the rising wind might increase to a storm, would turn back to the caravan route with its certain bearings and known destination.

Bator, Mendo and I would therefore make our way

back to camping-place No. 34 at Odakhroi, while Matai Lama and Tsereat would start in the direction of the caravan route a good bit to westward of camp No. 35.

And after wishing each other good hunting we separated.

My patrol now rode twelve miles through sand and desolation only to find that the most recent tracks at Odakhroi were those made by our own caravan during its stay there two days earlier. On lame and exhausted camels we then had to cover the whole distance of our march of the day before, and by the time we were once more back in camp at Hurun Dorgoi we had been thirteen hours in the saddle.

Tsereat and Matai Lama had not yet returned, and heated discussion of the affair went on in the camp. But Bator and I were dead tired and only wanted to sleep.

Next morning, however, we came in for more cursing, and when we heard that Matai and Tsereat had still not returned, we too became worried.

Had the two Mongols gone astray in the desert? Conceivable, but not likely, considering their deeply rooted instincts and skill in finding their way in the desert. Had they been captured, perhaps murdered by Oborgon's possible fellow-criminals? Not unlikely. Had the two Mongols caught Oborgon the day before but so late that they had to spend the night in the desert so as to find their way back to the camp by daylight? This possibility seemed altogether too wonderful for us to dare speak of it aloud. But in that case we reckoned that the two Mongols ought to be back in camp before eleven.

The chief, who was upset about the occurrence, gave orders that, in the event of the two Mongols with the thief and the stolen goods not being back in camp at eleven o'clock, I was to take an expedition consisting of three Germans and two Mongols, all on foot to spare the animals, but with three camels for the transport of water and provisions for four days. This expedition was systematically to search the surrounding country with a view to capturing the detested Oborgon. As an incentive, certainly unnecessary but nevertheless welcome, a reward of a hundred and fifty dollars was promised to the Mongol who should catch the robber.

The whole of the arrangements were entrusted to me, and at the appointed time three camels stood laden with sleeping-bags, water, rice, chocolate and cigarettes—all of which we fortunately were soon able to unload again. For suddenly Mendo let out a yell of delight.

" They're coming, they're coming ! " And out of the dunes three men and four camels were approaching.

The whole population of the camp ran towards the brave Mongols and their prisoner, and the last bit of their strenuous expedition became a veritable triumphal march.

The robber's hands were lashed together behind his back, and round his neck was fastened a rope, the two ends of which were held tight by his proud captors. And Oborgon displayed no great delight at the reunion with his former travelling companions. He knew how his crime was judged in the land of the Mongols. With tottering steps and bowed head he was dragged to the Chief's tent where he threw himself down with his forehead on the ground.

It was lucky for Oborgon that the tribunal that sat in judgment at Huron Dorgoi consisted only of the Chief and Professor Hsü, that the court sat under the Swedish flag, and that the Chief was not a Mongolian chieftain. It fell to me to act as interpreter and to retell the following tale.

AFTER parting from me on the previous day Tsereat and Matai had set out in the agreed direction, which at last brought them in among lower and lower dunes. Then they came to a rock, from which at a distance of a few hundred yards they discovered Oborgon sitting in the sand, busy with his boots, while the two camels rested near by.

Tsereat, the more bloodthirsty of the two pursuers, instantly galloped towards him. But the way led through a hollow in the ground, and when at last he reached the crest of the dune which hid the thief, the latter had mounted again and was riding on. Presumably he was unaware of the nearness of his pursuers, for he rode at an easy pace, and Tsereat gained on him more and more. But in his eagerness Tsereat used his whip a little too forcibly on his quite exhausted camel, and this produced a loud bellow of distress which Oborgon heard and which warned him of the approaching danger.

The distance between pursuer and pursued again rapidly increased and soon Oborgon once more vanished behind a high dune. For long he was invisible, but he could not get away from the fresh tracks in the sand.

At length the Mongols came to a large area overgrown with tall reeds where the trail disappeared. When, however, they found that no trail led out of the reed thicket the Mongols climbed an eminence so as to descry any movement in the reed stems, which were several yards high and must disclose the slightest movement of the camels. The search soon produced the desired result, and a bullet from Tsereat brought the thief out of his hiding-place to resume his flight.

Again the chase went on through heavy sand, and soon Tsereat's camel could do no more, but threw itself down, defying the whip and the torrents of abuse from the Mongol who once more saw his prey escaping him and about to vanish utterly among the dunes. Running on foot this "zealot for the desert laws of his forefathers" reached a dune from the top of which he was within rifle-shot of the fugitive until he disappeared behind another sand wave.

MEANWHILE Matai, the gentle lama, had also been obliged to abandon his exhausted camel, but when he came up with Tsereat's mount lying on the sand where it had had a few minutes' breathing-space, he succeeded in getting it to its feet again and on to the place from which Tsereat had just seen his prey disappearing. Fatigue and the wild excitement of the chase had made Matai forget completely his strict monastic vows, and the wild blood of their forefathers was by now hot in the veins of both the men. Each hung on to a stirrup and they whipped on the camel between them. In this way they were dragged up the next dune from which they could see

Oborgon in wild flight through a hollow towards a new hiding-place. Both men were now almost at the end of their powers and realized that this was their last chance. The first shot from Tsereat's trembling rifle made Oborgon let go the led camel, but he still went on, though the bullets whistled closer and closer and threw up the sand round him like bursting shells.

By this time Matai had caught up the loose camel, and pursuer and pursued were equally well mounted. At a bare hundred yards' distance the unarmed priest roared at Oborgon a frightful Mongolian death sentence to be carried out if he did not give himself up at once, but it was a last and alarmingly close shot that convinced the Chinaman that the game was up. He slipped slowly down from his camel, which was trembling with terror and fatigue.

No beast of prey could have thrown itself with greater gratification on its prey than our two Mongols when they got their claws into the wretched Oborgon. Luckily for him Tsereat's magazine was empty when they came up with him, but he got a taste of their heavy whips.

This, however, did not satisfy Tsereat's lust for vengeance, and he wanted to reload his rifle so that full justice might be done. But on that the lama, now somewhat appeased, suggested that they should first ponder the matter for a while and with the cooling of the heated blood the power of religion asserted itself once more and with it the fear of destroying life. The teachings of monastic life gave to the priest power to convince the hunter that, even if Oborgon merited death, the right to take his life was not theirs, since the stolen camels were the property of another. Vengeance belonged to the owner of the camels and no man might deprive him of it.

With the bound thief between them they had then started the homeward journey on foot, and there they all three stood after more than thirty hours of unexampled exertion and violent excitement. Oborgon was yellow and blue and completely dull and used up. But so soon as he felt himself safe from the maltreatment of the Mongols and observed that he was treated with inexplicable gentleness he recovered his old effrontery. He refused to give any information about the rider who had been with him in the desert, would not say whither he had intended to ride and maintained that he had never been in these parts before nor knew anything of its robbers.

The Mongols declared that if only they were allowed to handle him for a while he would soon confess everything. It was lucky for Oborgon that they were not.

To the Mongols' annoyance sentence was not pronounced on the spot, but it was decided that the prisoner should be taken to Etsin-gol and thence sent to a Chinese tribunal at Kansu.

That afternoon a parade was held at which the Chief handed a reward of fifty dollars each to Tsereat and Matai with the promise of gold medals from the King of Sweden. Bator and Mondo, who had also done their part, received twenty-five dollars each and the promise of silver medals.[1]

Later in the day all the Mongols in the camp climbed a wind-swept dune to perform the ceremony expressive of their racial contempt for the camel-thief. The whole of their personal belongings which had come in contact with the thief were smashed or torn to pieces and scattered on the sand, and the stolen provisions, precious though they were in the desert, were crumbled and thrown to the winds with many execrations. For goods stolen from a fellow-traveller are defiled by contact with one capable of so foul an action and are never after touched by honest folk.

Before nightfall Oborgon lay in irons, and that evening I was bidden to a feast in the Mongols' tent, where I came in for a bombardment of importunate questions as to the size, appearance and significance of the promised medals.

And the end of this eventful day was good, for when I went to my tent the Mongols were pleased and proud, the stars were twinkling softly in the night sky and Oborgon was sitting in his chains consoling himself with a " Chesterfield " cigarette.

[1] Swedish Medals of Merit in gold and silver were ceremonially conferred upon the fortunate Mongols in November, 1930.

CHAPTER XI

THE OPPRESSION OF THE DESERT

AGAIN we trudged on in the unending desert. Day by day our weariness increased, the sand grew heavier, the heat more insupportable, and I observed with concern how the distance between the marching camels increased. Their necks which earlier had swung so proudly were stretched forward in line with the tautly strained ropes connecting the wooden peg through each beast's muzzle to the saddle cantle of the one in front. More and more frequently the rope broke when the camel stopped or threw itself down overcome with exhaustion. And when that happens a caravan leader knows that his animals are suffering torments, that his ship upon the desert sea is heading for shipwreck.

"The camel goes till it drops dead," they say, and it is very nearly true.

When a camel has thrown itself down for the first time one can still get it going again by relieving it of its load. Only when a camel begins to sweat on the hairless inner side of its hind legs and throws itself down a second time is it doomed. When that happens neither orders nor blows are any use, for a camel that throws itself twice on one march has reached the end of its journey. It may be in the neighbourhood of a water-hole—neither rest nor fodder nor water avails to arrest the fugitive spark of life. The fallen martyr has trodden its last step in the sand and lies there like a malediction upon its tormentors. It is a torture to witness such a sight, a torture which removes all ambition to perform feats for one's own credit at the expense of murdered caravan animals.

The fallen camel's death-agony is long, often lasting

for many days, but this his last struggle is seemly. Silent and resigned he lies in the sand, his gaze seeking to pierce beyond the remote horizon. Without a tremor or a complaint the proud beast offers up his life—a new tribute to the hostile powers of the desert.

Why not shorten his agonies, extinguish the restlessly flickering spark of life? One must not destroy life, must not deprive the desert of its prey. The crafty ravens shall stab the lustre of the eyes, the birds of prey shall rip the reeking entrails, and wolves and wild dogs shall gorge upon the yet warm carcase. It seems cruel, but the laws of the wilderness are harsh.

To kill a doomed animal with the knowledge of the natives may have the most serious consequences. The caravan people would await with nervous tension the punishment of the savage powers for such a crime. The caravan would lose confidence in its leader and his inherent flair for success, and if that happens the very conditions are established for the misfortunes they expect.

One must therefore employ artifice if one would mitigate one's future memories of a dying camel, must pretend a shooting expedition as a pretext for getting away from the caravan and to provide a plausible explanation of the sound produced by the merciful shot. Now and then one lets oneself be deterred from carrying out such an intention by one's own inertia or weariness or by the aroused suspicions of the caravan folk, but it is a neglect which one regrets often and for long.

We were all now going afoot to spare the riding camels and let them relieve those of the pack animals which showed signs of giving up. In the morning the reveille was sounded in camp while it was still dark, so that the caravan should be ready for the start when the first faint flush showed in the eastern horizon. These early morning hours were the easiest in the day's march, but so soon as the sun had been baking the sand for a few hours our sufferings began anew. The worst was to watch the camels' wavering, dragging gait and the far-seeing look in their unfathomable eyes—that held a presentiment of the nearness of the valley of death which so many of them were soon to tread.

Like the doctor who takes the patient's temperature I let the long string of camels file past me so that I might ascertain how low the walking pace of the caravan had sunk. Forward we must go, but it was a question of straining the animals to breaking-point. The river valley of Etsin-gol, the paradise where lay all that we were now sighing for, seemed more and more remote, an almost unattainable goal. Through the hottest hours of the day we lay stretched under our blue tent, shielded from the sun but not from the heat. One day it was at Ohyr'en Ossu (the Waterhole of the Ox), the next at Ding'en Hotak (the Well of the Lamp), and between them there was no resting-place, but only a dry immensity of barren sand.

The sensations of these hot days were the reflections in the air. One day we observed a large lake to the southward whose cool blue waters and fresh green verges began suddenly to be effaced and were swiftly filled with the hot colours of the sand. Another time it was the view of a gigantic mountain in the north-east that deceived us. The mountain lay there so true to nature, and the spectacle lasted so long that we were at last convinced of its actuality. Then all at once the mountain divided into two parts, and its foot rapidly disappeared, while its two proud pinnacles remained floating in the air. And in the end the whole thing was no more than a pale blue reality of hot quivering air.

But one day there appeared an astonishing sight and one that was not to cheat us. Ever since the early morning we had observed far away in the west two dark strips, and gradually we became able to distinguish through glasses a multitude of great trees. Spirits rose, the pace was increased, and at the end of the day's march we walked into the shade of leafy poplar trees.

The sun went down, and the day's heavy stupor was dissolved by a wild desire to celebrate. The blue wood-smoke from the giant fire curled playfully up towards the tree-tops, and the surroundings took on the un-bounded beauty of imagination.

The " firewater " soon inspired our musicians to

unsuspected feats, and the soughing of the desert wind sounded like a caress as it swept through the wealth of illuminated leaves waving above our heads like millions of blood-red and golden-yellow hearts. Now and then a great splendid star peered down through our many-coloured roof of leaves. The same star was staring at the dead, sand sea that surged around us. We knew it well from many a night march, that great white desert star.

But the music of strings and minstrels' song kept all thoughts of sand and heavy-footed marching at a distance, and soon the stimulating notes of the gramophone were heard. Songs from home, that called for ready peals of laughter were succeeded by grave words to airs by the great masters. Our whole repertoire was dragged forth from the depths of dust-choked cases, and I came upon a flat parcel which recalled a half-forgotten memory.

I set the record going. The prelude sounded like a summons, and its notes invited silence. Then suspense was resolved by a powerful male voice singing. And the words were attuned to the longing of our hearts ; they spoke of that which fills the minds of journeying men—the more persistently the further the journey goes.

> " . . . keep right on to the end of the road.
> If the way be long,
> Let your heart be strong . . ."

I saw with joy how the melody captivated. Eyes gleamed with rapture in response to the unseen singer's voice which rang out like a challenge from the boundless expanses, like a cheery greeting from something loved and longed for, like a stirring bugle-call to action.

And we chose it for our caravan song.

Then I told the others about the girl who had brought us the record, and we all sent grateful thoughts to Morrison Street in far Peking.

The simple but clear import of the song often became the exhortation that spurred our will to endure and our hearts to conquer. And when we needed to hang on to the extreme limit of our energy, we whistled the tune through our clenched teeth.

The sound of bells from a caravan in the distance brought the morrow's march into our thoughts, and unwillingly we turned in.

How was it the song ended?

> " . . . if you are tired and weary,
> Still journey on till you come to your happy abode,
> And all you love and long for will be there
> At the end of the road."

CHAPTER XII

ETSIN-GOL AT LAST

THE next eight desert marches brought us into the
district once dominated by the powerful Tanguts.
Marco Polo, in describing his travels in these
parts, relates that the fertility of the soil and the
abundance of the cattle rendered the people independent of trading; but now, six hundred years later,
this same country is a sea of sand whose heaven-
aspiring waves surge right up to the territory of the
Ordos Mongols.

Now and then we passed a niggardly well which with
its surrounding tamarisks and reeds provided sustenance
for some few nomad families and their flocks of thrifty
goats and camels. These dwellers in the wilderness
bore the marks of their life-long terror of the furious
omnipotence of surrounding nature. They whispered
tales of all that they heard and saw when the forces of
nature raged about them ; sighs and lamentations and
savage howls arose from the warriors buried beneath the
sand, and when the storm whirled the sand from off the
ground they could see the bloody weapons and costly
ornaments of the slain. But when the storm laid itself
to rest, the flying sands solidified again, and the terrified
nomads found the whole face of nature changed into
new shapes.

And then I began to hear legends of Khara Khoto,
" The black and dead city ", which once was ruled by
Khara Bator Janjyn, " The black Hero-chief " and his
brave warriors.

" Once our country was rich and fertile and our forefathers were many in number and powerful. Their
ruler was Khara Bator Janjyn who dwelt at Khara Khoto,
and he was a brave warrior who bore the name of Khara

because he could talk *Khara ugge*" (black words—magic formulas).

Khara Bator's power grew so great that the Chinese Emperor feared him and despatched a mighty army to subdue the "Black Hero", and before the Chinese army's greatly superior force Khara Bator was finally compelled to withdraw within the walls of Khara Khoto.

The Chinese siege endured for long, but there was abundance of food and forage in the town, and below a watch tower in one of the walls was a deep well connected underground with the river outside, so that the inhabitants of the town need never suffer thirst.

Before the Chinese army encircled Khara Khoto, Khara Bator had succeeded in sending couriers to tribes in the west which were well disposed towards him, and the besieged awaited with confidence the arrival of succour in order to deliver the attack which should crush the Chinese. But the latter, whose weapon ever is guile, had foreseen this and had set up a row of watch towers between Khara Khoto and the country to the west and in this way had cut off the auxiliary forces from the beleaguered town.

Yet, in spite of this, Khara Bator withstood all assaults upon the walls of the town, and the Chinese had again to resort to guile. The Emperor himself threw a magic stone into the river which gave water to the besieged, and the stone, falling between the town and the sources of the river, caused the water to leave its ancient bed and break a new course for itself far to the westward of the town. The new river created by the Emperor is Etsin-gol, and it took its name from him (*Etsin Khan*—lord and king).

Khara Bator, who with his people was now without water, determined to die fighting at the head of his brave warriors. He prepared for the attack, but his favourite daughter prevailed on him to save his life. After a parley with the Chinese emperor it was decided that the Chinese should be allowed to enter the town unopposed on the following morning by the gate in the west wall.

During the night the whole Chinese army assembled

before the western gate impatiently awaiting the pillage of the coming day. But under cover of the darkness of the night Khara Bator and the remnant of his army left the eastern gate of the town, and the chief's favourite daughter stayed behind alone to open the western gate at daybreak in fulfilment of the promise given.

The warriors, once so proudly mounted, were obliged to escape on foot, for all their horses had died of thirst. Only a single ass was still alive and on this Khara Bator rode at the head of the melancholy remnant of his proud

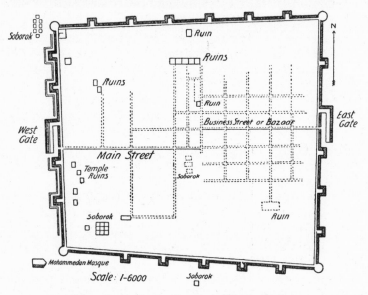

SCALE PLAN OF THE RUINS OF KHARA KHOTO.

army. All the while during the flight the chief spoke " black words ", and the country about the fugitives was transformed. All natural life died. The trees of the forest threw themselves to the ground, outstretched in the direction in which Khara Bator was disappearing and storms arose which soon buried the country in sand.

The " Black Hero " and his warriors went never again on victorious campaigns, for they encamped upon the boundary between their ancient land and that of the Chinese to let themselves be buried under the advancing wave of sand.

But during the night, before the Chinese obtained entrance to the town, Khara Bator's daughter threw its remaining treasures into the dried-up well. In the morning the Chinese found to their consternation that what at sunset had been forests and fertile grazing-grounds was now transformed to barren desert. Raging they stormed into the town to seek vengeance and to plunder, but all they found was one lonely girl who sat weeping in a watch tower.

Khara Bator's treasure was never found by the Chinese, for the girl was slain without having revealed its hiding-place, and the soldiers had to flee hurriedly from the dead town and its barren surroundings if they were not to perish of thirst and hunger.

Since that time many treasure seekers have tried to bring to light the assembled treasure of the town. On certain nights it may be seen lying in a great pot deep down in the well, but so soon as anyone approaches flames rise up for its protection. Shamans and Tibetan lamas have been brought to frustrate the magic power that protects it. But all has been in vain. The " Black Hero's " spirit still guards the riches of the town.

On September 26th our column encamped by the ruins of Etsina, the flourishing Tangut town described by Marco Polo, the ruin around which the Mongols' legend of Khara Khoto has arisen. The solid walls and weathered remains of the town still rise above the sand despite the powerful and malevolent assaults of the surrounding desert. A well-preserved Mohammedan mosque still stands in the shelter of the western wall of the town, on grey-violet windswept plateaux traces of the irrigation system of the cultivated fields still appear, and upon innumerable clay figures we found the finger-prints of those who shaped them.

Here, where a tribe once lived from generation to generation, our little community could only make a stay of a few hours in our eagerness to reach the life-giving waters of Etsin-gol.

This dead human memory had slept for six centuries in the desert's embrace when Koslov discovered it in 1909.

After a month's work, during which he had to maintain

constant camel communications with the Etsin-gol river,
Koslov found, deep beneath the sand, a vault filled with
treasures of art from a long-vanished epoch, banners,
marvellous paintings, cult objects and quantities of ancient
manuscripts. The treasures he excavated had been
preserved undamaged through the centuries in the dry
desert climate, and the colours glowed with their pristine
brilliancy.

We, too, during our brief stay at Khara Khoto, unveiled
memories from long-past times.

THE first pale streak that announced the dawning of a
new day aroused the heavily sleeping camp, and before
five o'clock the caravan was in motion.

We marched across hard sun-cracked clay-land. The
shapes of " The Dead City " and the last sand waves
stood out behind us against the bright background of
the sunrise, but receded farther and farther with every
step and were soon lost in a blue mist.

Like sun-dried mummies, dead, naked and grey, the
fallen tree-trunks lay about our path. Over a vast area,
once shady forest, they lay in thousands. We passed
the yellowish-grey ruins of deserted strongholds. Their
stout walls still withstood the havoc of wind and weather,
but in many places the flying sand had driven in, and the
south-eastern walls were buried.

We passed other ruins of deserted strongholds, and
with strange sensations dug up objects that no human
being had touched for more than six hundred years,
sword-belts and amulets of patinated bronze, images of
gods and plaster moulds for the casting of images. In
the former dwelling of a commandant of the fortress I
came upon a woman's comb of bamboo elaborately carved.
It was with strange feelings that I took it up from the
place where it had lain for so many centuries and I
wondered whether it had last been used by the smiling
daughter of some stern commander or by his lovely
blackhaired mistress.

The camels of the caravan dragged themselves laboriously forward, but all its men felt cheered by the thought
of the beckoning goal. After some hours' march our

cartographers announced that we had covered six hundred miles since our departure from camp No. 8. Just then we met a small Chinese trading caravan, and its people confirmed our surmise that the river of many legends was quite near.

This small caravan consisted of one Mongol, two Chinese, eight camels laden with hides and a big black dog. The two Chinese were traders on their way to Kwei-hwa Ch'eng with the produce they had bought by Etsin-gol. The Mongol was the owner of the camels and the caravan leader. In the west whence they came and whither we were bound rose a lengthy ridge, and at the place where the line of march crossed the ridge we saw the spiky outline of an *obo*.

"Up there," muttered the young Mongol regretfully, pointing to the *obo*, "up there one greets and up there one takes leave of Etsin-gol."

All the members of the expedition were gathered by the *obo* long before the slowly pacing caravan reached it. And there it lay at last, the river. Through our glasses we could distinguish the movement of the tree-tops, and the sight gave promise of water, shade, fuel and rest. It called up kindred thoughts in all of us, and all of us rejoiced.

The Chinese caravan's big black dog had attached itself to us at sight and remained persistently at our side. With lifted muzzle it sniffed in the direction of the river and its bushy tail wagged in delighted circles. We tried to drive the deserter eastward after its departing masters, but the dog's obstinacy was greater than ours. So the expedition acquired a new member, and the newcomer soon won for itself a position of dominance among our own dogs. We christened him "Etsina", and Etsina later accompanied us away from Etsin-gol and far into the west.

THE nearer we came to the river-bed the more vivid were the sensations of our desert-weary caravan. We were soon walking up to the waist in scrub, and leafy poplars threw their shade over our heads. The camels grunted with repressed craving for food, and it was difficult to drive them forward. The Mongols slapped their thighs with delight and made the welkin ring with their shouts at the discovery of a dwelling-house and sheep grazing among the trees. There was a brightness in front of us, it chuckled, it roared and rushed, and suddenly we were standing by open running water, unlimited quantities of fresh, clear, cold water.

On the opposite side of the river, scarcely a hundred yards away, Larson's column was encamped. The blue tents at the edge of the wood seemed to smile at us from the luxuriant foliage of the brushwood. The caravan dogs first perceived us and began to bark furiously. They threw themselves into the river to rush to the attack and were met in midstream by our no less infuriated dogs. Then they recognized one another mutually and howled with delight. And the men too on either side of the river were enraptured, shouted and waved with delight at the reunion.

But our camels from the deserts were hesitant and suspicious at the sight of all that water. It was with the utmost reluctance that they allowed themselves to be dragged out into the river, anxiously and uncertainly that they moved their feet the two hundred paces across to the opposite bank. Many of the animals were too feeble to withstand the swift current, though the river was scarcely three feet deep, and threw themselves down in the water with a bellow of self-abandonment. We were obliged hastily to organize relief expeditions with stronger camels, and it was many hours before some of the brutes and their loads were in safety on the western bank of Etsin-gol.

FOR the first time for many weeks our camels were now relieved of their heavy pack-saddles. They rolled in the grass to rub the itching saddle-galls on their backs. They groped with eager muzzles in the succulent reeds of the bank, and the caravan leader himself enjoyed the relief of seeing his weary animals at recreation. But there they were, our column's ninety-six camels. The tribute of the " scientific column " to the desert had been only one camel.

Then we lengthened Larson's picturesque row of blue tents with our own, and the two columns, so long separated, were one again. The cooks dug fireplaces and slaughtered fat sheep, and the rest of us hurried them on impatiently. We bathed and lapped up water from the river, we buried our faces in the soft grass and gazed up, fascinated, at the red-gold mosaic of the leafy vault. Delicious scents of the most varied kinds reached our greedy nostrils and added to the joy of living.

The great day when we reached Etsin-gol was the twenty-eighth of September. Larson's column had arrived five days before us at this the main caravan's camping-place No. 49, and his rested people as a matter of course undertook the arrangement of the day's festivities. We felt ourselves to be honoured guests that day, gorged royally upon heaped dishes of fresh mutton and drank fresh tea with the avidity of men long accustomed to strict rations.

Dusk fell without our having noticed the sunset, which the masses of foliage screened from our camp, and we gathered round a crackling log fire. The flames, a yard high, lighted up the whole of our happy circle, the fragrant veil of wood-smoke drifted back and forth like a flag over the camp and upon the headlong waters of the river the new-lit stars threw vibrant points of light. We crept early into the tent, for we were weary from much marching. For a while the dogs bayed at the echo from the forest verge on the opposite bank. The river chuckled sleepily on its hurrying journey to the north, and the night wind sang in the tree-tops an ancient melody, but one that we desert travellers had forgotten.

The dream of Etsin-gol had come true.

CHAPTER XIII

LIFE BY THE RIVER

NEXT morning we slept long, and not until the sun appeared above the tree-tops to the eastward and lighted up our westward forest verge did the camp come to life. The meadow between the wood and the river lay strewn with dew diamonds in the chill autumn morning, the sky was clear and the wind blew fresh along the stream.

And, inspired by the purity of nature, we human beings were moved to clean and tidy up ourselves. The Mongols sat, two by two, washing, combing and plaiting each others pigtails and pulling out each others disfiguring facial hairs with clumsy tweezers. Along the river bank the cook-boys were scouring pots and washing clothes, and the surface of the water was dotted with the grinning heads of Teutons and Mongols.

Only one man in the camp was out of humour despite the lovely day, and this was the camel-thief Oborgon. Nor was this difficult to account for, since on this day he was to answer for his crime. The old rascal had in fact had a very tolerable time in recent weeks, for as a prisoner he had been relieved of work and yet had had the same food as the other caravan men. The heavy iron shackles had long since been exchanged for a thin rope, a mere formality, since he himself could take it off and put it on before and after meals, and for the matter of that whenever it suited him. This had aroused no remark at all among the Mongols who had earlier been so avid of vengeance, for lasting malice is alien to their impulsive character.

The court sat in judgment in front of the Chief's tent, and he was prosecutor, counsel for the defence and judge in one. The assembled members of the caravan com-

munity stood drawn up in a circle round the judgment
seat, and the prisoner was brought in by his two warders.
The Mongols were once more seized by the dramatic
gravity of the moment. They stamped and gesticulated
with rage and with angry cries reminded both Oborgon
and one another of the enormity of his offence.

For the occasion of the trial the delinquent was extra
well bound, and in face of this rekindled hatred his sour
humour quickly changed to fear. He threw himself on
the ground with lamentation and wailing and besought
the great white man for protection and mercy for himself
and his defenceless family.

And he got both protection and mercy, and with them
an emphatic exhortation to begin, for the sake of his
family, a better life and one that would be a better
example to his children. He was provided with a little
food and money and was to be taken that very day sixty
li to the southward whence he could later proceed along
the river to the neighbouring district where there were
Chinese settlements.

But before Oborgon left our wandering company for
ever the dramatic scene of his capture in the desert was
to be re-enacted and to be filmed by Lieberenz. To
provide verisimilitude in the setting, Oborgon was taken
by Tsereat and Matai Lama a little way out into the
desert. Lieberenz took up his position on a sand dune
with the camera, and I stood beside him as interpreter.
The performers had orders to behave exactly as they
had done when the episode occurred in reality, but the
maltreatment of the prisoner by the Mongols was, of
course, to be simulated. And Oborgon was to try to
play the same extremity of terror that he had then
felt.

" *Tsa, tsa,*" yelled the Mongols eagerly ; they quite
understood the position. Oborgon regarded us rather
wonderingly and looked suspiciously at the Mongols out
of the corners of his eyes, but at length assented doubt-
fully that he too understood what we wanted.

I gave a shrill whistle, and the Chinaman galloped
off as fast as his strong camel could carry him. But the
Mongols had not patience to wait for their starting-signal

and were at once on his trail, giving tongue like a pack
of hounds. There was plenty of speed and life in the
picture, and Lieberenz cranked away happily.

Entirely according to programme the thief was now
dragged down from the camel and, to delighted shrieks
and yells, was bound hand and foot, and a little touch of
genuine Mongolian justice had been photographed before
Lieberenz finished the reel. But the actors did not
hear my thundered orders to stop, and it was not until
we arrived right on the stage that we succeeded in making
them understand that the scene was over. Oborgon's
terror-stricken face was by that time extraordinarily true
to nature and the Mongols looked a bit ashamed of
themselves but utterly content.

Then we took leave of Oborgon, who under guard
of the Mongols continued his sixty *li* journey to the
south.

WE counted on having to stay on these lush river banks
for at least a month before our worn-out camels would
be able to continue the journey to the west and we all
wished to employ the long wait in as profitable a way as
possible.

Doctor Hedin, assisted by the German Muhlenweg,
wished to attempt to follow the course of the river by
boat northwards to the place where it discharged its water
into the salt lakes Socho-nor and Gashun-nor. Neither
river nor lakes had been in any way explored hitherto
and the scheme now was to chart them accurately and
investigate the nature of their waters and ultimately of
their animal life. As our expedition did not possess a
boat the Mongols under Larson's direction were to build
a little craft for the purpose.

Hummel and I were to make an excursion northwards
along the river to examine the flora and get into contact
with the inhabitants of the district. At the point where
the river ran into Socho-nor we were to meet the boating
party.

ON the first Sunday in October Hummel and I set off
with a small caravan consisting of five strong camels and

two horses which we borrowed from a neighbouring Mongol camp. As servants we took Tsereat and Suidor.

Through dense groves of trees and across open meadows we followed the winding course of the river. The beauty of the landscape was untouched and entrancing, and in the end we felt obliged to pitch our camp in order to turn our new impressions to account.

In the neighbourhood of our camping-ground we found the remains of an old watch tower. The Mongols called the place " The last watch tower ", and according to their legends this ruin is the remnant of the most northerly of all the many watch towers which the Emperor of China once erected to the west of Etsin-gol to stop the Tangut chief, Khara Bator Janjyn, from obtaining support from allied nomad races in the west.[1]

Sun-gilded pheasants screeched in the trees and we caught sight of unknown birds of varied hue flitting through the chequered light and shade of the copses. We worked our way through thickets of thorny *jujube* (zizyphus) and liquorice plant down to the river, as the setting sun was casting its mellow tints across the willows and poplars of the bank. Silent and absorbed we sat by the water's edge and watched the life around us. Families of wild duck swam quacking by at a few yards' distance, pheasants, keeping a watchful eye on the opposite bank, walked down for a drink, and behind a boulder a heron stood on the look out for fish.

With twilight came the sound of passing birds following guidance of the river. First came the steppe grouse, circling above the tree-tops in their thousands, then the wild duck, and last of all, when night had almost fallen we listened to the flute-like, long-drawn notes of the wild geese and swans. From time to time, against the background of the starry sky, one even caught a quick

[1] It appeared from excavations carried out later by Folke Bergman that this row of watch towers, of which the one by which we were encamped was the most northerly, derived from the Han dynasty. About six miles to the west lay the watch towers which appeared to belong to the period referred to in the Mongol's legends about Khara Khoto.

glimpse in silhouette of the proud formation of a flock of swans in flight.

The camp fire called us back from the darkness and there we found two newly arrived guests sitting in a corner by the fire. Tsereat, who was a smart lad and knew very well what we were after, had visited during our absence a neighbouring Mongol camp and had succeeded in bringing back with him a couple of hunters, father and son. They were Torguts.

The younger man's curiosity was aroused by this meeting with white men and the elder talked willingly of ancient traditions and told stories of bygone days.

The Etsina Torguts cherished the tradition of the great mother race far away in the west and knew that their supreme ruler was the chief of this great tribe. But the leader of their own tribe was of the same " *tsaran yasse* " (white bone) [1] as the Khan of the mighty mother tribe. Neither they nor their ancestors for many generations had come before that mighty ruler or visited those far-off grazing-grounds that he administered as deputy of the gods.

But the tradition of these Torguts about their relationship with a distant main stem in the west was more than a memory handed down through many generations, for as recently as two years ago a proud mission had come through the desert to seek out the chief of the Etsina Torguts with a message from the Khan of all the Torguts.

Both our guests had met these messengers from far away and had learned from them much about their kin. Particularly they had heard described the wisdom and goodness of the great prince who now held the Khanate. And everything that the Torgut Khan's ambassador had told them about the affinity of the two tribes was corroborated by the traditions handed down from their fathers, and this had made the Etsina Torguts proud and glad.

---

[1] The Mongols are divided into four social orders, *tsagan yasse* (white bones)—nobles ; *khara yasse* (black bones)—socagers ; *darkhan* —a not numerous middle class, arisen from *khara yasse* but exempt from socage ; *lama*—the religious order, exempt from both socage and military service.

On one point only there was some confusion. There fathers had told them that their forefathers had left the pastures of the main tribe by the Ejil-Tsar river (Volga) far away in the land of the Shara-oros (Russians), but these messengers of the Khan came from habitations on the other side of the Black Gobi and had not passed through territory in Russian occupation.

THE Etsina Torguts came to their present grazing-grounds with the young chief Arab Jur who, with his people, separated from the main tribe by the Volga in order to perform a mass pilgrimage to holy Lhasa. They travelled in the true Mongolian way, taking with them tents, women and children. During this time, how-ever, when Arab Jur and his people were living in the high-lands of Tibet, a feud had arisen between the Manchus and the Dzungars, and when the pilgrim caravan on its return would have crossed Dzungaria it found the way barred by the Manchu-Dzungar battle-front.

Unable to reunite with the main tribe by the Volga, Arab Jur, who had remained to the south of the fighting line, decided to proceed into China instead and beg the help of the Manchu emperor. Thus he arrived in Peking in 1705. He was assigned grazing-grounds for himself and his people by the emperor and later on was given a Manchu title. His son and his descendants received a grant of the fertile land by Etsin-gol, and the little Torgut tribe settled down by the green banks of the river in 1732.[1] Half a century later the chief's family was given the rank of *Beile*, and the present chief of the Etsina Torguts, who is a direct descendant of Arab Jur, bears like his father the title of *Wang*, a dis-tinction which the family received in consideration of its loyalty to the new Chinese republic.

THE present Torguts by Etsin-gol live in great and fatal isolation from their kindred, and their existence is ever

[1] In the neighbourhood of the Chinese town of Maomo on Etsin-gol, about sixty miles south of the expedition's camp No. 49, there is said to be a stone whose inscription shows that it was erected in 1750 to mark the boundary between Mongolian and Chinese territory.

growing more precarious. For a long time hordes of
soldiers and officials from the neighbouring over-
populated territory of China have brought pressure to
bear on them, and Chinese colonists are crowding in
from the south, damming up the river to improve their
newly cultivated lands and thereby robbing the Torguts
in the north of the greater part of their pasturage. At
times the river is almost dried up, the belt of fertile
ground is narrowing and the desert creeping closer, from
both east and west. Owing to the scarcity of fodder
the Torguts' herds of cattle, horses and sheep are also
dwindling every year. And their chance of expanding
northwards is entirely cut off, for there hovers Soviet
Mongolia with ideals and regulations incomprehensible
to the freedom-loving Mongols.

One can see in these Etsin Torguts that they are putting
up a hopeless fight. They are often timid in their
bearing and their faces bear the stamp of tragedy. And
by Etsin-gol I saw for the first and only time Mongols
who rode by preference upon asses.

At all times the Torguts have been in constant contact
with the dwellers in the north, for the people from Sain
Noyen Aimak [1] and the Buryats from the shores of Lake
Baikal have always used the track along the river for their
pilgrimages to holy Lhasa. The high-spirited Buryats
and the vigorous northern Mongols regard these Etsin-
gol people and their country with contempt. They are
used to trees which provide far better timber and fuel
than the poplars along the river, and they cannot regard
an ass-riding Mongol as a good Mongol. " Just as the
poplars are the poorest of all trees, so are the Etsin-gol
Torguts the poorest of all Mongols," they put it.

Now, as ever, Tsereat was invaluable to us as our best
introduction to the camp fires of the Mongols. He was

---

[1] *Aimak*—old Mongolian denomination for a chief's territory, consisting of one or more principalities. The *aimak* is divided into
hoshun (banners) which are independent and go by inheritance to
younger branches of the family, but the alliance within the *aimak* is
maintained, and the oldest prince of the family who rules the principal
hoshun is regarded as head of the tribe and leader of the whole *aimak*.
The *hoshun* is divided into *sumon* (arrows).

popular everywhere, for he was well-bred and courteous besides being amusing and full of news from the world beyond the desert. We too were made welcome everywhere and often received the impression that we were guests long awaited by the inhabitants of the tent.

At the time of our visit the Etsina Torguts consisted of only one *sumon* (arrow) of ninety-six tents. I visited most of these tents along the river bank and generally found the people friendly and hospitable, smiling and songful in spite of their troubles. Sometimes too I came across sturdy and tradition-loving hunters and shepherds who were proud of being true Etsina Torguts and loyally upheld their local chief.

We had no great difficulty in persuading the Etsina Torguts to let us take anthropometric measurements, and we were soon able to form a conception of this interesting remnant of a people. Most of these Torguts showed traces of mixed blood, and the fact that several of their legends concerned events and persons from the time (four hundred years before the Torguts came to Etsin-gol) when the dead city of Khara Khoto was a flourishing metropolis, indicated that on their way hither the Torguts had absorbed a part of the country's original Tangut population.

There is a scarcity of native Etsina Torgut women and they are practically sterile. Many of the marriageable young men have to make journeys to other tribes to find tent-mates, and the stock is to a large extent losing its racial characteristics. Especially in the southern parts we found that many of the Torguts had mothers from other tribes. And among the present wives those who had been brought from other parts of Mongolia and especially from the Eastern Mongolian tribes were even more numerous.

All the women, however, native or imported, wore the proper Torgut clothing and ornaments and did their hair in the Torgut fashion. And later on I was in a position to ascertain that the dress of the Etsina women accorded in all essentials with that of the women of the far-distant main stem although it is two hundred years since the tribes separated.

One day Tsereat informed us that a *hutuktu* had his place of meditation not far from our camp. Tsereat had already paid his respects to the *hutuktu* and had had a long conversation with him. The holy man was friendly and had expressed a desire to see Tsereat's white masters.

We were constantly discovering that Tsereat was deeply devoted to us and proud of being in our service. And a devoted Mongol finds it easy to see his master's merits and makes excuses for the defects of his character. To Tsereat it was a sacred duty to facilitate the fulfilment of our wishes, and the parting prophecy of Yolros Lama stood for him always as a conclusive assurance of good fortune. When the Mongols believe in something they do so blindly and uncritically and often with such firmness and fervour that they make even the most fantastic prophecies come true.

Before we set out to pay the holy man a visit, Tsereat eagerly pointed out that there was no certainty that he was the *hutuktu* whom Yolros Lama had prophesied we should meet. Tsereat himself was convinced that although the man in whose presence I should soon be standing was a holy *hutuktu* the visit would not be of any deeper significance.

We forded the broad river and rode across the open, sunlit, wooded land. On a couple of the trees a number of shoulder-blades of sheep and oxen were hanging, all inscribed with Tibetan texts. These bits of bone rattled in the wind but nothing else disturbed the serenity of the landscape. Unfrightened hares scuttled about in the green undergrowth, several times we passed by calmly browsing antelopes and near us we heard the gentle cooing of wood-pigeons.

Our way led across the fertile tongue of land which divides Etsin-gol into Obo'en-gol and Dondur-gol, and the *hutuktu's* dwelling lay where the eternal rushing of the two streams sounded like the subdued harmonious notes of an organ.

The *hutuktu* of the Etsin-gol Torguts lived far from any monastery and remote from the strife of mankind. Three white tents in a sunny woodland glade constituted both his sanctuary and his home. The camp was like many other orderly Mongol camps and its life differed little from theirs. Horses and other animals grazed on the surrounding pasture and we found the *hutuktu* sitting outside one of the tents placidly regarding his sheep and the little lambs that gambolled round like white balls of cotton wool in the wind.

He lived in these three white tents in company with a few devoted disciples and some shepherds, for the *hutuktu* had become a Mongolian nomad. He was not Mongol by birth, however, for Tangert Gegen's last rebirth had taken place in Tibet and the *hutuktu* had undergone his spiritual education in the remote monastery of Kumbum. But at the age of twenty he had had a call which took him far to the northward, and for more than three decades now he had had his place of meditation in the leafy poplar groves of Etsin-gol.

In the tent which he himself inhabited there were a number of holy books and religious objects, and on an altar stood a few images of gods, but otherwise there was nothing to distinguish the interior of the tent from that of the ordinary mortal. Tangert Gegen had lived here for more than thirty years and God's green earth suited him far better than the heavy gloom of the monastery.

The Torguts used to say that Tangert Gegen understood the language of animals, and they had seen the *hutuktu* feeding with his own hand wild beasts of the forest which ordinary men only regarded as human food. No huntsman dared to hunt in the neighbourhood of his camp and all wild creatures throve and multiplied.

Tangert Gegen had not become a famous *hutuktu*, because he had not surrounded himself with the mysterious atmosphere of inaccessibility of a Mongolian divinity. He himself never sought anyone out, but lamas needing advice and Torguts oppressed with sin came often to him, and he was always ready to help with counsel and blessing. His prophecies gave an immediate impression of wisdom, for his ear was tuned to the divine in nature ; he had learned of its wonders, listened to its voices and had grown aware of many profound truths.

We talked for a long time with him and he was exceptionally human.

The going down of the sun made us all silent, for just as the ball of fire sank behind the heads of the poplars in the west, the trunks at the edge of the wood glowed like the pillars of a temple.

CHAPTER XIV

ASIA'S BIRDS OF PASSAGE

ON our first journey to the north we passed by Ser-Sonche, the residence of Etsina Torgut Wang.

The chief's abode consisted of one large and several smaller houses constructed of limewashed sun-dried bricks. The roofs were flat, the architecture on simple straight lines reminiscent of the houses in Algiers. Round the precincts ran a wall from the top of which fluttered banners inscribed with various texts and prayers.

In the south wall was an enormous red lacquer door. This was closed and would remain closed, for on the ground in front of it were laid three great tree-trunks in such a way that with the threshold on the fourth side they formed a rectangle. This might signify that the prince was ill or afflicted with some trouble, but it might equally well imply that the lamas were in this way shielding their lord from " the evil eye ".

The surroundings of Ser-Sonche were desolate and grey. The buildings lay on a stony plateau which trailed away to the west, but with sharp eyes and in good visibility one could make out the band of woods which indicated the course of the river's two branches, Dondur-gol and Obo'en-gol. Not far from the residency in the direction of Obo'en-gol lay a little temple from which issued the melancholy notes of some wind instrument. Otherwise all was silent and deserted.

A few hundred yards beyond the princely abode lay a row of tents and thence three men approached us. They were finely dressed, dignified people, and one of them wore in his hat the peacock-feather insignia of nobility. The latter bowed courteously to us and pointed to the tree-trunks symbolizing the impassable rectangle in front of the house, but at the same time gave us to understand that we would be welcome guests down in the tents.

We accompanied him into the largest tent and were regaled with tea and pipes by the fireside. From the wealth of books, papers and writing materials which lay in piles upon the red lacquer shelves, we came to the conclusion that we were in the prince's *yamen* (council chamber).

With indirect and courteous formalities our hosts learned of our errand and our wishes, and they deeply lamented the circumstances which made it impossible for the prince himself to receive us. But he was old, both his body and his soul were frail, and he could only see his nearest kin and the lamas who helped him when the spirits occasioned him distress.

They were three extraordinarily fine and pure Mongol types that we had before us. The highest of the officials had the rank of *Tushmit* and was married to one of the Torgut chief's two daughters. The ailing old man had besides two sons, of whom the eldest would be his successor and bore the rank of *Kung* [1] while the younger was Geling Lama at the neighbouring monastery Dageling Gompo.

During the conversation the tent curtain had often been pulled to one side to admit inquisitive Torguts and the circle of men round the fire grew ever closer. And many others came and stood by the walls of the tent behind the sitters so that soon we had a large audience.

Among those who were standing quietly in the background, a young man attracted my special attention.

[1] The Mongolian Chieftains' ranks are :

Prince of the first class	. . .	*chin wang*
Prince of the second class	. .	*chün (jy) wang*
Prince of the third class .	. .	*beile*
Duke of the first or second class	.	*kung*
Noble of the first or second class	.	*taiji*

The insignia of the various ranks consist in part of oval buttons on the official hats, formed respectively of ruby, red coral, sapphire, blue opal and rock-crystal, and in part of the peacock feathers, with from one to three " eyes " hanging backward from these buttons.

He was of a large build and seemed in some way untamed, and he was more marked by wind and weather than any of the others. He stood far apart in a corner but all the same he appeared to dominate the others. When he looked at me I was aware of his eyes, and when the others smiled he laughed heartily and without restraint. But as soon as he noticed that he had drawn special attention to himself he grew shy and distressed and tried to make himself small and unnoticeable. When he was serious he looked savage, but when he smiled he looked like a happy child. The tent seemed too restricted to give him space.

The others chattered with him in Mongolian, but many of the words he himself used I did not understand. His dress was unlike any I had seen before on Mongols—simple, free from all ornament and clearly made by himself. On his feet he wore a kind of moccasins of ox-hide fastened with leather laces twisted up the leg and tied under the knee. But what astonished me most was that he had a silver ring in one ear, because I had never before seen this in a male Mongol. When I spoke to him he did not answer and when I signed to him to draw closer he hurriedly disappeared from the tent. I asked the others who he was and whence he came, but their answers were uncertain and evasive. All I got out of them was that he was a Mongol and belonged to a tribe far off in the west.

A LOUD cry from outside the tent brought us all to our feet and most people rushed out into the open. A man appeared in the opening of the tent. He was a tall, well-set-up Mongol and to judge from the reception he received from those who had remained in the tent he was a personage of rank. He stood just inside the opening of the tent with his face turned towards it waiting for the visiting Mongols to crawl out. Then he swung round and faced us. The three Mongolian officials approached him and I watched eagerly how they would greet him so that I could thus estimate his rank. But he dismissed them with a wave of the hand and quickly seated himself by the fire.

The man had a bold and prominent nose but the lines of his face bore witness mainly to a gentle melancholy. Over his shoulders he wore a long red cape of Tibetan wool and on his head was a huntsman's cap trimmed with a squirrel's brush. Thus it was nothing in his garb to indicate who he was, but his demeanour and his way of speaking were those of a man accustomed to command and be obeyed.

To begin with, the conversation was formal and meaningless, and we had plenty of time to observe one another, but later in the afternoon we learned that he was called Puntsuk and was the son of the old chief, the man who one day would take his place in the line of the chiefs of the house of Arab Jur.

He gave us to understand in what a precarious position he was placed when so great a number of armed foreigners suddenly appeared in his country. " To the north and south lie mighty lands both of which send their agents hither to lure us to them. We hear of civil wars and revolutions and hatred between peoples. But we Torguts by Etsin-gol are too weak to wage war and we want no revolution. All we desire is to live our own life without foreign interference, since for us there is only one kind of life : that which our forefathers lived before us."

Puntsuk told us that his good old father was so full of years that the wisdom he had acquired during a long and blessed life had once more left him. Until a few years before, the princely family had had its residence four miles farther south in a beautiful district of forest and water. But one morning the old chief had awoken blind, and from that day the sounds of the gurgling river and the fluttering poplar trees had become unbearable to him. He could not concentrate his thoughts to say the prayers which would prepare him for the next life, and at night he could not sleep for grief that he could no longer see the works of nature which he loved and heard about him.

For this reason they had built this new residence for him on the quiet desolate gravel plateau far from the bustle and purl of wood and water, and now

The Expedition's camels assembled before the start from Hojertai-gol

[face p. 128

Photo Lieberenz

The genesis of "Long Snake"

Photo Lieberenz

Landing of the boat expedition after the voyage on Socho-nor

[face p. 129

the old chief lived in deep retirement, listening only to the lamas who would prepare him for the next world.

Before the prince withdrew, I tried to obtain some information about the main Torgut tribe, but as soon as I brought that question into the conversation, Puntsuk showed himself either ignorant or unwilling to answer.

Next day Hummel and I continued our journey along Obo'en-gol, and after a twelve-mile march came to the northernmost poplars. The night was black and silent, and from the north-west the cold wind blew unchecked. Once or twice we heard the barking of dogs from somewhere south of us on the other side of the river and our old Torgut guide told us that there lay the most northerly settlement of the Etsina Torguts.

At daybreak we crept out of the tents and received an entirely new impression of our surroundings. To the north stretched the vast salt-exuding steppe that surrounded the two salt lakes. The eye lost itself in immense distances and the rising sun shed an utterly colourless light upon monotonous, empty, dead expanses. But due north one could just make out a faint line of blue mountains.

As our guide declared that it was only two hours' ride to the southern shore of Gashun-nor, we decided not to strike camp but merely to make a day excursion up to the salt lake.

The outer bushes of the scrubby tamarisk thicket were encrusted with salt and shrivelled by their eternal conflict with the north wind. Where the growth ended, the naked, dried-up, fissured earth began, with its innumerable little volcano-shaped hummocks.

The river split up into an extensive muddy delta and as this was quite impassable we were forced to go even farther north-eastward. Slowly the sunlight stole over the unbroken, cheerless waste until suddenly it reached the mirror of the lake, for there, a bare half-mile away, lay the dull lustre of Gashun-nor, reflecting the pure azure of the sky.

The ground near the lake was powdered with little

white sparkling salt crystals, and in many places the salt had piled itself up into yard-high formations like pack ice. At the south-eastern end of the lake rose blocks of salt like gleaming marble hills.

We turned our horses towards the highest point of the beach and soon our ears grew aware of the life of the lake. From the air came the warning cry of wheeling gulls, and from out on the lake could be heard the ceaseless babble of a thousand birds. Alarmed lapwings flung themselves down at us with hoarse cries and flapping wings.

From that high white mountain of salt we saw an unforgettable sight—that of Asia's birds of passage gathered together to rest during their journey to the warm countries of the south. Swarms of aquatic birds floated like dark islands on the blue surface of the lake. Flocks of mandarin ducks, motley as parrots, looked like flower beds among the dull grey of the wild geese, and far beyond the " archipelago " snow-white swans rocked in dignified seclusion. On the edge of the beach black storks were strutting, and cranes trod out their high stepping dance.

We fired a shot into the air and the report had scarcely died away before the murmur of that chorus of a million birds rose to a wild crescendo. The whole flock rose from the lake and dispersed in the air, new thousands rising from the water as soon as they found wing-space, and the air was dense with flapping wings. Ever farther and higher spread the multitude, while the lake sent up fresh hosts. In a moment the very sky was blotted out and the air trembled with the clamour.

But soon there began to be order in the confusion. As if under command the various species began to arrange themselves in different groups which kept on circling over their respective territories from which they had risen. And since no further danger was observed, the boldest swooped down again to the lake and the flocks soon followed the example of their leaders. Only a bevy of swans continued their rising circles of flight, captivating us with their entrancing song. For a long time the clamour could be heard out on the lake. It was as if the birds were scolding one another for having sounded the alarm without cause.

THE old Torgut guide sat deep in meditation with his face turned to the north. Away there lay the chain of blue mountains, and beyond them one could make out three majestic pinnacles rising to heaven. This view was the old man's earliest memory of childhood and now he revived the impression which had been his daily inspiration throughout a long life. " Now the sun of a new day shines on Boro Ola (the Brown Mountain), on Kukshin (the Old Man) and on Noyen Bogdo (the Divine Prince)," he said slowly and dreamily. " Wisdom one learns among men, but the higher qualities of the soul one acquires in the mountains."

OUR expedition through the district of the Etsina Torguts might now be considered complete. We had pushed forward to the most northerly of the two salt lakes into which the branches of Etsin-gol river poured their water, and we had reached a No-man's-land lying north of both humanity and vegetation. But we had not encountered the boat expedition as according to plan we should have done, and we therefore decided to make a quick return on our tracks, keeping an eye on the river the whole time.

But the boat did not come. The bubbling mass of water rushed by us, scornful and unnavigated, and we got right back to the main camp without having met the first subjugator of Etsin-gol.

CHAPTER XV

SAILING ON UNCHARTED WATERS
WITH THE CHIEF

IT was silent and deserted in the camp, for many of our companions were away on minor expeditions, and all the caravan folk were out with the camels looking for better pasturage along the river.

At the " dockyard " lay the vessel destined for the navigation of Etsin-gol and the salt lakes, and its build looked imposing and inspired confidence. It had been fraught with difficulties for the steppe-trained Larson and the Mongols, who knew nothing of marine matters, to construct a seaworthy craft from the available materials and with the few tools there were.

First of all the idea had been a sort of canoe, and a long tree-trunk had consequently been hollowed out. But in spite of excavation and ballast the trunk rolled over in the water and that idea was given up. After this the present raft-like vessel had been constructed consisting of two hollowed-out tree-trunks three feet apart, joined together by a deck of planks. But such a quantity of intensely sappy wood was too much for the river's scanty depth, and on the trial trip the ship lay immovably on the bottom.

If the proposed voyage was ever to take place we should have to get hold of a far more buoyant and seaworthy craft. And it was urgent, for the water level of the river was growing ever lower, it had already dropped from twenty-four to twenty-one inches. New islands and spits of sand were creeping up out of the water and with every diminution of water the risk of grounding increased.

The greatest difficulty was that the only building material at our disposal consisted of heavy new-felled tress. However a Scottish explorer of Africa had once told me how the negroes transformed the sap-laden tree-trunks of the tropical forests into light vessels, and we decided to try their method.

For two days and one night Tsereat and I worked, with Gombo, who was a good carpenter, as assistant, at a construction which attempted to follow both the directions given by the chief and the African model. The clumsy vessel in the " dockyard " was pulled to pieces, the heavy deck was discarded, after which the roughly hollowed out pontoons were filled with smoking embers from the week-old camp-fire. The outsides of the pontoons were kept wet the whole time to prevent any possibility of the wood being burnt through.

After a few hours interval the embers were emptied out and the insides of the charred logs were scraped away. Then the pontoons were re-filled with hot cinders. Each time the thickness of the pontoons was reduced by a fraction of an inch, and all the while the moisture evaporating from the tree-trunks smothered the place of our labour in steam. Every other, or every third time we scraped away a new layer of charred wood fibre, and during the whole process someone had to keep watch to see that no holes appeared from the wood being burned through.

By the afternoon of the following day we had two light canoes. Their breadth at the water line was scarcely eighteen inches and the sides were curved inwards so that the opening at the gunwale was only twelve inches. These two canoes were now joined parallel with one another, fifteen inches apart, by means of two light but tough cross pieces.

In the bows between the two canoes the lid of a chest was fixed as a desk for the captain, and behind it a narrow plank to be used as his writing-chair. The " crew " was relegated to the branches connecting the canoes.

And so the nerve-racking moment arrived for this remarkable vessel to be launched. All who were at home were gathered on the bank, and the efficiency and solidity of the boat were critically discussed. Slowly it was lowered down the steep bank and with a thud and a splash landed in the river. And the exultation was great for the boat floated away on the swift stream until the mooring ropes checked its further movement. And there it lay rocking on the swift stream, a little ungainly but as solid as a broad-breasted goose.

We christened her *Ormen lange*,[1] our famous boat that took so long to build but had at last materialized. And then we went on board for a trial trip. With one leg in each canoe we sat on the narrow thwarts. On the " desk " in front of him the chief had his compass and other map-making gear. My only tool was a two-bladed oar, a kind of makeshift paddle.

On the bank stood the Mongols speechless with amazement, while our delighted companions ran along the edge of the water—but we sailed proudly past them.

After an hour and a half's sailing it began to grow dark, and as we had set out with absolutely no provisions or sleeping equipment, we decided to regard the trial trip as successfully accomplished. It proved to be exceedingly difficult to paddle the light craft against the rapid stream, so we drew *Long Snake* up on land and returned to the camp on foot.

The same evening the boat expedition was planned in earnest, and it was arranged that this should start the very next morning. So as not to load the boat more than necessary, a camel-corps under the leadership of Larson was to set off northwards at the same time, to carry the mariners' baggage and prepare the camp for the night.

I turned in that night completely happy, for it had been decided that I should be the one to accompany Sven Hedin on the boat expedition through the rivers and salt lakes of the Gobi desert which had never before been navigated.

THE sources of Etsin-gol are far down in the south at the foot of Nan Shan, the Tibetan border range. After having drunk from several lesser oases on Chinese territory, the small watercourses unite at Maomo, after

[1] *Long Snake*—a famous Viking ship.

which the river carries its waters farther north and into
Mongolia. Here the river splits into an eastern and a
western branch, and these themselves divide again into
smaller branches which all discharge and disappear into
the two alkaline lakes, Gashun-nor and Socho-nor.

The eastern of the two great branches of the river
is called by the Mongols Etsin-gol or Ikhe-gol (the great
river), and this in its turn splits into an eastern stream,
Dondur-gol (the central river), and a westerly, Obo'en-
gol (the river of the Obo). These two branches empty
themselves into Socho-nor with the exception of the
body of water which is carried by a lesser tributary of
Obo'en-gol over to Gashun-nor. That the most easterly
of these watercourses is called "the central river"
would seem to be a relic from the time when the whole
of that now completely sterile district round Khara
Khoto was an irrigated and fertile land. The western
of the two great branches is called Murin-gol (the
winding river) and all its water is carried into Gashun-nor.

The main camp of the expedition lay by the one of
the two great branches that is called Ikhe-gol, and the
boat expedition was to follow its course northward till
the stream divided, when it would follow the eastern
branch up to Socho-nor. On the seventeenth of October
we struck camp and in company with our little auxiliary
caravan journeyed to the place where we had left *Long
Snake* the evening before. It was a glorious morning,
still and full of sounds, and the sun cast warming beams
which within the wood were transmuted into colour.
The river wound about, and from time to time we were
carried by the current into its inner concave bends
towards the sheer eroded banks and sometimes swung
at an easy pace between long tongues of land and sand
islands. There were often men and beasts on the
banks, for all came to the river for water.

The Mongols stood as if fallen from the clouds with
astonishment at the passing vision and were in no state
to reply to our greetings, and the animals forgot either
to drink or to be afraid. At a sharp bend we took a
flock of swimming wild geese by surprise, and I had
never imagined that wild geese could express such dumb

and idiotic amazement. They forgot both to warn each other and to fly although we passed them only twenty yards away.

The river ran through whole avenues of whitebeam and poplar ; at other times the winding banks were bordered with thickets of tamarisk and clumps of yellow reeds. We passed the camping-place of the camel men whom we had sent out from the main camp. The camels were crowding down by the river to drink. At our coming they lifted their heads as if at the word of command, and their eyes were filled with an astonishment even greater than the normal astonishment of camels.

The pull of the current often ran from one bank to the other and it was when we had to follow this cross-wise line that we most often ran aground. Each time I had to jump out into the ice-cold water, but the job of hauling the boat across the shoals was a warming one, and we were soon floating gaily and freely again with the current.

At three in the afternoon we came to the point where the river divides, and glided into the eastern branch, Dondur-gol. Towards evening the river suddenly nar-rowed into a channel scarcely fifty feet wide squeezed into a tunnel of steep wooded banks. Poplars leaned over the water at a sharp angle, the stream ran silent and unruffled, but dark and opaque as a bog. Rays of warm colour from the setting sun pierced through the golden-red mosaic of the vault of autumn leaves, and a drinking fox stole away at the sight of us. Shortly afterwards the smell of smoke drifted across us and soon our cosy blue tent loomed up on the bank.

Larson served *shaslik* and other nomad delicacies in honour of the day. The fire spread its kindly warmth over our circle, and Banche sang sweetly in tones which for all their softness carried far. The night whispered and rustled and the wind crooned quietly in the tree-tops. Another of the Mongols played the flute and drifted from theme to theme while Banche sang of the worlds of phantasy. One heard, as if in a dream, the beating of the earth's very pulse, and it was late before anyone wished to sleep.

During the night a fierce north-easterly gale arose. The trees moaned and creaked, and leaves from their autumn-weary tops fell rustling on the canvas of the tent. Early next morning the boat expedition and its land auxiliary set out simultaneously. The river was covered by a carpet of leaves that drifted with the stream. Sometimes it seemed to us that our vessel stood still on the leaf carpet, but the banks glided past, and they were lovelier and more gorgeous in colour than ever.

Our next camping-place was at the south-eastern edge of the vast steppe in which lay the palace of the blind Torgut prince.

As soon as the news of our arrival reached the palace, the prince's son, Puntsuk, came over to our camp on a visit of courtesy. He showed great interest in all that he saw at our camp and minutely examined our weapons, equipment and provisions. But what impressed him most of all was *Long Snake* which was lying tugging at her moorings. And both he and his retinue of attendant Torguts stayed at the camp to see the start and convince themselves that it really was true that two grown men could ride over the water in that wonderful object.

The Torguts were exceedingly anxious to know if the vessel was to sail on Socho-nor, and we told them that we intended to attempt this. I was drawn aside by Puntsuk who confided to me a desire that lay close to his heart. Would I, when I came out on that great lake, keep a look out for *socho* and afterwards tell him how they looked at close range and how they behaved ? Many had seen *socho* from the shores but their accounts of what they saw were so diverse, and, since *socho* kept right in the middle of the lake, no one had really been able to get a near view of them.

I had no notion what *socho* were, but after an anxious glance towards the lake the prince gave me this description :

" Where the lake of Socho-nor now heaves there once stood a great and wealthy city. Its inhabitants lived a sinful and unrighteous life which called forth the wrath of the gods. In order to punish the people the angry gods one night caused the whole city to sink into the earth, and in the hollow made by this they created a lake into which they cast alkali and salt so that no people would be able to live in its proximity. But the innocent cattle were not to suffer for the sake of their sinful owners and the animals therefore were transformed into *socho*, the water cattle, who could live and multiply on the rich pastures of the lake's bed. Sometimes one could see them rise to the surface of the water, but always right out in the middle of the lake. Sometimes, when the water level was specially low, early morning hunters had seen their tracks on the brink, and old folk could remember their parents telling them how sixty years ago, when the lake was dried up after a very dry summer, the mysterious water cattle had been seen disappearing into the interior of the earth through a hole in the bottom of the lake.

The lake was ruled over by *socho* and was therefore known as " The Lake of Water Cattle " and *socho* were in intimate contact with the gods. Once upon a time, many generations before, men were better than they are now, and in those times it could happen that a poor huntsman who lived a pure life would hear at night the tree-tops whispering a mystic formula. And if this poor huntsman on the next night led a cow to the edge of the lake and laid himself down to sleep beside it after having cried the proper formula out over the lake, during the night the cow would be visited by *socho* and soon afterwards would become pregnant and give birth to a calf whose productivity was equal to that of a herd of many hundred animals. But nowadays, when people were less good, these miracles occurred no more."

On the morning of the twenty-first of October the water level in the river showed itself to have sunk another couple of inches, and it was therefore necessary immediately to break camp, since a further slight fall would make all boating impossible. We arranged to rejoin the caravan at the point where the river flows into Socho-nor, and after a cordial parting with Puntsuk and his Torguts, we let the stream bear us farther north.

The river grew broader and divided into many branches, and the shallows were frequent. We often ran aground, and the water was cold and so salt as to be painful. The surroundings were the most dismal imaginable and remained just as dismal, grey and cold for hour after endless hour. The air was damp and saturated with salt, and the grey-blue sky hung low and heavy. So as not to risk foundering right out in the boggy area of the delta, at each new branching of the stream we steered in a westerly direction and thus had an ever-increasing stretch of bog to the right of us but firm land in sight to the left.

In the end we were brought to a complete standstill by a wide barrier of sand blocking the delta's outflow. There beyond it the Lake of the Water Cattle waited, unknown, frightening and unreal. We lay now helplessly stuck fast in the treacherous sand. The depth of the water was only six inches, and I wanted to try to reach the strip of firm land a bare hundred yards away to the west, but scarcely had I got out of the boat and let go of it when I was sucked down. And it was only by a mighty effort that the Chief hauled me on board again.

At last our caravan came in sight. Rapid measures of rescue were now taken, and we were able to walk ashore over an improvised bridge of case-lids. After this the boat was hauled in by the camels to the bank. A hundred yards beyond the western edge of the delta the lake shore was comparatively firm, and thither the vessel was dragged. And then it was launched on Socho-nor.

The wind had risen, the misty grey air grew clearer, and soon the sun's rays broke through the clouds. The surroundings seemed less repellent as soon as we grew less cold. The surface of the water in front of us took on a clear greenish-blue colour which clearly defined the line of the shore to east and west until this disappeared in grey-blue haze. To northward the lake stretched farther than the eye could see and seemed to melt into the distant horizon. Some screaming lapwings tried to drive us away, and out on the little white-crested waves groups of water-fowl were floating.

The vigorous south-easterly breeze invited an attempt to convert *Long Snake* into a sailing craft, and she looked fine with a wooden mast forward and the Chief's waterproof cape bellying like the sail upon a viking ship. Our friends ashore looked apprehensive, but we reassured them and ourselves by announcing our intention only to make a little trial trip close inshore.

Lightly and elegantly we rocked forward over the waves, and the speed at which the shore behind us disappeared and the figures of our friends were obliterated assured us that we were moving at a good rate. The Chief was occupied with compass bearings, lightning calculations and notes, and I took soundings. The depth varied between five and eight feet, but with a long pole I could feel that the bed consisted of bottomless mud.

Suddenly we were out of sight of land. On all sides there was nothing but swirling water and a hemisphere of blue-green sky. Since everything now seemed equally remote, we determined to continue our northerly course. The wind freshened to a gale and ragged clouds scudded across the sky ; the waves dashed with headlong force against *Long Snake's* sides, and she began to take in water. So as not to meet the weather broadside on we took a westerly course and got the waves astern. The Chief bailed incessantly with an aluminium bailer, but in spite of his efforts the water slowly rose in both canoes, and *Long Snake* laboured more heavily.

I knew exactly the limit to the ballast the boat could take in and that it would not be long before the whole thing would go to the bottom with a gurgle. Our friends ashore were certainly uneasy, but not in a position to bring us any help, since *Long Snake* was the only vessel " within seven leagues ".

If the boat sank, there was nothing for it but to swim for our lives in one direction or another and hope that the nearest land lay in the direction chosen. For the rest the important thing was to keep our feet away from the clutching mud of the lake bottom when we got into shallower water.

All at once the Chief began to sing " Black Rudolph "

in thundering emulation of the clamour of the elements, and I believe we both laughed heartily. Soon afterwards we made out a dark line of shore and, just as the last light of day was about to die, we landed upon the northern shore of Socho-nor.

It was a grey and desolate land upon which we set our feet, and soon all was submerged in black night. We were freezing in our saturated clothes, and we were hungry after all our exertions and had a raging thirst from all the salt exhalations we had imbibed. But except for a small piece of chocolate, a few biscuits and a drop of brandy we had nothing to relieve these discomforts. We froze like dogs, and to get a little warmth into our bodies we began running about in the night. We often lost one another in the pitch-black darkness. Sometimes we stumbled over little shrubby plants or bits of driftwood, and these we eagerly collected so as to try to get a fire going. Fortunately we had dry matches, but all our fuel was so damp that we were obliged to use *Long Snake's* mast to help us kindle a short-lived fire.

We peered out into the darkness for an answering blaze, but saw only the cold indifferent stars. When the fire burned down we went down to the shore to cool our burning tongues, but the water was so salt as to make us retch. We put a very little lake water and the whole of our brandy into our common cup, and it both warmed us and improved our spirits. The twinkling of the stars seemed more friendly ; the lake sang a song of the sea and inspired us to strike up new sailors' chanties.

Then a living flame arose far out in the darkness, and we hurriedly looked at the compass by the light of a match. Our friends' signal lay to the westward, twenty degrees north, and it seemed to throw its warmth across the intervening lake through distance and darkness. We sent a bit of *Long Snake's* writing-table and a hastily gathered supply of scrub up in flames, and the answering flame rose higher.

Our little pyre soon sank to embers, but the distant fire burned on. It seemed so near and palpable that it conveyed a profound feeling of security. The night was cold and still young, and we beguiled its hours with making plans for a new day.

Next morning there was a dead calm, and we were compelled to row the heavy craft back to the camp. But across the vast surface of the lake lay a guiding sun-path.

Long Snake had ended her voyage and fulfilled her mission. But to preserve the craft for contemplated future excursions we drew her up on to a hillock above high-water mark. She had a primitive look, like a museum piece of some remote period, and the discoverers of later days might take her as evidence that the ancient dwellers on Etsin-gol had been seafaring folk. To prevent any such mistake I carved in big capital letters on her wide stern : " *Long Snake navigated Etsin-gol and Socho-nor in the sixty-third year of Sven Hedin's life.*"

CHAPTER XVI

WE TRAVERSE BLACK GOBI

ON our way back to the main camp we passed great herds of cattle and horses, the well-fed appearance of which induced in our Mongols a tender longing for their own horses and cattle far off in distant Chahar. They often had to stop to point out some particular horse to me. " Look at that black with a coat like velvet." " Do you see that one ? He's just like my *Kiling Saghan* at home." Now they wanted to know how many foals I thought they had in their home camp, now whether the wolves had been troublesome, now whether it was to be expected that their horses were as fine, as handsome and in as good condition to withstand the coming winter as the animals we saw here.

Around the Torgut camp joy in work and infectious gaiety prevailed. They were slaughtering to complete their winter stores and gorging on the offal. Children were gnawing bones, infants were sucking juicy entrails, sewn up in hide bags, and the dogs stood fawning at the tent openings and almost forgot their obligation to be fierce and wary.

The Torguts had begun their great autumn slaughtering, and this meant that the beasts were now as fat as they could become that year, and that the long hard winter was standing at the door. The summer had been good and bountiful, and both man and beast could meet the winter with confidence.

All were happy and friendly ; there were none who did not wish to share with others their happiness and their superfluity of meat and drink.

But for us the approach of winter brought the signal for departure from settled and inhabited regions. It meant that our camels' time of rest and recreation was

143

over. The forces they had now collected must last them for at least the next seven months, for seven hard winter months would intervene before the vegetation of a new year would burst forth. During that time the beasts of burden were to carry our great expedition on many a long march through dead and unknown deserts.

We went home by way of the place where the men in charge of the expedition's camels were encamped. The Chinese camel-drivers were busily engaged in making warm stockings and mittens of camel wool, but the Mongols just sat and looked melancholy.

In the reed beds in front of the faded tents hundreds of camels were grazing, happily unconscious that soon they would again be laden with heavy burdens and driven over arduous desert marches. The saddle-galls on their backs were now healed, and their humps had risen somewhat, but their thighs were still flabby and thin, and the animals seemed broken down, cowed and weary of life. I tried to startle them with a revolver shot, but they scarcely responded; they only gazed stupidly in my direction and at once resumed their munching. Many of the camels seemed too exhausted to be able to sustain a winter at Etsin-gol, and I wondered how many of them would be fit to get through the winter's strenuous marches through Black Gobi.

The thoughts of the Mongols did not go out towards the west. The late autumn is the time of all others when the nomad on a caravan journey is seized with longing for his home tent.

The happy feelings, which, in us, are born with the spring and culminate on a light midsummer night, are faint, almost non-existent in the Mongols. For in spring the cattle are famished, the grazing on the steppes is scanty, the cows are without milk, and the store of meat devoured, and spring storms kill many winter-worn and exhausted beasts. Not until the midsummer rainy season has restored luxuriance to the dried-up grasses of the steppe do the animals begin to recover their lost forces, the milk supply to increase, cattle and sheep to put on flesh and the horses to regain their spirit.

To watch his cattle thriving and daily improving in

condition delights the Mongol more than anything, and his happiness is greatest in the late autumn, for then his horse can gallop faster and farther over the steppes than at any earlier period of the year, the cattle are in good flesh and their growing offspring vigorous.

And now here sat our Mongols far from their dwellings in the east, full of wonder as to how everything was going in their own tents, full of longing to witness the happiness of their own people and full of dejection at having to go in the opposite direction. Go they must, out into the unknown wilds, still farther from their native Chahar.

At the end of October the various groups of the expedition were once more assembled in the main camp, for the time had come for a further advance towards the west. The banks of Etsin-gol, lately so splendid with autumn foliage, had been transformed into a black lattice of naked tree-trunks, and drift ice was grinding in the river.

The four hundred and thirty miles that lay between us and Hami, the easternmost oasis town of Sinkiang, was the most intimidating stage of our long journey, and the preparations for it were made with care.

Our caravan was divided into three columns. The largest, consisting of a hundred and twenty-seven camels was to make its way along the northern edge of the desert so as to avail itself of the probably existing water-places. With this column the chief and eleven of the expedition's staff would travel, and the conduct of it was entrusted to Larson. Norin and Bergman with a caravan of thirty camels were to follow the southern edge of the desert, while the third column was to cross its very heart. The middle column was made up of the meteorologists Haude and Li with Dettmann, Hempel and Kaul, who were respectively to take astronomical observations, to map the route and to maintain wireless communication with the German station at Nauen for checking the time factor in their calculations. The oasis town of Hami was the common goal at which the three groups counted on meeting in the middle of December for a joint celebration of the expedition's first Christmas.

The leading of the middle group was entrusted to me—a task both alarming and alluring. The feebleness of the camels and our ignorance of the position of the water-holes in that vast sterile tract were our handicap, and to steel my column against its hardships I brought forward a plan which was enthusiastically accepted by my travelling companions.

All the servants' and caravan men's work was to be done by ourselves, and we should take with us only two Mongols so that in critical situations we might be able to avail ourselves of their strongly developed desert instinct. The number of camels was to be reduced to twenty-four which was the minimum. No dogs were to be taken, since these as well as men and camels need water. A hundredweight of the least necessary cargo was to be taken from each camel's load and replaced with the same weight of beans. By allowing each camel four and a half pounds a day of this nutritious fodder we hoped to be able to maintain their working capacity for the twenty-five days which we reckoned it would take to reach less sterile territory, while each camel-load would be diminished daily by that amount.

The middle column was the first to start, and we left Etsin-gol followed by the cheery wishes of our friends for a successful journey and a quick reunion at Hami. Only Tsereat, who was to be attached to the northern column, seemed depressed, and at parting he handed over the two objects which Yolros Lama had entrusted to his keeping on my account, for, he said, *now* I might find a use for them.

The first march on the new long trail brought us to Murin-gol, where we camped on the threshold of the desert. I spent the whole of the following day with our Mongols in visiting the surrounding Mongol camps in the hope of finding a guide. But it was all in vain ; neither kind words nor payment could induce any of them to go with us through Black Gobi.

We met with Mongols who had been a day or two's journey to the west on the track of strayed cattle, and all they had seen had been waterless stony wastes. But they had heard from passing caravans which had later gone by Etsin-gol on their way between the markets of China and the oases of Central Asia that the crossing of Black Gobi was made possible by the presence of two wells which divided the most perilous part of the desert into " the four dry " and " the three dry " marches. If one but found these wells the camels suffered no lack of water ; if one found only one of them one could get through, but if one found neither the caravan was lost.

Far into the desert would lie a fortress which until a few years ago was controlled by the notorious robber chief Dambin Jansang. It was he who had dug both the wells to entice the caravan traffic to pass through the No-man's-land which he dominated. The rich merchants had willingly paid the tribute exacted, for, since the Soviet had closed the northern caravan route through Khalka Mongolia and the southern route had been made impassable by the Chinese robber bands infesting it, Dambin Jansang's route was the only available communication between east and west.

But now Dambin Jansang was gone, and his disciplined robber band was transformed into a pack of unscrupulous bandits, and the road through Black Gobi was consequently accursed both by gods and men.

THE tales of the local Mongols were little calculated to arouse an optimistic temper for our start. I pondered long over the responsibility laid upon me and the chances of finding the water-holes.

Gombo, who shared my anxiety, suggested that I should open the two packets which had been Yolros Lama's parting gifts to me, and when the Mongols saw their contents they at once became convinced of the happy issue of our undertaking.

The packets contained a document inscribed in Tibetan characters and a prayer-flag, and when we set out at dawn the next day the prayer-flag was fluttering gaily above the leading camel of the caravan.

For three days we wandered, and our camping-places

were nameless specks in the desert. The nights were cold, and the days' dismal impressions haunted our brains. Etsin-gol was infinitely far, and uncertainty lay in front of us. The country we traversed was empty of life, but each morning we had heard for a short while the song of a lark, which enchanted us in the great stillness. We persuaded ourselves that it was the same lark accompanying us, and the Mongols were convinced that it was the reincarnation of a good spirit that was leading us through the desert.

But on the fourth morning we lay long in our sleeping-bags vainly awaiting the bird's glad morning greeting.

All through the day the glances of the Mongols were often turned on Yolros Lama's prayer-flag in expectation of a new sign to support their hopefulness.

On the following night our despondency kept sleep away, but suddenly our ears caught the faint sound of bells from some approaching caravan. We leapt up, and the Mongols and I galloped out into the night to meet the sound.

We found a Chinese caravan in terrified flight to the eastward. In vain we tried to persuade the leader of the caravan to camp in our neighbourhood; I could only get him to stop for a moment to answer our eager questions. Two days' march to the westward they had been attacked by robbers, who had maltreated the caravan men and robbed them of both camels and goods. They had passed both water-holes, of which the nearer lay one and a half day's journey to the westward, but I did not succeed in getting the leader to spare any of his boys to show us the way thither.

The caravan's growling dogs were circling round us, but one of them sneaked up to me in friendly fashion. While I was patting him the idea struck me that this dog had certainly many times slaked his thirst at the two water-holes on caravan journeys through Black Gobi. And despite the savage curses of the caravan leader I swung the dog up in front of me on the saddle and galloped back to our camp.

We christened our new acquisition Khara Sain, " Black Goodness ", and hoped he would do justice to his name. When we went on towards the west I rode at the head of the column leading the dog on a strong cord, and on our arrival at the evening's camping-place he was kept without water.

During the next march we followed the same tactics, and we intently observed the thirsty dog's behaviour. Towards afternoon he began to act uncertainly and, after having long led us in zigzags, tore himself loose with an unexpected jerk and disappeared in a northerly direction.

But Gombo was almost as swift, and after half an hour he came grinning back to bring us to the water-hole to which the dog had guided him.

We were overjoyed for now we regarded ourselves as saved, and when four days later Khara Sain led us in the same way to the second water-hole we blessed him, and he was regaled with the best we could afford.

149

CHAPTER XVII

A ROBBER'S STRONGHOLD IN THE DESERT

THE Chinese caravan men's hysterical account of an encounter with Dambin Jansang's robbers loomed the larger in our thought that we were on our way to the desert tract in which it had occurred.

The savage desolation of the country prompted us to stringent precaution and the utmost readiness for defence. All was sterile desert ; no trace of life was to be seen, but none the less we had often an anxious presentiment of the proximity of lurking dangers.

The heavy silence of the night was frequently dispersed by Khara Sain's furious outbursts, and by day it would happen that the dog, growling and bristling, would fix his eyes on some object invisible to us on the hazy horizon.

Every now and then we made reconnaissances off the caravan route and found fresh and indisputably human tracks. We thought and talked of nothing but robbers, and I fancy we almost hoped for some violent release from this monotonous preoccupation.

Our imagination filled the crevices in the savage hills with every conceivable danger, and we approached every pass, every outcrop of rock, with eye to sights and finger on trigger. We startled one another by taking aim at inanimate objects, and we often wished a grey stone had been a swarthy bandit's head.

At last our suspicion that the bandits were hanging round us was confirmed, for early one morning we caught a glimpse of a number of dark silhouettes of mounted men against the grey-blue dawn. The sight made us forget all our prearranged counsels of prudence, and in a wild lust for vengeance we entered on a hopeless pursuit of the swiftly galloping figures, which were soon swallowed up in the drab landscape.

On the sixteenth of November the temperature fell to
— 16°. We were passing through desolate stony desert ;
only to the north and north-west a grey line of hills
was dimly visible. At nightfall we began the descent
into a wide depression, and the pale light of a multitude
of stars threw a ghostly gleam over the unknown contours
of the landscape.

We were dead tired and longed to pitch camp, but
sought in vain for an inviting spot. The dragging gait
of the camels aggravated the horrors of the darkness, and
the hours of the night were eternities.

Suddenly a new silhouette appeared against the starry
sky to the southward, and the caravan pulled up. We
seemed to be standing before an immense stronghold
of darkness, and since the caravan could not risk having
its hidden danger in its rear, we halted.

Our distance from the fortress was greater than I
reckoned, and I counted over nine hundred camel paces
before the surmised contours were transformed into the
astonishing reality. In front of me lay a huge stone-
built fortress with towers and walls, a colossus reared
by human hands in the midst of the unpeopled desert.

Cautiously I rode along the wall until the acrid smoke
of Chinese *dunsa* [1] suddenly tickled my nostrils. I pulled
up my camel. Four horses stood tied up behind a
projection in the wall, but their smoking riders were
invisible. I was just going to give my companions the
agreed signal of distress, three rapid shots, when my
camel rushed off bellowing loudly. I had lost one stirrup,
and felt a heavy living being attach itself firmly at the
back of my saddle.

The camel's wild plunge quickly relieved me of the
assailant behind me, and during the gallop we put up
three dark figures, but when the beast finally stopped I
was again surrounded by blank darkness.

Three shots from me were answered by nervous salvos
from the rifles of my companions, and we gathered for
a conference. We all agreed to camp at the foot of the
fort, for we had to clear up its mystery by daylight.

[1] *Dunsa* (Chinese Tung-shen)—tobacco imported from China which
the Mongols smoke in their long pipes.

With some of the others I returned to the place where the four horses had stood, but the only sign of life there was the still-glowing plug from a Mongol pipe.

The rest of the night was apparently peaceful, but no one in the camp slept, and Gombo's time after time repeated : " This is an evil country, not fit for honest folk," kept returning to our minds.

But daylight returned, and a warm sun smiled on us, and the camping-place on which we had chanced in the darkness proved to be an oasis of surprises. After those many days of oppressive monotony we found ourselves in a scene which was beautiful, though its vegetation had suffered from the frost. A little brook wound through the valley and at the point where this flowed into the lake which was its goal, a few hundred yards below, we saw a sight as completely lovely as the sunlight itself.

There were five *kulans* [1] playing on the shore, magnificently beautiful in form and movement. They drank at the edge of the ice, nudged one another amicably, nipped one another's necks, rose on their hind legs and chased one another at a gay gallop over the steppe, to resume later their morning drink. From time to time they stopped to peer at our camp. Their asses' ears flicked with curiosity, their noble, proudly carried heads swung up and down in the untamed freedom of the wilderness, and the sun gave a brilliance as of gold to their pale yellow hides. In size and build they reminded one of big ponies, but their ears and tails were those of the ass.

We enjoyed this splendid sight for a long time, until the horses disappeared with a thunder of hooves between the hills towards a new No-man's-goal.

The fortress of the night before was still there in the daylight, and our camp lay in its shadow.

This was the centre from which mysterious power had until quite lately overspread the whole of Central Asia ; this was Dambin Jansang's late chief stronghold, a place which few honest eyes had seen, but which was the focal point of thousands of the tales whispered by the camp-fires of the Mongols. To judge by its appearance

[1] Kulan—*Equus hermionus.*

this desert fastness with its charred woodwork might have been a thousand-year-old ruin. But in actual fact many of the men who here laid stone on stone are still young fellows whose deeds of violence awake echoes of terror from the stronghold's time of greatness among the caravan people who cross the Black Gobi.

In the sober light of day the fortress lay dead and deserted ; not a trace of life was to be seen. From the highest turret room of the citadel we looked out over the land which once was swayed by Asia's dreaded lama bandit. To the south and west the view was cut off by the blue chain of the Ma-tsung mountains, but to the north the glance could pass freely over the low rocky hills of the desert to Northern Mongolia's infinity of steppes.

At the foot of the fortress flows the stream which made it possible for Dambin Jansang and his horde to live in the midst of the stony desert. The Mongols call the place Baying Bulak, " the rich spring ", but the Chinese Kung-p'o Ch'uan, " the spring by the duke's precipice ". Down in the valley there were traces of irrigation canals, and everywhere there were remains of fireplaces bearing witness to the life which not long since had prevailed in the stronghold.

Dambin Jansang is one of those forceful figures that have arisen again and again in Asia's vast expanses and by remarkable personal qualities have acquired a mysterious power over the Mongols. Legends of the dreaded fighting lama are innumerable, and new variations of them are constantly arising, but from them arises a vivid picture of an adventurer who re-enacted on the steppes the savagery of an earlier time.

The Mongols' real knowledge of the man is of the slightest, and to this day they waver in uncertainty as to whether he was an instrument of divine vengeance or the incarnation of an evil spirit in a robber chief.

The Polish professor, F. Ossendowski, met him in 1921 under the name of Tushe-Gun Lama, " the avenger lama ", and describes his enormous force of will and hypnotic power.

Dambin Jansang constantly appeared in new disguises

and made a practice of giving as his domicile some place far remote from that of the persons in whose company he was at the moment. But by collating the observations of those westerners who have encountered him it is possible to determine the main features of his adventurous career.

The man was born in Russia and derived from the Western Mongolian *Durbet* stock which lives a nomadic life by the Volga. As a result of his virulent revolutionary activity he early found himself in a Russian prison, but succeeded in escaping and went into hiding in far Tibet. There he devoted himself for several years to the study of Buddhistic metaphysics and the mystic formulas of the *Tantra* system, and he himself asserted that he had acquired in India the supernatural qualities of the fakirs.

Europeans who have met him say that he had mastered Sanskrit as well as Tibetan, Mongolian, Chinese and Russian. He had served in the Chang-chia *hutuktu's Yamen*, the ecclesiastical institution in Peking which draws up the Mongolian calendar and is occupied with other astronomical and metaphysical problems.

It was about the year 1900 that Dambin Jansang began his struggle for power. The Russian professor Pozdneef, relates that at this time he heard him spoken of as a young lama travelling magnificently dressed through the Mongolian steppes. He then called himself Ten-pei Jalsang and claimed to be the son of Temursana and descendant of Amursana, the great champions of liberty among the West Mongols.

Later he proclaimed himself as the reincarnation of Amursana, come to free the Mongols from the Chinese yoke, and wherever he went on the steppes he was received as a divinity. His travels extended from Astrakhan to Peking, from Siberia to India. In 1910 he appeared among the Khara Shar Torguts in Eastern Turkestan and in 1912 in the Durbet chief's camp at Hageltsik.

Among the nomads the conviction long prevailed that Dambin Jansang was the re-incarnation of the great Amursana, and the prophecy was whispered in their camps that the time had now come for the new war that should assemble the tribes and re-create the ancient *öret* confederation. All who know the power of prophecies over the primitive lamaists of Asia should be able to understand Dambin Jansang's success. He was worshipped as a divine warrior, and soon hosts of savage fighters gathered round the new leader.

He was the most prominent of those who inspired the Mongols' national struggle for freedom in 1911 and 1912, and he commanded the horde of West Mongols that attacked the Chinese garrison of Kobdo. After the town fell Dambin Jansang had the Chinese and Mohammedan inhabitants massacred, and himself slaughtered ten persons according to an occult ritual and with their blood painted tokens of victory on the standards of the troops.

For his great services to the newly formed Mongolian nation Dambin Jansang received profuse gratitude from the authorities at Urga. He was invested with the title of *Kung* and was proclaimed as *hutuktu*, and as military governor of Western Mongolia he soon became one of the richest and most powerful chieftains in the country.

He was cruel to his enemies and was feared by his adherents. The Mongol chiefs behaved towards him as though they had been his servants and on several occasions he humiliated them to the degree of making them hold his stirrup when he mounted. Any who dared to disobey were annihilated ; none could escape the fighting lama's terrible vengeance.

All were convinced of his supernatural power. I have heard eye-witnesses relate how he would throw himself into the thickest of the fight, and how afterwards his cap was pierced through and through with bullets, but he himself was unwounded, and when he shook his clothing the bullets fell in quantities to the ground.

In 1914 reports of his deeds of violence reached the Russian Government, and a strong force of Cossacks was sent to capture the disturber of the peace. When they took him by surprise in his tent they found the seats of honour in it covered with human hides, those of his two mortal enemies whom he had had flayed alive.

For several years he remained in a Russian prison, but

with the revolution he obtained his freedom and soon appeared again in south-western Mongolia among the people of the Tsagechin Beile tribe.

When the Chinese An-fu troops under General Hsü reconquered Outer Mongolia in 1919, Dambin Jansang got another chance. He occasioned heavy losses to the Chinese and was hailed on the steppes as the champion of Mongolian freedom.

Later he co-operated with Baron Ungern von Sternberg, who besieged Urga in 1921. After the fall and execution of Ungern in the same year, Dambin Jansang became the central figure among the defenders of the old regime in Mongolia. The "Red" Government in Urga feared the "avenging lama" and sent a force to take him dead or alive, but Dambin Jansang escaped and took refuge in an unknown oasis in the heart of Black Gobi by the well which he called Baying Bulak.

Mongolia's adored hero was now transformed into a formidable robber chieftain, but so great was his power over men's minds that he was soon in command of a numerous band of fighters. Many against their will followed the outlawed fighting lama out into the barren No-man's-land he had chosen as his base of operations. They brought with them their families and cattle, and soon five hundred tent-dwelling families were established round the robber's tent by Baying Bulak.

Chinese prisoners of war were made to build the robber's stronghold, and new effective fighters were impressed into his army.

The lama bandit became the most dangerous enemy of the newly formed Mongolian Soviet State, and in 1924 a strong expedition was sent out from Urga to make an end of his power. This expedition, which was made up of Mongols and Russians, was commanded by Baldan Dorje, a Mongolian chief renowned for his valour.

The closing scenes were later described to me by the young chief of the Tsagechin Beile, who had long been Dambin Jansang's assistant and right-hand man.

Baldan Dorje left his six hundred fighting men in a cleft of the hills several miles from the robbers' stronghold, and himself with two selected chiefs, dressed as high lamas, went on. At Dambin Jansang's outposts they explained that they had come on a weighty errand from the Living Buddha at Urga who sought the assistance of the "free Mongols" in a revolt against the Russians.

The three disguised warriors were well received in the fortress, and for several days they devised plans with the leaders of the bandits. Meanwhile they reconnoitred the strength of the fortress and, when they realized its impregnability, Baldan Dorje put his daring plan into operation.

For two days he did not leave his room, and visiting Mongols saw him lying dying on his bed, while his two friends read over him the office for the dying. On the third day a message was sent to Dambin Jansang that Baldan Dorje lay at the point of death and that his last wish was to receive the *hutuktu's* blessing.

And the lama robber came, but as he bent over the ostensibly dying man, the latter drew a revolver from his yellow lama's robe and emptied it into the brigand's body. It was the work of a moment, and before the hurrying soldiers reached the guest-room the severed head of "the immortal" had been flung through the door into the courtyard.

Next moment Dambin Jansang's murderer stepped forth to the panic-stricken warriors and before their eyes swallowed the dead leader's bloody heart. At the sight of the robber's lifeless head and in the belief that by devouring his heart Baldan Dorje was now in possession of his invincible qualities, the garrison of the fortress took to flight. Many were killed and others were cut off by Baldan Dorje's force, but many more escaped to places of refuge known only to themselves in Black Gobi, whence they continued to spread terror among peaceful travellers in the desert.

Among those who disappeared was Dambin Jansang's lieutenant, the young chieftain of the Tsagechin Beile.

The Urga Government afterwards had Dambin Jansang's severed head carried on the point of a lance throughout the length and breadth of Mongolia, but the Mongols are nevertheless still unconvinced that Dambin Jansang is dead.

It is whispered round the camp fires of the nomads that the fighting lama's arrow-swift black horse had vanished from its place in the stable before the general flight from the fortress and that his magnificently chased silver saddle was not among the booty which Baldan Dorje took back to Urga. And it is said that the savage watchdogs that used to be fastened by stout silver chains before the fighting lama's dwelling still lurk in the neighbourhood of the fortress awaiting their master's return.

CHAPTER XVIII

PRISONERS

THE temperature was falling daily. We struggled against the desert's bitter winds, but it was not until the nineteenth of November that the Siberian winter seized upon Black Gobi with storm and snow. For thirty hours we lay cowering in our sleeping-bags, and no one spoke.

When the gale at last died down we awoke again to life, but round about us nature lay cold and terrifying. The camels were deeply buried in the snow. Two pregnant ones had slipped their foals during the night, and we were obliged to shoot them. The tents were fluttering in rags, our watches had stopped from the cold and it was difficult even to simulate optimism.

When the grey of the sky grew less dense and the sun became visible as a pale disk we made a start. The loads of the two dead camels were transferred to riding camels and we all went on foot.

Day after day we hastened westward, driven by longing for the security of Hami, fleeing from the brooding menace of the desert.

At last, on the twenty-seventh of November, twenty-eight days after the start from Etsin-gol, we came in sight of vegetation. We fell to cheering, for now we believed that all our troubles lay behind us. We camped under some poplar trees and hastened towards some houses with smoking chimneys, filled with longing to encounter human beings.

But we never reached the inviting human dwellings, for we were checked by the thunder of hooves. Suddenly we were surrounded by a wild troop of horsemen whose fierce cries we did not understand, but whose faces expressed obvious hostility. They shrieked and howled, and several hundred rifle muzzles encircled us.

The Chinese-speaking leader, a wild-eyed, black-bearded Sart,[1] informed us harshly that the Chinese Governor-General of Sinkiang, Yang Tseng-Hsien, refused us entrance to his domains, and that the soldiers had strict orders to drive us back into the desert whence we came.

This was nothing less than a death sentence on the caravan, and the impossibility of obeying the order confirmed our courage and our contumacy. We were now at Miao-go, an outlying oasis two days' journey from Hami, and there we were allowed to remain under guard. In the course of the following days we were often threatened with execution, but so much the oftener did we roar our battle song, " Keep right on to the end of the road."

Our queer behaviour was reported to the authorities at Hami.

On the fifth day our captors received cavalry reinforcements—which, however, were to become our help and deliverance. Fanfares of trumpets announced their arrival, and soon we discerned in the red cloud of dust a dense mass of galloping horsemen. A sharp word of command brought the troop into open order, and we were ringed round by eight hundred fierce-looking soldiers.

We stared in amazement at the newly arrived warriors, for they were all dressed in Cossack uniforms and their evolutions were carried out with western military precision. And I was even more astonished when the young leader of the troopers walked into our tent, for his bearing was stamped with dignified grace and his words were Mongolian.

Two days later we were in Hami where we were brought before the Chinese commandant of the town, an opium-ravaged human wreck, and before the commander of

[1] Sart is the name given to the town dwellers of Eastern Turkestan. They are Mohammedans and are often of mixed Turkish and Persian race.

Photo Hempel

"In the red cloud of dust a dense mass of galloping horsemen"

[face p. 160

Mongrolda Noyen, the young leader of the Khoshut Mongols with his bodyguard

Tsagechin Beile

[*face p.* 161]

the whole eastern front of Sinkiang, a man of about forty in the uniform of a Chinese Marshal. The few words the Marshal uttered were in Mongolian, and his eyes had a friendly, enquiring glance. I met with the young Mongol officer who brought us from Miao-go to Hami, a number of times, and we arrived at relations which were friendly if also strictly reserved. From him I learned that our hostile reception was due to unfavourable reports received, concerning the expedition, by the Governor-General of the province but that he thought everything would be satisfactorily arranged.

In response to our anxious enquiries as to the northern column's fate he told me what the Mongolian scouts had reported. The column had been pursued by ill-fortune ; many of the camels had died ; and the rest were no longer fit to carry loads ; the Chief lay sick with a few members of the expedition at the water-place of Sebistei far within the desert ; the remaining members were on their way to Hami on foot, since there was not provision for the prolonged stay of so many people in the desert.

This was depressing news, and we tried by every means we could think of to get leave to carry the succour to our colleagues. But every attempt stranded on the refusal of the Chinese Governor-General in distant Urumchi.

We celebrated Christmas in the shelter of a house in Hami, but with sentries outside our door—and our friends were still out in the vast cold desert.

Our imprisonment in Hami lasted for more than a month. We were in daily negotiation with the local authorities for permission for the expedition to enter Sinkiang and for relief to be sent to the northern column stranded in the desert. We so far succeeded that an order came from the Governor-General that a relief caravan with fresh camels and provisions was to be sent to Sebistei and ourselves conducted under escort to Urumchi, the capital of Sinkiang.

On the twenty-third of January, after seventy-three days in Black Gobi, the last remnants of the northern column arrived in Hami, but by then the central column's members were already on their way to the capital. We travelled the whole way under guard of the young Mongolian chief who had brought us from Miao-go to Hami. I soon came to know that he was Mongrolda Noyen, the leader of the Khoshut Mongols, and that among his soldiers there were Torguts belonging to the great tribe that I was seeking. The chief and his people treated us with friendly courtesy, but I never succeeded in getting from them any information about their native country.

The morning before our arrival in Urumchi, Mongrolda Noyen had disappeared and had been replaced by a Chinese escort, and when we made our entry into the Governor-General's *yamen*, we passed through a guard of honour of soldiers presenting arms.

The old Governor Yang soon became filled with inquisitive interest in our project, and from that time onward he was to become the protector of the expedition until his death which, alas, occurred before its task was finished.

CHAPTER XIX

FACTS AND MUSINGS ABOUT A COIN
AND A WOMAN'S DRESS

THE expedition's headquarters were situated in that part of Urumchi which in the time of the Tsars was a " factory " concession for Russian subjects. The greater number of our neighbours were White Russians, mostly old people and women with children who had not ventured out into the regions, terrifying and difficult of access, which separated their isolated place of refuge from more civilized parts of the world. After the defeat of the White Guards in Siberia, thousands of those soldiers and their train of refugees who were faithful to the old ideals passed through Sinkiang on their way to China and India, and the few hundred exiles among whom we lived there were a little troop left behind by the fleeing hordes.

Immediately in front of us lay the large park area surrounding the Russian consulate and the Russian church. The red flag now floated over the consulate building, and its offices were the centre of Soviet activity in Sinkiang. They had tried to turn the church into a place of amusement, but the pious Chinese governor of the province had intervened to prevent this vandalism, and from its onion-shaped cupolas the Byzantine cross still shone as a unifying symbol for those who still were able to believe.

The last consul of the time of the Tsars had eschewed the sight of the Soviet flag over the domain which for many years had been his home and field of work, and had sought refuge in a little mud hovel deep in the Chinatown of Urumchi. It had come to my knowledge that throughout his long service in Sinkiang the old consul had been possessed by a veritable passion for

Central Asiatic ethnography and still had in his possession
a great many rare and interesting objects which he had
collected on his long journeys.

One day I went to see him in his hut. We went
through his large collections together, and he explained
them and told stories about them for hours on end.
Among other things he had an extensive collection of
coins which he had dug up from various sources or
purchased from the natives. The many lead-soft silver
pieces and patinated copper coins threw gleams of light
on the chequered history of Central Asia, and we read
in them the epochs of the dominance of foreign invaders.
I listened fascinated to the aged consul's expositions and
theories which lent to these old silver and copper coins
the attraction of gold itself.

Suddenly I gave a start, for in the collection of those
impressed with oriental hieroglyphics lay a silver Swedish
coin. It was a Caroline *daler*, and in its upper edge
was a cord-worn hole indicating that it had for long
been used as an amulet. The consul had bought this
coin from a Mongolian prince, the chief of the Tsagechin
Beile tribe, who had stated that it came from the tribal
treasure chest inherited from his father.

How this Swedish silver *daler* more than two centuries
old came to crop up in the heart of Central Asia the
consul could in nowise explain, and we both cudgelled
our brains over it without finding a likely explanation.

The prince of Tsagechin Beile was among my most
interesting acquaintances in Urumchi. He too was a
fugitive from the Red Power in the North, for the lands
that were his and were still inhabited by the people
whom he was appointed to lead lay at the foot of the
Altai mountains and were now incorporated in Khalka
Mongolia, the territory annexed by the Soviet.

Nevertheless, Tsagechin Beile by no means regarded
himself as a fugitive emigrant ; he was very much a
chieftain, having people and cattle with him, and he
was at home wherever there were grazing-grounds.

He and I were born in the same year, and the sign of
the " Fire Ape " floated above both our tents. When
one saw him approaching in the dress of his tribe he

made the impression of a veritable nomad chieftain, irradiating health, but when visiting the town he often wore an ill-fitting Russian costume, the homespun colourlessness of which robbed him of his captivating charm.

In the company of strangers he was silent and abstracted and appeared embarrassed and impatient, but his clear brown Mongol eyes were watchful and critically observant.

Tsagechin Beile was extremely well read both in secular Mongolian and Tibetan religious literature, and he could write in both those languages. While he was yet a young hereditary prince his wide learning and prudent counsels had been famous on the steppes.

But these very merits of his had been the cause of events which left dark memories upon his life. One night he had been taken unawares by the dreaded freebooter Dambin Jansang, who took him captive and soon made use of his valuable abilities on his staff. For years the young prince had sat as coadjutor in the false *hutuktu's* council tent and had been one of the leaders of the robber band. For so great was Dambin Jansang's mastery over men's minds that he could persuade honest folk against their will to perpetrate deeds of violence and attach them to his wishes by a mysterious compelling power.

But at the same moment that Dambin Jansang fell Tsagechin Beile had become himself again. The sight of the freebooter's severed head had released him from the hypnotic influence which had dominated him for years. And in the confusion after the fall of the chieftain he had succeeded in getting hold of the desert stronghold's swiftest horse and had fled on its back out into Black Gobi. No avenging pursuer had been able to overtake him, for the horse he rode and the saddle under him had belonged to Dambin Jansang himself. He had turned loose the horse when he reached his father's tent, but the saddle he still had in his possession.

This saddle, which had carried Dambin Jansang, the incarnation on earth of Amursana, " Mongolia's strong man ", on so many bloody journeys, was the most valuable

165

I ever saw in Mongolia. One day I succeeded in acquiring both it and its heavy silver appurtenances, and now the whole equipment is preserved in a glass case in the Ethnographical Museum in Stockholm.

During the time when the young prince was performing enforced service under Dambin Jansang, the old Tsagechin chief had died, and on his return Tsagechin Beile assumed his father's inheritance. But the time of peace on his native steppes was not of long duration, for soon " Red " soldiers were threatening his boundaries. He had fought gallantly to preserve the grasslands conferred upon him by the gods, but the odds had been too great. He had then dismissed his still efficient army and ordered his riders to return to the home camp to resume their peaceful nomad life, and himself had migrated with one of his *sumon* to Chinese Turkestan to await the victory of justice.

The *sumon* which Tsagechin Beile took with him into exile consisted of eight tents, and he had migrated in Mongolian fashion bringing with him the whole families of these tents and all their cattle. He was in constant communication with the tribe, for his old mother had remained as a poor and obscure woman to look after the interests of the family. And she let him know that his remaining subjects had never ceased to be loyal to him, but that their forces were of no avail against the new rulers.

The young chieftain and I often spent whole days hunting together, and in the evenings we would sit by the fire in his silk-draped chief's tent.

Tsagechin Beile was a typical representative of the wide-awake young upper-class Mongol who has been seized by the spirit of a new era. He was quite ready to adapt his views to the new ideas in so far as these were compatible with certain traditions which he regarded as inseparable from his family and race, and in the course of our conversations he tried to arrive at a solution of many problems.

For me he and his people constituted an interesting subject of study as belonging to an obscure Mongolian race and line of chieftains, and the study of their history was facilitated by the prince's fund of knowledge and his willingness to impart it to me.

SEVEN generations back Tsagechin Beile's direct ancestor had been a young chieftain of the *öret* Mongol horde. He had lived during the period when the *öret* Mongols were so powerful that with increasing success they combated the combined forces of the emperor of China and the four Khalka Mongol Khans.

The great Khan of the *öret* Mongolian confederacy had ordered the young chief to go with a thousand of his youngest and bravest warriors to the borders of Khalka Mongolia there to establish an outpost. The young man had left his native steppes by Ili and reached the distant boundary by the Altai mountains where he erected a defensive tower. According to Tsagechin Beile's account, that watch-tower still exists, and the present flourishing trading town of Guchengtse has grown up under its protection. But a Manchurian army, which penetrated to Ili by a more southerly route, had cut off the line of retreat of the thousand warriors and these had been obliged to seek refuge in the Altai mountains. The battle down on the lowlands ended in the victory of the Manchus, and the *öret* Mongols, formerly so numerous and powerful, had been almost exterminated. The mother race of the thousand detached warriors had completely disappeared.

Tsagechin's ancestor and his thousand warriors had remained in the Altai mountains and had never again seen the steppes of their fathers by distant Ili. They had taken to themselves wives from local tribes, but the present generation of Tsagechin Mongols nevertheless count themselves as pure descendants of the parent stems that once lived a nomadic life by the Ili river. The women who in past times had married into the tribe had adopted the dress worn by the women of the men's tribe, and to this day the Tsagechin Mongols, men as well as women, wear precisely the same dress and follow the same tradition as the long-vanished original tribe.

The dress worn by the married women of the Tsage-chin tribe is particularly interesting and differs materially

167

in cut and in many details from that of all the other Mongolian tribes that I have seen. Its most striking peculiarity lies in the stiffened shoulder pieces of the outer cloak which are cut as a wide collar out over the shoulders and project noticeably beyond them.

Before I left the hospitable tents of the Tsagechin Beile Mongols I succeeded in acquiring a number of valuable ethnographic objects for the expedition's collections. And on my departure I received from the chief two dresses with complete garniture of silver ornaments and sword belt, all used by himself and his *Khatun* (consort).

But before handing over the gift he cut from each dress one silver button and kept it, to ensure his being able to reproduce the dresses.

Four years later, in Stockholm, I learnt of facts which may with some propriety be considered in connection with the circumstances I have just described. But before I try to bring forward my hypothesis, which embraces both the Russian Consul's Swedish *daler* and the woman's dress which I got from Tsagechin Beile, the story of two Swedish lives in that country's period of greatness must be briefly sketched.

AMONG the Carolines who found themselves in Russian captivity after the defeat at Poltava was a certain young Renat.

Renat belonged to a family of Jewish immigrants from Germany who with other Jews were baptized in the German church in Stockholm on September 29th, 1681. The father, Moses Jacob, became a Swede and a Christian under the name of Gustaf Michael Renatus, and the family, impoverished by the migration, came gradually to enjoy, thanks to persistent petitions to the city and the Government, a certain degree of prosperity in Stockholm.

The son, Johan Gustaf Renat, enlisted at the age of eighteen in the artillery, was at Narva, Dyna and Poltava, and was taken with other prisoners of war to Tobolsk in 1711.

Among the prisoners of war from Poltava there was

A Mongol salutes his Chief

[face p. 168

also a young Swedish woman who was later to share the same cruel fate as Renat. But even before this time her life had been like a tempestuous sea.

She had first seen the light of day three years after the Jew baptism in the German church of Stockholm mentioned above and received upon admission into " the fellowship of Christ's dearly bought congregation " the name of Brigitta Christina Schertzenfeldt. Her parents, " the Lieutenant of a Regiment of Horse, the noble and well-born Herr Knut Schertzenfeldt and her Dear Mother Fru Brigitta Tranander ", died while she was still an infant, but her mother's sister and " several distinguished relatives " gave her a careful upbringing.

At the age of fifteen the young lady was married, but the great war widowed her after a few years. Fru Brigitta had, in order to be near her husband, migrated to Riga, and there she later entered into a new marriage with a Caroline soldier. Him she accompanied on the army's march into Russia, and after Poltava she was taken with her husband as a prisoner to Moscow where in 1711 she again became a widow.

Fru Brigitta, now twenty-seven years old and still beautiful, entered for the third time into matrimony with another of the Swedish prisoners of war, the Mecklenburger, Michael Sims, and with him was soon after transferred to the Swedish war-prisoner colony at Tobolsk.

Tsar Peter had plans for extending his boundaries in the direction of Turkestan with its rivers rich in gold-dust, and to that end Lieutenant-Colonel Johann Buckholtz was commissioned to equip an expedition to the steppe territory of the independent Dzungars. In this Russian expedition a number of Swedish prisoners of war from Tobolsk experienced in artillery and fortification took part, and in 1715 the expedition was conveyed up the Irtysh to Jamyshev where Buchholtz erected a fort. Among the Carolines who took part were Michael Sims and Johan Gustaf Renat.

As the surroundings seemed peaceful, several officers of the expedition sent for their wives, but before these arrived " the fort at Jamischoff was hemmed in by

Kalmucks and all the country round ravaged by contending parties which attacked also these travellers . . . Captain Sims was slain. . . . The women . . . fell into hard and miserable slavery."

AMONG the Dzungars' prisoners were Fru Brigitta and Renat, among the killed Fru Brigitta's husband Sims.

The Dzungars into whose hands the Swedes fell belonged to the *Khoit* tribe, and after having annihilated the Buchholtz expedition and thwarted the Tsar's plans they fell back again to the territory by Ebi-nor.

In her thirty years of life Fru Brigitta had suffered many trials, but in the autumn of 1716 she passed through the most frightful suffering of her life. She was a slave in the hands of the Dzungars, those barbarians who were the brothers of Ayuk Khan's Torguts who, according to a contemporary writer, swarmed about the Swedish army " like ravening hounds ". The Asiatic barbarians subjected her to merciless treatment " in that they not only stripped her of all her clothing but also bound her so harshly and for so long with iron and strong ropes that she bore the marks of those same bonds on her arms and legs to the day of her death ; and when she was finally brought into Kalmuck territory she was forced to perform divers hard and infamous tasks, such as fall to the lot of bondslaves, and must needs be content with vile, scanty and often unclean food such as is unwonted and held to be intolerable among civilized nations ".

The chief of the *Khoit* tribe handed over his white captives to the Dzungar general Dukar, who in his turn was to bring them to his ruler, Tsewang Raptan, the mighty warrior chief of the Dzungars, " the supreme ruler of the Kalmucks, who by his subjects and the people who are of one race with them is called a sovereign King, but by the surrounding powers is recognized as a Prince or Grand Duke, is entitled Surructu Erdeni Batur Contaigi, which signifies a valiant noble hero and exalted prince ".

Tsewang Raptan allotted the Swedish lady as a slave to his elder consort who was a *Khoshut* princess from the Kuku-nor region in Tibet. And now Fru Brigitta's condition became somewhat more tolerable in that " she was given some old skin clothing wherewith in some measure to cover her hitherto completely naked body ".

By degrees the Swedish slave won the love of her princess, for besides being well behaved she was skilful in women's work, " particularly in crochet-work and cloth-weaving ". And the favour that Fru Brigitta came to enjoy at the court she employed to the advantage of other Christian prisoners who had fallen into slavery with Mongolian private persons.

Among the slaves she helped and whose lives she perhaps saved was Renat.

The apple of Tsewang Raptan's eye was his young daughter Seson, whose mother was the chief's second wife, a daughter of Ayuk Khan the powerful chieftain of the Volga Torguts. Since Seson now conceived a particular desire to do crochet-work, she demanded the Swedish slave as her instructress, and Fru Brigitta was transferred to the lesser court. Here too she contrived to win great favour, and soon obtained everything she desired.

When the young princess Seson was betrothed to Ayuk Khan's grandson Donduk Ombo, Fru Brigitta was given the confidential mission of purchasing a suitable trousseau for her mistress, and to that end spent two years at " Gerken " in " Little Bucharea " (Jarkent in what is now Eastern Turkestan).

Renat, the former Caroline Sergeant Major of artillery, who, through Fru Brigitta's intervention, had succeeded in escaping from his slavery, also enjoyed much favour at the Dzungarian court. He himself, in his petition for discharge delivered to King Frederic, states that he had set up artillery " with guns and mortars and taught 200 Kalmucks the same Art ". He also relates that he had taken the field with the Dzungars against the Chinese.[1]

[1] In the proceedings of the Russian Academy of Science, 1732 and 1733, it is stated that Renat also taught the nomads to print from movable type instead of from woodcut blocks as they had learnt from the Chinese.

Renat finally persuaded the sovereign of Dzungaria to send him as ambassador to the King of Sweden, but a war which at that time broke out with the Cossacks necessitated the postponement of the " embassy ".

On her return from " Little Bucharea " Fru Brigitta, with the sanction of the princely family, entered into matrimony with her countryman Renat and was thus relieved of her office as lady-in-waiting. This was to be her salvation, for when, in 1727, Tsewang Raptan suddenly died it was suspected that he had been poisoned, and his Torgut second wife and her daughter Seson were tortured into a confession and were executed with their whole household.

During the latter years of Tsewang Raptan the Emperor of China had completely broken the power of the Dzungars, and the former's successor, Galdan Tsering, became ruler of only the shattered remnant of a once great and powerful people.

With this prince too the Swedish couple enjoyed great favour, and soon the hour of their deliverance struck. For although he released unwillingly " these two so useful and agreeable persons ", the chief did not wish for his own benefit to hinder their " pleasure and desire ". On March 22nd, 1733, the Renat family took leave of their benefactor, having then sojourned seventeen years among " these Barbarians ", of whom the biography of Fru Brigitta says that " in uprightness, mutual Love and several other virtues they compare with many Christian Nations, if they should not in certain respects with reason be preferred to them ". After having set out upon the journey Fru Brigitta received as a token of the love they bore her " several handkerchiefs, one after another, whereon were seen signs of the tears which these Princesses had let fall on account of her departure ".

The Swedish couple had succeeded in obtaining the release of eighteen Swedes and a hundred and thirty-four Russians from Dzungarian slavery. On the journey home our travellers were accompanied by the eighteen Swedes and also by twenty " Cottonian Slaves " whom Fru Brigitta wished to bring home to Sweden in order to convert them to Christianity. Of these some died on the journey and others were detained by the Russians, but Renat and Fru Brigitta arrived in Stockholm with the rest of their following on July 6th, 1734.[1]

Only two years after her return, on April 14th, 1736, Fru Brigitta closed her eyes " after she had lived in the world 51 years and 9 months ", and her tired body was laid to rest in the Royal Artillery Church of that time.

Renat on his homecoming was appointed lieutenant in the Ordnance Company in Stockholm and promoted captain in the Royal Artillery Corps. In scientific quarters he became the object of great interest. Several maps of Central Asia, not, judging by the execution, drawn by Renat but by Mongols, as well as a magnificent dress which he brought home from captivity were acquired by Uppsala University; the learned Bishop of Linköping, Erik Benzelius, procured copies of the maps ; and Dean Olof Celsius, the patron of Linnæus, received seeds brought home from Dzungaria which were planted in the Academy's garden at Uppsala.[2]

After having mourned Fru Brigitta for three years Renat married Elizabeth Lenström, widow of the silk manufacturer, Isac Fritz, and lived with her until he died in 1744.

AFTER my arrival in Sweden I chanced to hear that there was a " Kalmuck Chief's dress " in the Armoury collections. This had been handed over sixty years before by Uppsala University with an ancient servitor's dress from the earlier days of that seat of learning and had even been taken for a similar one. It was later identified as the dress brought home from " Calmuckia "

---

[1] Three " Calmuckesses ", Altan (Gold), Sava (Moongleam), and Gurban (Three), were examined in the Christian doctrine and baptized on the third Sunday in Advent, 1735. A ten-year-old boy, son of the Scanian dragoon M. Brant and his Mongolian wife, was baptized in Katarina Church, October 6th, 1734.

[2] " I have now obtained several species which have come from Calmuckia with H. René, who has brought with him many kinds from thence."

CELSIUS TO LINNÆUS, 1736.

(Dzungaria) by the well-known Caroline artillery officer Johan Gustaf Renat.

This dress, brought home by Renat from captivity, I found to be a Mongolian woman's dress, and to my amazement it completely coincided with the peculiar woman's dress which had been given to me by the Tsagechin Beile chieftain.

Then the fascinating theory suggested itself that, inasmuch as Renat states that in 1718 he took part in the Mongols' campaign against the Chinese, he may have come in contact with the forefathers of the Tsagechin Beile tribe, who seven generations back were also fighting the Chinese, and have acquired the dress from them. And this supposition is confirmed by the fact that this peculiar dress is worn only by that tribe. It is tempting to assume that the dress was worn by Fru Brigitta.

It is also easy to connect with the Renat family the Caroline silver coin which the Russian consul at Urumchi obtained from the then chief of the Tsagechin Beile and which belonged to his hereditary treasures.

CHAPTER XX

NEW FIELDS OF WORK

ON the last day of February the northern column of the expedition at last arrived in Urumchi and for several days our headquarters was the scene of a joyful reunion. But Tsereat and our other splendid Mongols I saw no more on that journey, for Governor Yang's permission to enter his province had not included them, and they had turned back from Hami into the desert winter of Black Gobi to return to their homes in distant Chahar.

We were all avid for contact with the new country, and soon we would be dispersed in various directions to seek new tasks in its mountains, deserts and steppes. In the beginning of March Bergman and I set out southward to penetrate through the Lop Desert into the Tibetan highlands. We found productive fields of work at Singer and Shindi, and summer heat was upon us before we reached the northern edge of the desert.

As the month of April wore on the heat increased, and midday marches were gradually replaced by early morning and late evening stages. When the morning sun got round to the south-east its power was so intense that further marching became a torment for both man and beast. The heat lay upon our bodies like an inescapable weight impeding every muscular movement, the reflected light from the white sand sea was a torture to our eyes, and every attempt to think revolved dully round the longed-for *water, shade, lethargy*.

The whole caravan searched the horizon with their eyes for the dark flecks that indicated vegetation and its accompanying water-place. Thus at times we camped on fields with luxuriant reeds or in low thickets of tamar-

175

isks and wild olives. Sometimes a few poplars thrust up their tall scraggy crests above the dwarf vegetation, and one evening after a hot march we pitched the tent and put the camels to rest in the inviting circles of shade which the poplar leaves traced upon the sand.

But during the night that followed we came to learn one of the Lop Desert's rules of travel. We spent many sleepless hours fighting against biting sand-ticks, and when morning broke we found the restless caravan animals profusely festooned with these pests. Before the start we had to scrape off and pull away hundreds of them from the camels' hairless bellies and the inner part of their thighs, and the insects had sucked so much blood during the night that they were swollen from their natural size of ladybirds to bladders of the dimension of a ripe chestnut. Sand-ticks are one of the dangers of the Lop Desert, for in many places they occur in such multitudes that they can kill the strongest caravan animal.

There is always a risk of meeting with them under poplar trees, and one thanks one's star if one can camp in places where a caravan or a flock of sheep have recently been resting, since the pests often leave the place with the departing animals.

Our route frequently crossed the dried up Tarim river, and we camped beside mud-filled lagoons or water-filled hollows in the former river bed. But the farther south we went the rarer and more insignificant these bodies of water became, and the vegetation round them grew ever more scorched in its hopeless resistance to the drought and the encroaching desert sand.

Once we came upon an abandoned Sart village, where newly thrown up dams and uncompleted excavations bore witness to the departed population's desperate struggle to retain the vanishing water. When the river ran dry the fields had not been able to produce crops, and the people had had to subsist on the rapidly diminishing herds of cattle in the patient hope that the river would soon again be filled with water.

But a day had come when there was no more water to be had. The animals stood by the watering-places and sought in vain for moisture, the women wept in the houses, and the men gathered in the mosque to pray to Allah for the miracle which alone could save their many homes. But no miracle happened ; the village got no water, and in the last extremity of famine the people had thrown their most indispensable possessions on to the remaining horses and donkeys and hastily left their homes and the lands of their fathers to follow their *aksakal* [1] out into the parched country around on a desperate search for water.

The dwellings in which there had been such abundant life now lay desolate and dry as the desert around them, and numerous traces bore witness to the hurried flight. In the houses lay abandoned household gear and articles of clothing, in the lanes saddles, agricultural implements and tools were scattered about. All was reminiscent of life ; at every corner one expected to come upon living beings ; in each house one fancied there must be a blazing hearth. But neither in the houses nor in the silent lanes did we encounter a soul who could tell us the name of the place or recount the fate of its inhabitants. All was silent and dead, for the place lacked water—one of the conditions of life.

Outside the abandoned village lay the field in which the living had been wont to bury their dead. On the many clay-smeared graves stakes had been thrust in on the tops of which long horns of wild animals or grinning skulls of oxen were fixed. On some were bushy yak tails which fluttered like funeral plumes in the hot desert wind. But no prayers were any longer said in the mosque for the departed.

Later on we sometimes met with small parties of these former agricultural villagers, who now drifted about out on the steppes as unhappy nomads. The fugitives had been obliged to divide into small groups, since no one water-hole could accommodate them all. They told us of their last troubled year in their native place, when Allah had punished them by taking away their river, but even more willingly they returned in memory to the happy times when Allah was with them and crops and cattle

[1] *Aksakal* (Turkish *ak* = white, *sakal* = beard)—village elder.

flourished and gave them sustenance. Now their will to live was cowed, and they had no plans for the future. But, with oriental submission to Destiny, they did not complain, but prayed their persistent prayers for a flood of water between the banks of their ancient river.

It was with a sense of relief that we left the dried-up river area with its dying vegetation and luckless human beings and returned to the eternal sameness of the unchanging sandy desert.

The most blessed moment of the marching day was when after some hours of marching in the early morning we came to a place that invited us to camp. So soon as the camels had been unloaded and turned loose, the servants would begin to pitch the tents, and Bergman and I set to work on the fitting up of our own canvas home. This was set up every day in new surroundings, but met us every day with the same interior that we had come to love.

We had gradually exchanged the whole of our original American camping outfit for objects, less practical but far more attractive and beautiful, which had captivated us on our visits to various native dwellings. The floor of the tent was spread with genuine Khotan rugs which copied nature herself in delightful combinations of colour. Our sky-blue sleeping-sacks lay like ottomans on either side of a low Chinese lacquer table. By getting rid of camp-beds, chairs and a long-legged table and lying and sitting on the rug-covered ground itself we had gained a good three feet of space. Our tea was served in ancient, nobly shaped copper jugs and we drank it out of silver-mounted birchwood cups.

And so soon as the tent was furnished and homelike, I threw myself down on my blue ottoman to fall into a doze, and Bergman performed his daily ritual. From its protective paper he unwrapped a framed portrait which he carefully hung up on the inner tent-pole facing his half of the tent. And then he said to me : " Henning, look at Hanna ! Isn't she sweet ? Don't you think I'm a fool, tramping round here in Central Asia while she sits at home in Sweden ? " To begin with I had actually made an effort to look at her, and as she was blonde and

sweet and smiling I had heartily agreed to both proposi-
tions. But as day and months went by and everything
changed except his ritual, he forced on me the irritating
thought that perhaps it was I who was a prize idiot who
had not a portrait to hang on the tent-pole. And I went
through a new mental experience.

Between the hot days we had the boon of cool nights,
and we threw ourselves on the cold sand to rest our sun-
tormented eyes in the dim remoteness of the gentle stars.
The dogs lay in a circle about us ready with friendly
waggings of their tail on the slightest glance from their
masters. The servants slept, and the camels breathed
deeply and heavily in the great stillness.

Every month came the full moon, and then we experienced a strange intimacy with all that was obliterated
in the sober light of day. Slowly the round moon glided
across a star sprinkled sky, we felt a blessed sense of
mental relaxation, the night was timeless and filled with
sleepless rest. Occasionally we exchanged an idea, and
in the gleaming silver mirror of the moon's disk we
interpreted the dreams of our longing. In my desert
moon I found the picture of a girl. I knew her attributes
and understood her meaning. But Bergman could never
see her, and so we kept each his own, and the two girls
were equally near to us and almost equally distant.

One day, when we had been without letters for nearly
six months, we were lying—as we often did—wondering
how everything was going on at home. The caravan
was taking its midday rest, and the sun shone vertically
down. Outside the tent two of the servants stood
sluicing the sides of it with water, and to our brains
dulled by the heat this gave the impression of quantities
of cool running water. The thrown back tent-flies
framed a view of rolling sand waves the outlines of whose
crests trembled in the heated air, and far off between
the desert and the sky the horizon danced in flaming
tongues of light. In the middle of the picture stood one
straight, proud poplar. Its shadow moved with the
hours like a desert sundial, and a flapping shadow
betrayed an eagle seeking prey.

Suddenly the sleeping camp was woken by the barking

of our dogs, and soon after the shouts and hallooing of the caravan men were heard. Drunken with sleep we tumbled out of the tent and were fully awakened by the unwonted sight of an approaching camel rider.

There was no breaking of camp that evening, for the rider was a courier from headquarters at Urumchi and had brought four saddle-bags full of letters from the outside world. For long we read and took out and read again, and for the rest of the night we talked. Warm woollen mufflers and camel-hair gloves were welcome in the tropical heat, and we did not reflect that the oldest of the letters were more than a year old. Nor did we know that one of the friends who sent us news of himself and his people had then been dead nine months.

CHAPTER XXI

THE OASIS BEYOND THE DESERT

THE landscape changed, and we travelled through desolate, dead, stone steppe between belts of undulating clay-sand. The ground was covered with a white powdering of salt, and long ridges of loose sand formed obstacles across our way. Signs of organic life were of rare occurrence, and the bad quality of the scanty water was a trial both to temper and physique. For three days a heavy hot haze lay over the desert, and when it cleared a new panorama lay before us of gleaming blue mountains to the southward. This increased the pace of the caravan, for nearer than the mountains lay the oasis for which we longed.

The mountains in front of us grew larger, and trees became visible at their foot. Towards noon we met human beings in the desert. A mounted patrol came galloping towards us and came to a halt at a few hundred yards' distance from our caravan. Three tall men dismounted and slowly approached us on foot. They bowed deeply and ceremoniously and in courteous phrases bade us welcome to their country. "*Assalam aleikum*," they murmured, and deferentially stroked their long grey beards.

Two of the men wore Sart caps, which were edged at the bottom with a wide border of fox skin. The third was a learned Mullah, well versed in the Koran, and wore a muslin turban wound round his embroidered skull-cap. All three were dressed in long, tight-fitting coats of black satin and long-legged riding-boots. They were of imposing stature, and their movements were elegant and graceful. Above their tremendous beards their noses projected with Aryan vigour, and their big light-brown eyes gave us a feeling of racial kinship.

They addressed us as "excellency" and treated us like princes, and we blushed when we contemplated their venerable beards.

We were now conducted in ceremonial procession to the place where they had dismounted. Their servants had meanwhile spread a richly embroidered black rug upon the sand, and on it had laid out all manner of splendid things to eat and drink. We stood staring paralysed at this vision in the desert sand.

On the rug were earthenware bowls heaped with sour milk, mutton in various forms, newly baked bread, melons, almonds and raisins. We were capable of committing a crime to come by such a spread, but there was no need. The three greybeards took off the leather slippers which they wore like galoshes over their soft heelless boots, then knelt down on the outer edge of the rug and, with eyes turned heavenward and outstretched hands, murmured a prayer. Having thus asked a blessing they drew back a little and bade us fall to and eat. It was for us, all of it.

We ate, and we gave our caravan men to eat, but even when we had reached the stage of repletion, the rug was still so covered with food that we could not trace its embroidered pattern. We gasped for breath, stretched ourselves and, full and happy, gazed at our hosts. Their expression was well hidden behind their bushy beards, but their eyes smiled at us amiably.

With the three Sarts as guides we now went on to the oasis town of Charklik. The town was preparing for us a most unexpected and most magnificent welcome of which we had cognizance beforehand, for several times we were met on the way by messengers with refreshments. And when we approached the oasis itself a large deputation was standing to receive us under the outlying poplars. The obsequious manner of the men and their friendly words of welcome really gave us the impression that the whole oasis and all that it contained was now committed to our hands.

The oasis of Charklik is situated beside the river of the same name which has its source among the Altyn-tagh mountains in the south and at its height discharges into

Cherchen-darya. I am told that Charklik signifies
" wagon-wheel ", and I have heard two different explanations of the name. Some say that the oasis was so
named because an early inhabitant was a wheelwright
renowned for the construction of wheels specially suited
for desert regions. Others again considered that the
name had arisen from the resemblance of the shape
of the oasis to a wheel.

When Prschevalski, the first European traveller to do
so in modern times, visited Charklik in 1876, it was a
new community, and among its eight hundred and fifty
inhabitants some of the original settlers were still living.
They had been hunters from the oasis town of Kerya
who had come here by way of Cherchen, Gas and
Altyn-tagh and had found in the oasis the ruins of a
little town. On the return journey to Kerya these
hunters followed Marco Polo's long-forgotten route, and
they came upon ruined towns which at the time of the
Venetian's visit had been flourishing places. At the
time of our visit the population of Charklik had been
considerably increased by immigration from Niya, Kerya
and other oases in the west, some even from Lop-nor
who had fled hither from the dried-up banks of the
Tarim.

There was luxuriant growth in the fields and gardens
of Charklik and everywhere there was the delicious sound
of murmuring water from the numerous irrigation canals.
Cooling fruits and all kinds of appetizing products of
the soil lay in the open shops, and the bazaar was full
of contentedly smiling people.

An enormous distance separates the place from the
nearest outposts of civilization, and we had a strong
sense of the charm of living in conditions which seemed
unchanged since the days of Marco Polo. It was good
to be here, so we sent the desert-weary camels to graze
in the cooler foothills in the south. We ourselves prepared to enjoy the novelty of our surroundings and
imagined ourselves living in long-vanished times.

One day the Chinese *amban* came and begged us to
visit his sick wife. The harmless patent medicine which
we prescribed in doubtful cases soon relieved her pains,

183

and our reputation as physicians was at once established. Next day a large part of the population were suffering spasms, and the patients crowded our courtyard. Our equipment included a well-assorted travelling medicine chest and a medical book, and Hummel had worked out a concise explanation of the ailments commonly occurring in Turkestan with a list indicating which of our medicines we should employ in each case. We were fully conscious of the limitations both of our stock of drugs and of our medical ability, but it appeared that we alleviated the affliction of many.

Our medical receptions brought us into intimate contact with the natives, and thus our knowledge of their language and customs increased, and since I arranged for the examination of each patient to be preceded by an anthropometric measuring we at the same time gathered interesting scientific material for the expedition.

It was easy to distinguish quite different racial types among the native population.

Some were well grown and had Aryan features, light-brown eyes, red-brown skin and a vigorous, often reddish, growth of hair. A number of people measured six feet six inches or more in height, and their indistinct beardless faces recalled no other race that I had seen in Central Asia. In the wild Mongolian types that differ so strongly from the Sarts we could trace descendants from the twenty Mongol women brought here a generation earlier as spoils of war from the *däde* Mongol tribe in north-eastern Tibet. Of these twenty women two were still alive and were living in the neighbouring oasis of Abdal.

The quietude of a hot midday siesta was broken by a noisy hubbub. A crowd of natives in the courtyard were gesticulating and pounding their feet in their eagerness to impart their weighty news. A *white* man, a man who looked like us, had turned up in Charklik.

We sought out the white newcomer at Selim Bay's poor *sarai* and found a Russian sunk in a melancholy so profound that it was heartrending to witness.

Smigonov and Makejef had been chums for many years and so strong had their friendship been that the

184

Sart Musicians

The Sart *aksakal* and Chinese *amban*

[*face p.* 184

Photo Bergman

The Däde Mongols' *Khuruldei*

After the Hunt

[*face p.* 185

one only lived for the other. During the days of the Great War they had both been carefree students at the University of Tomsk, but then came the revolution, and Siberia too had been split up into the supporters of Red and White ideals. The two students, who enthusiastically embraced the latter, drifted into Ataman Annenkov's renowned Cossack corps.

For several years the bloody front wavered over the snow-fields of Siberia, but the Reds had the better of it, and a day came when Annenkov stood with the remnant of his shattered army at the point where Holy Russia ends and the Middle Kingdom begins. Those who contrived to cross the boundary escaped death at the hands of their fellow-countrymen, but fell instead into Chinese captivity.

The period of captivity had been full of trials, but the day had come when Smigonov and Makejef had all roads open to them—except that which led home. They had wandered southward through steppes and deserts until they reached the " Snow Country ", and in the peace of the mountains had sought to forget those scenes of blood. For five years the two friends had lived isolated from all that had constituted their old life ; they had lived close to nature and among simple nomads, and this had restored their faith in mankind.

These years had deepened their old friendship and made them inseparable. Nevertheless, they were divided now. Makejef was gone and Smigonov left alone to mourn his friend.

Makejef had been on his way with a Kirghiz from Tibet to Charklik to sell five camel loads of wool. They had surmounted the perilous " Stone Pass " and were descending, when the avalanche came which swept the little caravan into the depths. Smigonov, who was travelling the same road a week later, had been attracted to the scene of the disaster by the appearance of a lone horse. The horse was carrying Makejef's saddle, but the rider and the rest of the caravan lay in the abyss.

May came to an end, and the stifling heat of June lay heavily over Charklik. But high above the vibrant heat of the lowlands Altyn-tagh raised his mighty grey-blue spine with glacier-crowned peaks gleaming white against the bright blue Tibetan sky. In the mornings little cloud formations arose over the mountains in the south-east, and we followed with longing eyes their westward passage through the limpid air. In the last rays of sunset the mountain pinnacles took on the brilliancy of jewels, and the clouds were like gold-tipped dream-ships sailing towards the wonderland of colour.

We must go! Away from all this down here and up to all that!

And on the same day that we realized this we started.

CHAPTER XXII

ADVENTURE IN "THE SNOW COUNTRY"

THE caravan consisted of twenty camels, three donkeys and my *Buran*. Our goal was the source of the Cherchen-darya river in the Tibetan highlands. During the journey Bergman was to look for places for archæological excavation and I to examine anthropologically such people as we chanced to meet with.

We took a cordial farewell of the dwellers in the oasis, and the old *aksakal* furnished us both with provisions and with friendly counsels and warning. And we received them with gratitude, particularly the latter, for we had never before attempted such elevations as we were now to climb, and the entry to the Snow Country was by the notorious Tash-Dawan, the " Stone Pass ", where Makajef had met his fate.

We toiled for days through heavy sand until we reached the rain and glacier-water furrowed glens among the foothills. We advanced slowly and with many interruptions, for as the gradient grew steeper the camels, accustomed to the desert, became more and more unmanageable on the strange ground.

For three days we ascended twelve hundred feet daily, and our hearts and lungs began to labour heavily under the strain of the rarified air. Our ascent went in curves along a steep hill-side which to the left of us plunged between sixty and a hundred and sixty feet to the bottom of the canyon we were following. The camels pressed, terrified, against the hill-side, and every time the baggage bales bumped against some inequality the animals were pushed out towards the edge of the precipice. The caravan men shrieked that we must turn back, but the track was too narrow to permit such a manœuvre.

We succeeded in passing a dangerous projection of

rock, but on the other side of it came upon a highly
dispiriting sight. We were now only a few hundred
yards below the horizon line between the mountain and
the sky, but in front of us rose a steep slope. The rush
of water from the melting snow had etched three yellow-
ish white streaks which pointed from the abyss beneath
us up towards three saddle-shaped gaps in front of us,
and down in the depth the bottom of the widened canyon
was covered by a chaos of fallen masses of rock.

The caravan was out of breath and nervous, and when
one of the camels stumbled, disquiet spread along the
whole long file, and we were on the verge of panic.

Our salvation was a ledge on which the camels could
be unloaded five at a time. The baggage was piled along
the hill-side, and then all available men were set to
leading the unloaded camels two by two over the remaining hundred yards to the top of the " Stone Pass ". But
to get the exhausted and helpless camels up these hundred
yards took more than four hours, and the many minutes
of those hours were crowded with perils and anxieties.

At last we were standing at the top of the pass, high
up in the blue ether and looking out over a sea of jagged
mountain ridges. Nothing but snow-powdered peaks
and glittering glaciers raised their heads above us, and
all our lofty kingdom lay bathed in the colours of an
alpine sunset. In the gap between two mountains to the
southward we caught a glimpse of a broad watercourse.
The camels were saved, for the dangerous threshold of
the highlands had been crossed, and before us there was
water and vegetation. But the caravan's baggage, all our
instruments, all that we were to live on during the coming
summer up here still lay to northward of the pass.

Dsuk was coming on, and it had to be dealt with.

One tent and a small supply of provisions were carried
by the caravan men to the top of the pass where they
were loaded on to one of the camels, and then Bergman
went on with the rest of the unladen camels to seek
such safety as he might find beside the blue-green lake
to the southward. I myself stayed with two caravan
men, *Buran* and our three donkeys to solve the problem
north of the pass.

A Charklik Beauty

Seng Chen's earthly father, Tu-yen Meng-ku Khan

[face p. 188

My pony and the donkeys were good climbers and together were up to carrying the weight of one camel load. Thus they should be able to transport the twenty camel loads over the pass by crossing it twenty times. But it took time, for all the heavy cases had to be emptied and repacked with only a quarter of their original contents, and on a platform south of the pass we had each time to empty them all so as to carry back the empty cases to the starting-point where they were again packed with another quarter load.

We were able to make four journeys there and back daily, and thus crossed the pass forty times in the course of five days. We learned every secure foothold and came to know the rate of progress which allowed of our hearts' maximum performance in the rarified air.

But the accursed donkeys never learned anything. They were capable of straining after a blade of grass at the most perilous places, and the animal which for the moment was out of reach had a way of falling into protracted meditation on the very edge of an abyss. During those five days yells and curses echoed between the " Stone Pass's " mountain walls. And day-long yelling and bawling is hard on the heart and lungs when one is thirteen thousand feet above sea level.

Eight times a day we rested at the top of the pass, and each time the vast panorama lay under new conditions of light. I could have sat up there for eternities forgetful of all except the beauty of the views.

At night we scrambled down to the bottom of the canyon, to let our hearts and lungs recover themselves during rest in a more normal air pressure.

AT the bottom of the canyon lay the remains of Makejef's caravan.

Three of the camels had their nose-pins wrenched out, but that of the fourth was still in position, and the rope which was made fast to the nose-pin was tightly noosed at its other end round a human hand. The man lay buried on a sheltered ledge near the top of the pass, and in a heap of stones a lance had been planted with a bushy yak's tail waving hither and thither in the shifting wind currents of the pass.   This was Smigonov's homage to his dead friend.

I made a Russian cross out of a spare saddle, and on the cross I carved a sentiment.   The Christian emblem now stands beside the Asiatic yak-tail symbol, both visible in summer, but in the winter embedded in the purity of snow.

At last the whole of the baggage was on the south side of the pass, and I galloped to Bergman's camp by the river to send back the camels for it.

That night I had an attack of mountain sickness. Pulsations thundered in my temples, and my heart galloped until it suddenly stopped altogether for seconds that seemed eternities.   I gasped for breath like a drowning man and was convinced that I was going to die.

But next morning I was fit again and the mountain sickness never returned, although later on we were to travel in far higher regions.   But I cursed and swore no more at the donkeys, at least not so violently as to strain my heart.

Our immediate goal was Temirlik on the mountain lake of Gas-nor, where we expected to meet with Mongols of an interesting tribe.

We marched for days through magnificent mountain solitudes, and absolute silence enfolded us.

We were constantly on the look out for the animal life of these regions which includes such interesting varieties as the wild horse (*Equus Prschevalski*), and the *kulan* (*Equus hemionus*).   The wild horse takes its Latin name from the explorer N. M. Prschevalski, who was the first Westerner in modern times to come on the tracks of that elusive animal.   We ourselves never saw any wild horses, though we often came across their tracks.

The *kulan*, which in appearance suggests a yellowish-brown mule, is far commoner and is often hunted by Mohammedan hunters, who regard its flesh as a great delicacy.   The hide of the *kulan* is also much sought after, for it surpasses all others in wearing qualities and is used in preference for the making of sandals and boots. The *kulan* is enormously tenacious of life, and the hunters assert that even after the animal has been flayed and its skin dressed its tail still goes on lashing at the flies !

Now and then we saw leaping *tekhe* (wild goats, ibex, *Capra siberica*) and *argali* (wild sheep, *Ovis Poli*). The sheep often kept to the most inaccessible peaks and their colossal horns stood out silhouetted trumpet-shaped against the sky. They shot over the abysses like winged creatures, and we saw them climb the steepest mountain-sides with playful ease.

The farther south we went the oftener we saw the tracks and droppings of *kulan*. We were very anxious to procure a handsome specimen for the expedition's zoological collections and had made many excursions to that end, but had not hitherto succeeded in getting within range of any. When therefore one afternoon I met a Mohammedan hunter who had shot a *kulan* that same morning, I persuaded him by the promise of payment to take me to his hunting-ground which lay a few hours' distance from our camp.

We set out at midnight and rode through darkness and silence. Beside a little mountain lake we pitched camp in high reeds. When the first streak of dawn appeared in the east there was a crackling among the reeds, and my companion stiffened in his watchful attitude. Dark silhouettes were stealing forward out of the grey dawn. There was a splashing in the water, and we crawled cautiously in the direction of the sound. When we reached the edge of the reed bed we could distinguish seven horselike animals at a distance of scarcely three hundred yards. They had stopped drinking and were standing with heads erect sniffing in our direction.

" *Kulan*," whispered my companion and pointed out the two which ought to be dropped first.

Suddenly disquiet arose in the herd, and our shots sent them all in thundering flight into the morning mist. But two had fallen, and I ran to the edge of the lake to have a look at my first *kulan*. I was wondering at their resemblance to Mongolian ponies, and then I perceived that one of them was gelded—and I understood.

Raging I turned to my guide and saw that he was wild-eyed with terror. In a voice of supplication he asked if it might not be supposed that my bullet had killed both the horses, and seeing in his terrified eyes the importance he attached to my answer, I gave him a confirmatory nod.

I was now a criminal in the eyes of the Mongols. I had slain two sacred animals, and one of the horses was hit in the head, the very seat of the incarnation. The animals were powerful and glossy, and their stiffened muscles were still astrain for the leap that had never been taken. I felt myself a squanderer of splendid life, and I have never ceased to wish that senseless deed undone.

It was only later that I could think of the owner of the horse, whom I must seek out to explain my mistake and offer compensation for the loss he had sustained. My companion explained that the nearest dwellings were at Temirlik, and the caravan quickened its march thither.

After three days' journey we reached the little mountain community which consisted only of six Sart families living in caves dug out in the side of a steep clay slope. The Sarts had migrated from Cherchen to carry on trade with the nomads of those parts and the passing Mongolian pilgrims on their way to Lhasa.

I sought out the elders of the community and related my tragic experience in the mountains, but all the cave families had their horses with them, and none was aware of a loss. None of the nomads were occupying grazing-grounds so far north, they told us, so that the shot horses were either deserters from some passing caravan or Mongol horses which had run away from the herd to join the wild kulans. Such things happened.

As a last attempt to ease my evil conscience I determined to report the matter to the local Mongol chief. It is true I was vehemently advised against this course by the Mohammedans on the ground that it would raise a great fuss among the Mongols even if the horses did not belong to their herds, in which case the lamentable story would never become known unless I myself related it. I was not, however, so sure of this, since my hunting companion had levanted not long before our arrival at Temirlik and might be expected to have informed against me so as to divert suspicion from himself.

" Dressed in an ample cloak of lynx skin he was sitting against the
background of a black rug on which the image of a ferocious
tiger was inwoven "

Camel transport across the river

Torgut Soldier

[*face p.* 193

The six Mohammedan families were by no means on the best of terms with the surrounding Mongols, and a frequently recurring cause of contention was that the Sarts are eager *kulan* hunters, while the Mongols regard the *kulan* as a kind of horse, which it is thus a sin to hunt. It was an extremely awkward situation into which I had brought the expedition, since the enmity of the Mongols might render all work in these regions completely impossible for both Bergman and me. A conference between us convinced us that the only right course was honestly to report the occurrence and to make good the loss. And when the Sarts found that this determination was unshakable they sent for a friendly disposed *merin* [1] to ask his advice.

The Mongol arrived under cover of dusk and only indifferently succeeded in concealing under a mask of politeness the nervous disquiet he felt at being let into this melancholy secret. He advised us decidedly to report the matter and left us hastily.

Next morning the sun beat down upon the tent, and the country was resplendent with vivid colour. To the south and south-east lay a grassy plateau which extended to the gleaming of waters Gas-nor. The grass land was dotted with grey-white Mongol tents and vast herds of cattle moved in the neighbourhood of the lake. Soon inquisitive riders were attracted to our tent over which waved a blue and yellow and a red and white flag. It was our first encounter with Däde Mongols. The men looked savage and seemed to be completely lacking in the calm dignity and strict etiquette which commonly marks the demeanour of the Mongols. Loud voiced and unconcernedly inquisitive as untutored children they walked round inside the tents, and we perceived that if our stay among these people was to be productive of good results we must make ourselves respected from the first. We understood their dialect and exchanged friendly greetings while offering them tea and tobacco. The Mongols wore cloaks of Tibetan cut and had scarlet cotton handkerchiefs wound round their heads.

The same afternoon we received a visit from a sumptu-

[1] *Merin*—Mongolian magistrate.

193

ously clad elderly Mongol, Yetum, whose physiognomy and whole bearing filled us with evil forebodings. We gave him tea and showed him all the courtesy due to a guest, and the conversation turned on the route of our accomplished journey, its abundance of water and dearth of habitations. Suddenly the man asked in a sharp tone whether we were in the habit of shooting horses. I answered that we never did so knowingly, but that I had unwittingly committed one such action for which I was ready to make redress and offer compensation.

The old man's face was distorted with malice, and during our conversation I was constantly interrupted by his ungoverned outbursts ; we had killed his horses and it was with the intention of shooting horses that we had come there. And people who shot horses might at any time turn their rifles on human beings. We were thieves and murderers and it would be well to exterminate us before we committed more murders.

Then I thought we had had enough and drove the fellow out.

To forestall the indignant Mongol, who might persuade his chief to intervene precipitately in the affair before we had explained the facts of the case and put forward the circumstances which might serve for my defence, we galloped at once to the chief's tent a mile or so from our camping-place.

The chief's tent was of the most primitive description, and the man who occupied the chief's seat appeared completely unapproachable. Dressed in an ample cloak of lynx skin he was sitting against the background of a black rug on which the image of a ferocious tiger was inwoven. His glance was sullen, his bearing haughty, and the small moustache on his upper lip indicated that he belonged to the warrior caste.

With a commanding gesture he bade us be seated by the fire, and in silence and without interest he awaited what we had to say. This was the most arrogant chieftain we had anywhere encountered, and we exerted all our eloquence and charm without succeeding in producing any change of expression in his grim features. But he appeared to be just, and before we withdrew he declared that the *Khuruldei* [1] of the tribe should hear both parties and would then give judgment according to the law of the nomads.

All joy had deserted our camp in face of the doom which might cut short the expedition on which we had set out with such high expectations. We went through all my arguments in defence, but think as we would the fact remained that next day I was to be judged by Mongols and that by the law of the Mongols I was a criminal.

[1] *Khuruldei*—council of chiefs or magistrates.

CHAPTER XXIII

I BECOME A SHAMAN

THE court, which consisted of the chief and five grave Mongols, sat in judgment in our tent, and their train of soldiers and lamas filled the space around it. My antagonist was attired in costly lama's robes and arrived attended by his suite and a crowd of curious people who clearly showed their sympathy for him and against me.

Bergman and I took up a position in the northern corner of the tent, and my opponent and his suite sat opposite. The soldiers crowded the entrance, and outside could be heard the loud discussions of the anxious and angry crowd.

I based my defence on the facts that I was not a Mongol, had never been in those parts before, was ignorant of the laws of these people and therefore could not be judged according to them. I had shown my regret as soon as I perceived my mistake, as was proved by the fact that I had informed against myself and offered compensation to the owner of the two horses, although I might have kept the affair secret, in which case the owner of the horses would have been the poorer by their value.

I concluded my address by bringing out the compensation I offered, and the assembly grew silent at the sight of my silver *yamba*.[1]

The chief and his five counsellors carefully considered my words behind the cloud of smoke from their long pipes, and the soldiers in the tent-opening repeated my speech to the multitude outside and described the lustre and weight of the lump of silver. Yetum conferred in whispers with his suite, and then his greed

[1] *Yamba*—a lump of silver shaped like a horseshoe, weighing four pounds.

196

took the upper hand, and he declared himself willing to settle the matter for three such silver pieces.

This was an impudent demand for two horses which had long since run away from his herd, and if I gave in to his effrontery we would become a laughing-stock to the whole population and would certainly be subject to extortion throughout our stay.

I therefore declared that my offer was adequate and that I would not pay an ounce more. But at that my adversary's hatred flared up again, and he began his attack. In shrill tones he flung out the most venomous accusations against the white invaders, represented us as the incarnation of all evil come to disturb the peace of the grazing-grounds and plunge the nomads in disaster, and, incited by the applause of his followers, worked himself up into a violent rage. We had broken the laws of the steppe ; the punishment both of the gods and of the nomads was upon our heads.

The impressionable Mongols were fired by his fanaticism and, shouting for vengeance, they swarmed into the tent. Rancorous glances and threatening fists were directed at us ; they closed in on us, and it was impossible to make ourselves heard.

Our position was critical and might at any moment become disastrous.

My thoughts sought wildly for some way out of the situation. Images of shamans and lamas and their devices, which impress the nomads as marvellous mysteries, passed in review through my brain, and all at once I remembered the teachings of an old lama during a long winter spent in the forests of Northern Mongolia.

And then I became a Shaman !

Unending streams of Tibetan formulas rolled over my lips while with my hands I traced mystic figures in the air. Sometimes I mixed lines of European verse with my Tibetan text, and the lamas present marvelled at my knowledge of their formulas and made an effort to grasp the incomprehensible.

I fixed a piercing gaze on my enemy in the middle of his sweating forehead ; my chanting voice rose and fell and at times passed into wild shrieking. Dead silence fell over the multitude ; they sought my wonder-working gaze and followed its direction. My enemy shifted nervously, and his eyes looked over the crowd, but everywhere they met glances all of which were fixed upon his forehead.

Suddenly my prayers ceased, and I bent forward with outstretched arm so that my forefinger almost touched the point on his face at which all were staring.

"You see, " I shrieked, "you see the sign upon his forehead, the mark which signifies the curse of the gods ! "

And they all saw it.

My victim shook with terror and clutched at his forehead. And then I pronounced his doom.

" Desire has created your wealth and the power you have won among your fellows. But I am sent hither by mighty gods to prove your sense of justice, and I have found only hatred and desire. You are under the curse of the gods ; your punishment begins this day and shall continue until you have acquired the good qualities of the spirit. This day you shall pay me a sheep, and you shall continue to lose cattle until you amend your ways, and if you persist in evil, in two years you shall be a destitute man."

Then I commanded him to separate himself from all honest folk, and he fled from the tent followed by the scornful looks of the crowd.

I had drawn my bow taut, and it had stood the strain. For a while the atmosphere in the tent was charged with suspense ; the gaze of all rested uncertainly upon us, and no one spoke a word. But after we had handed the lump of silver to the chief, not as a fine but in token of friendship, and treated all those present to tea and tobacco, the tension relaxed, and they began to entertain us with stories of Yetum's sinful life which explained the punishment of the gods that had now fallen upon him.

Bergman and I spent the rest of the day in anxious expectation of the sheep which I had charged Yetum to deliver to me as a punishment for his offences. If the sheep came it would be a sign that the lama was afraid of punishment ; if it did not come it would mean that the fear I had inspired had subsided, and in that event the sympathy of the Mongols might soon return to Yetum's side, and new difficulties be in store for us.

The sun went down upon our anxiety, but with the darkness came the longed-for sheep. It was large and fat, and upon its horns was laid a costly *hadak*. The bringers of the beast were deferential men, and they presented their master's humble greetings.

By the pilgrim's way to Lhasa, not far from our camp a number of pilgrims were encamped, and I had heard that one of them was a highly esteemed *hutuktu*. Following an inspiration I dragged the sheep to the pilgrim camp and presented it to the Mongolian incarnation of divinity.

And the *hutuktu* proved to be Altai Gegen, one of the saints of the Torguts.

My fat sheep pleased the kindly man, and so did the story of how this beast from the covetous lama's flock came through me to find its way into his fleshpot. We ate the daintiest morsels of the sheep, and the *hutuktu* was convinced that in the critical situation of that day I had been inspired by some friendly divinity.

And then I seized the opportunity to elicit from him information about the Torguts, and he promised to show me the way to their country if I would attach myself to his caravan which would be resuming its homeward journey so soon as the horses were rested, and this he reckoned would take six weeks.

THE Sarts at Temirlik said that the place took its name from the primitive metal weapons and armour (*temir* or *tumur*—iron), which were found when the caves were excavated. This confirmed Bergman's hope of interesting finds, and we spent many arduous and happy days in these regions. The Däde Mongols proved helpful; they assisted Bergman in his diggings, and I carried out more anthropometric measurements among these Mongols than I had yet succeeded in obtaining from any single tribe.

The Däde Mongols (*däde*—dwelling in high altitudes) who now roam the regions about Kuku-nor and Teyiner-nor are descendants of the Mongols of the Dzungarian

Khoshut tribe which conquered these Tibetan territories two hundred years ago.

When in the beginning of the seventeenth century the great West Mongol coalition, Durbet öret, began its expansion to the territories outside Dzungaria, one of the four main tribes, the Khoshut, drifted to the south under the leadership of the valiant chieftain Turu-baihu. In 1637 the Khoshut Mongols took possession of the country round Kuku-nor. Afterwards they stormed Lhasa, drove out the last king of Tsang and set up the hierarchical dominion which still prevails in Tibet. For this service homage is paid to Turu-baihu throughout the lamaist world as " the defender of the yellow doctrine " under the name of Bogdo Gushi Khan.

The Khoshut Mongols of these regions are called Taburn tsaidam (*taburn*—five) and are divided into five *notog* (domiciles). The five *notog* are called Kuket-beise, Kurluk-beise, Barun-jassak, Jun-jassak and Teyiner. Each *notog* is subject to a prince who has several subordinate chiefs of whom each is the leader of a " banner ". The total strength of the Khoshut Mongols in these regions amounts to twenty-one " banners " numbering altogether about twelve hundred tent families.

The Däde Mongols by Gas-nor among whom we were now staying constitute one " banner " of Teyiner *notog*. The " banner " chief was the grim nomad leader who had his camp not far from our tent, but the prince of their *notog* resided by the lake of Teyiner-nor about two days' journey to the south-east of Gas-nor.

Descendants of the original Dzungarian Khoshut tribe are living in other parts too. Thus there is one " banner " in the Altai mountains south of Kobdo, and there are three at Khara Shar by the lake of Bagrash-Köl. There are Khoshut Mongols by the Volga, descendants of the three thousand tent families which at the end of the eighteenth century migrated under the leadership of Kondolen Ubashi from Dzungaria to Russia.

DURING our further stay in Tibet Bergman executed a map of our route, and here as elsewhere he added to the expedition's botanical collections. We visited the high-lying source of Cherchen-darya which lay imbedded in the massed flowers of the short-lived alpine summer, and when we turned northward again to follow the river to the lowlands, archæological finds began to crop up. At the oasis town of Cherchen Bergman acquired the first Stone-Age urn found in Sinkiang, and this epoch-making discovery led to his decision to devote prolonged investigation to the ruined towns and burial places of these regions.

THE time during which Altai Gegen was to rest at Temirlik before returning with his train of pilgrims to the land of the Torguts was now overpast by several weeks. I was seized with impatience to be off, for each day carried the *hutuktu* a day's journey farther to the north, and with him disappeared this chance of reaching the goal of my longing. But I hoped that riding alone and without heavy baggage I should be able to catch up with his slow camels on the desert road between Charklik and Toksun before the caravan disappeared in the Tien Shan mountains.

So I parted from Folke Bergman, the best of travelling companions on trying journeys, and rode out into the desert alone on *Buran*. For five days I traversed the same sand ocean that Marco Polo crossed six hundred years ago and of which he related that " it is a well-known fact that this desert is a haunt of evil spirits which entice travellers to destruction by the most splendid illusions ".

In Charklik I learned that Altai Gegen and his Torguts had passed the oasis ten days earlier on their way to Turfan, and I accordingly went on post haste to the northward. I passed the dead and dying regions of the Lop desert, froze while riding over the passes in the heights of Kuruk-tagh (5,500 ft.) and scrambled down the mountains' northern slopes to the tropical heat of the Turfan depression six hundred and fifty feet below sea level.

Here I overtook Altai Gegen the day before he and his train were to leave the caravan route and bury themselves in the trackless mountains that conceal the camping grounds of the Torguts. The *hutuktu* deferred his journey for twenty-four hours and during this time he listened smiling and with kind eyes to my wishes. By the end of the time I knew a good deal about the Torguts and had received the holy man's assurance that I should be well received by his tribesmen.

Altai Gegen told me that, in the evening following my departure from Temirlik, Yetum had visited the *hutuktu* to confess a number of his life's sins and to speak about the curse which "the white lama" had called down upon him. He wished to know whether "the white lama" really had such power and what, in that event, he should do to reconcile himself with the gods. The *hutuktu*, who had already heard my version of the affair, assured him that my power and my knowledge were such as the greatest shaman's and that the only way for Yetum to be rid of the curse was to deliver a sheep weekly to the tribal monastery until its prior found his life in better agreement with the Doctrine.

The prior had later informed Altai Gegen that Yetum's tale of sins was so black that it would take about two years to wash away. A hundred and four weeks was letting him off cheaply, Altai Gegen considered, for Yetum was the possessor of over two hundred sheep.

I WAS now obliged to go on immediately to Urumchi to fit out the expedition to the land of the Torguts.

THE four hundred and fifty miles between Charklik and Urumchi had taken two and a half months on the outward journey with the caravan, but my *Buran* galloped it in twelve days and nights, which on top of an arduous journey of three hundred miles was a proud performance on the part of my splendid horse.

I was met in Urumchi by tragic news. Old Governor Yang, the friend and supporter of our whole expedition, had been murdered during the summer by his own foreign minister who in his turn had been executed with certain of his adherents. The new governor, Chin Shujen, was ill disposed to the expedition's aims and had already begun the series of intrigues which were for long to hamper our work in his domains.

BOOK II

"Perhaps we are people who do not know much ; but all that is simple and natural, that we know and fully understand . . ."

From a Mongol's letter.

THE CAVALCADE OF THE WEST MONGOLS THROUGH THE CENTURIES

THE legend-interwoven story of the Torguts has long captivated my fancy, and I have in the course of years sought from books and original sources to evoke the historical background to the present condition of this Mongolian tribe. I have observed how its fate through the centuries has been linked up with that of its West-Mongol kin, and from many sources, of which the chief have been Chinese and Russian manuscripts and historical documents, I have tried to compose a tolerably clear picture of that fate so far as there is any record of it.

Most of these sources differ considerably as to the main features, and in respect of details they are far from agreement. But I have been able to check most of the facts here submitted in conversation with Torguts of the Khara Shar Khanate who were interested and well informed in the former history of their race. I obtained many data from *Toregut Rarelro* which was read and expounded to me by learned lamas in the Torguts' "Yellow Monastery" in the Tien Shan mountains. This ancient collection of documents, written in Mongolian and of purely Mongolian origin, is the Torguts' own highly coloured and imaginative account of the forefathers of the Khan and the people and of their exploits in the vanished centuries.

At the end of the fifteenth century several great West Mongol tribes united in Durbet öret, the fourfold alliance. The most important tribes within this alliance were the Torgut, Khoshut, Ölet and Durbet, to which were added the lesser tribes, Khoros and Khoit.[1]

This West-Mongol confederation arose in the extensive territory of Dzungaria, and the allied Öret Mongols' steppes stretched from the Ili valley in the west to Kobdo in the east. Southward they reached the sterile regions south of the Tien Shan mountains and northward the territory in south-west Siberia occupied by Kirghiz, Kasak and other non-Mongolian tribes.

The name Dzungaria (from *dzun*—left, and *gare*—hand) is explained by the Mongols as having arisen from the fact that the nomads of Dzungaria constituted the left hand or wing on the Mongols' long front against the non-Mongolian hereditary enemies in the north.

Under the warlike Öret Khans Mahmud, Togon and Essen the West Mongols dominated the whole of Mongolia and were a constant menace to the Chinese empire. Essen took one of the Ming emperors prisoner, but not long after, on the death of Essen in 1453, the West-Mongol confederation lost its political power, and for more than a century and a half the Dzungars (West Mongols) exerted little influence on Mongolia's destiny.

Towards the end of the sixteenth and at the beginning of the seventeenth century powerful leaders again arose among the Öret chiefs. Khara Khula united the West-Mongol tribes under his strong will and assumed the title of *Khun-taiji* (supreme chief).

His son and successor Batur Khun-taiji brought about an alliance between Western and Northern Mongolia (Dzungaria and Khalka), which was ratified in 1640 at a congress in which forty-four Mongolian tribes took part. The West Mongols were now approaching another period of greatness, and their Khun-taiji was a powerful ruler greatly feared by neighbouring peoples.

At the same time that Batur's policy united the free West-Mongol tribes in a strong combination, several Mongolian tribes, whose chieftains were too freedom-

[1] The four tribes which constituted Durbet öret are variously named in different sources. The names given above agree with the Torguts' own records.

loving to willingly subordinate themselves to the suzerainty of a neighbouring chief, emigrated from Dzungaria.

The most important migrations were those of the Khoshuts under Gushi Khan and of the Torguts under Boro Örölok (Ho-orlyk).

The Khoshuts plundered Lhasa and, in the beginning of the seventeenth century, took possession of the territory round Kuku-nor which their descendants the Däde Mongols still inhabit. The Torguts pushed out towards the north-west and went to meet the fate which I shall describe later.

The breaking off of these two nomad peoples from the Dzungarian alliance seems to have been in full accord with Batur Khun-taiji's policy of expansion, for both Gushi Khan and Boro Örölok maintained their connection with the West-Mongol block, and the seals of both chiefs appear on the ratification document of the forty-four allied princes. The migrations would appear to have been largely occasioned by the constant desire of the nomads for new grazing-grounds.

Batur Khun-taiji was succeeded by his son Galdan. Under the latter's leadership the West Mongols made bloody incursions into the steppes inhabited by the Khalka Mongols, and these turned to the Manchu Emperor K'ang Hsi with prayers for help. The Emperor, who lay with his army ready for battle behind the Great Wall, allotted to the fugitive Khalka Khans the steppes bordering on the grazing-grounds of the Sunits and Durbet Khuhets, and himself took the field against the advancing Dzungar hordes. But Galdan put the Emperor himself to flight and pursued the Manchus into China.

Not till they were within a hundred miles of Peking did K'ang Hsi succeed in checking, in a decisive battle, the advance of the Mongols. The Dzungarian cavalry, a hundred and twenty thousand strong, had taken up a position behind a barricade of ten thousand camels tied together and carrying on their backs felt-covered chests with loopholes through which the Mongols discharged their arrows and darts. K'ang Hsi, who had now received reinforcements of artillery, produced with this complete panic in the living camel-fortress, and the Dzungars were utterly defeated.

Galdan himself succeeded in escaping and before long collected a new army with which he encountered the Emperor by the river Gerelchi. After a fierce battle Galdan was again defeated, and among the fallen was his own *Khatun* (queen), Amu. According to the Chinese Amu Khatun was a fair Amazon who loved the game of war. Clad in a shining copper coat of mail she discharged death-dealing arrows and darts, and her mount was a fantastic camel-like beast. Under Amu's banner fought the pick of the warriors, and in the last battle they were all slain with her.

Once more Galdan succeeded in escaping, and he galloped back to the distant Ili in the hope of there being able to assemble the scattered remnant of his people. But his own kinsman, the chief Tsewang Raptan, had usurped the power during his absence, and Galdan was murdered by his own men in 1687.

Now followed a brief period of peace on the Dzungarian steppes. But under pressure from the Dzungarian nobles Tsewang Raptan resumed after a few years the obstinate war against the Manchus and the Khalka Mongols, with a view to reconquering the steppe territory in the east which the West Mongols had ruled during their period of greatness. For long they fought with success, but in 1719 the Emperor K'ang Hsi sent into the west two mighty armies which annihilated the power of the West Mongols.

Tsewang Raptan was poisoned in 1727 and was succeeded by his son Galdan Tsering.

This chief resumed in 1730 the attack on the Khalka Mongolian steppes and even penetrated into Chinese territory behind the Great Wall. The Dzungars were long successful, but finally in 1732 the united Khalka Mongolian and Manchurian armies contrived to lure them into an ambush, and Galdan Tsering suffered a decisive defeat which put an end to the warlike plans of the West-Mongol chiefs.

Durbet öret still existed, but the Manchus had exterminated nine-tenths, six hundred thousand, of the Öret Mongols.

In 1753 the Ölet chieftain Amursana gathered the scattered West Mongols for a last war of liberation against the oppressors, and for more than a year the nomads fought an embittered but hopeless fight against the superior Chinese forces.

The Chinese succeeded by political intrigues in the form of bribes and golden promises for the future in involving Mohammedan princes and ambitious young Mongolian chiefs in the struggle, and the result was a civil war of extermination.

Finally Amursana was obliged to flee to Siberia where he died in 1755, and the dominion over Tien Shan, "the heavenly mountain", and the ancient grazing-grounds of the West Mongols was assumed by the Chinese General, Chao Hui.

But by the nomads' camp-fires one may still hear the heroic exploits of Amursana extolled. The descendants of Amursana's warriors look stern when they tell the legend that the liberator Khan will one day reappear in a warrior figure inspired by the gods, and the mothers gaze with pride on the children of the tent when they sing of the heroes who shall one day rally round Amursana's coming incarnation on the steppes.

THE Torgut chief, Boro Örölok, who with five thousand tent families left Dzungaria in 1618, made war upon the nomad tribes of Western Siberia in the course of a systematic advance to the north-west. In 1630 he crossed the Ural mountains and followed by his six sons and twenty-five thousand Torguts he marched down upon the Russian steppes. After having completely subdued Nogai, Kipchak and other Tatar tribes, the Torguts took possession of the fertile steppe region between the Ural and the Volga and plundered the Russian towns and villages along the river even as far north as Samara. Then they turned against Astrakhan, but failed to conquer that city, and Boro Örölok was killed outside the city walls (*circa* 1643).

He was succeeded by his son, Shykyr Daichin. After a series of feuds with the Russians he agreed to a peaceful settlement and commissioned his son, Puntsuk, to swear, on behalf of his father and the people, faith and obedience to the Tsar. To show the sincerity of his oath Puntsuk called the gods to witness, kissed the Torgut book of law, *Bichik*, licked his knife and turned its shining steel against his throat.

But despite this solemn oath the Torguts continued to make incursions into Russian territory, to plunder their villages and to carry off the inhabitants as slaves. The Tsar, however, overlooked these deeds of violence partly because of his own powerlessness, partly because the Torguts readily stood by the Russians whenever the southern frontier was threatened by Mohammedan hordes.

Shykyr Daichin was succeeded by his son, Puntsuk, and during his time the Torgut horde by the Volga was increased by the migration from Dzungaria of three thousand tent families of the Khoshut tribe under the leadership of Kondolen-Ubashi.

Puntsuk's son and successor Ayuk is perhaps the finest chief in Torgut history, and the half-century during which he was leader of the tribe was the Torguts' period of greatness in Europe. He was a born leader and possessed all the stern qualities which go to make a great steppe chieftain. His person and the wild deeds to which he inspired his Torguts made the neighbouring people fear and respect the Mongolian hordes, and the renown of them and their chief was widespread.

Ayuk received the title of *Khan* from the Dalai Lama, and before the Tsar and other potentates of Russia the Torgut chief appeared as a free and powerful prince. Peter the Great visited Ayuk Khan by the Volga, and the two rulers entered into an agreement by which the Khan undertook, in return for an annual tribute of cannon, powder and lead, to furnish the Tsar with military support. The Torgut cavalry became the Russians' best defence against the Ottoman menace from the south, for " the turbaned heads " were as much hated by the Mongols as they were feared by the Russians.

In 1707 the Torguts took the field against the Swedish king, Charles XII, and the Mongolian nomads hung like hounds on the heels of his marching columns.

Some years later, in 1714, the ruler of the Torguts received an embassy from the Emperor of China. The Chinese envoys, who travelled from Peking through the immense expanses of Siberia, were met at Tobolsk by an escort of a hundred Russian dragoons who were to conduct them on their further progress to the west. A former officer of Swedish dragoons, J. C. Schnitscher, who was attached as an officer to this company wrote his experiences on the journey, and a copy of his manuscript reached Stockholm where it was printed in 1744.

On July 2nd, 1714, Schnitscher arrived in the train of the Chinese ambassador at Ayuk Khan's magnificent residence ten days' journey from Saratov. The visit lasted ten days. The official errand of the Chinese was to exchange demonstrations of friendship between the Emperor of China and the Khan of the Torguts, but the far weightier mission, and one kept secret from the Russians, was to offer to the Torguts the best grasslands of Dzungaria together with great riches if they would return to the land of their fathers and aid the Manchus in the conquest of the Öret Mongols living there.

Ayuk, however, rejected this proposal of treachery against his kinsfolk in Dzungaria to whose ruler, Tsewang Raptan, he had given his daughter in marriage. But he carefully preserved the secret document in case the Torguts should wish in the future to set up their tents again in Dzungaria under the protection of mighty China.

Schnitscher writes of the Torguts :

These people far surpass us Christians in mutual love, for they do not enjoy the least thing for themselves unless they have first shared it with such of their fellows as are present even though they be twenty or more. . . .

When they ride out, for they walk scarcely more than twenty steps on foot, masters and servants, yes, and the Khan himself, ride without distance between them ; that, however, may be so that they may always have him among them. The greatest honour and reverence that the Khan has of his household is that they always look him fair and square in the eyes.

They are as heroic, yes, as wary and swift as hares in cold

winters, but at the same time as cunning to plunder and steal as the hungriest wolf. When a famished wolf is chased he keeps straight on for a while, but stops and looks back that he may catch something. So also they; if one pursue them they run, but if one turn back they follow at one's heels.

DURING the time of Ayuk Khan the Torgut horde by the Volga was further increased in that several Öret chiefs, who had fled from the war-ravaged steppes of Dzungaria, attached themselves to their famous kinsman in the west.

After Ayuk's death in 1724 disputes about the succession arose among the Torgut princes. Finally they agreed to accept Ayuk's weakest and least ambitious son, Tseren Donduk, as ruler, but Donduk Ombo, a son of Ayuk's eldest son, contested his uncle's right to power and in 1735 succeeded in proclaiming himself chief, and such he remained until his death in 1741.

Donduk Ombo was succeeded by another of Ayuk's grandsons, Donduk Taiji, and it was in his time that the troops of the Khoshut, Durbet and Khoit tribes that escaped the Chinese massacres in Dzungaria came to the Volga. In order to assure his son Ubashi's right of succession Donduk Taiji in 1758 appointed him official heir to the chieftainship.

Three years later on his father's death the seventeen-year-old Ubashi ascended the throne in the Khan's tent of the Torguts, and took possession of the great silver seal that was the symbol of his Khanate. *Ubashi* or *Ubasha*,[1] the name given at birth to the princely son by the lamas of the Khan's tent, is the Tibetan form of a Sanskrit word. The young chief was proclaimed Khan under the Mongolian name of Obish Khan, and it is as Obish Khan that he is honoured by his descendants and by the Torguts who rally round them, as the great liberator of the tribe from the Russian yoke.

The Russian ruler with whom young Obish Khan had to deal was the shrewd and ambitious Empress Elizabeth. She perceived that the troublesome disturbances which were constantly inflicted on the Russians

---

[1] *Ubashi* or *Ubasha*—one who has given a promise.

by the Mongolian horde by the Volga were due in part
to the great mobility of the horde, and she accordingly
set herself systematically to alter these conditions.

She succeeded in inducing the young and inexperienced
Obish Khan to revise the horde's mode of government,
so that the Khan should share his executive power with
a council, and at the same time the Russians began to
surround the Torgut steppes with a ring of fortresses
and an increasing pressure of colonization which limited
the nomads' freedom of movement.

This caused great disquiet in the horde and the
terrible suspicion arose among the Torguts that the
Russians were trying to make house-dwellers of them
so as to change them into Cossacks obedient to the Tsar.

According to the Torguts yet another circumstance
helped to increase the tribe's growing sense of oppression,
namely their increasing isolation from the head of their
religion in Lhasa. The diligently travelled pilgrim's
way to the holy city of Lamaism had been more and
more barricaded by Russian Cossack fortresses, and the
steppes on the way thither, which earlier had been
dominated by their co-religionists, were filled with
hostile Mohammedan hordes.

Gradually in the mind of the people's leader the
fantastic thought matured that the horde should throw
off its more and more detested yoke in the land of
strangers and flee back to the steppes of its fathers in
Dzungaria. From the east came rumours of steppes
lying empty of people and fertile, and "the Son of
Heaven" himself, the great Emperor Chi'en Lung, who
was sensible of the truths of Lamaism, had invited them
to live there in peace and happiness.

Signs of unrest among the Torguts gave birth to
suspicions in Petersburg, and the Empress Elizabeth's
equally power-loving successor, Catherine the Second,
who was anxious to retain the vigorous nomad population among her faithful subjects and who was afraid of
losing her efficient Torgut cavalry, sent spies and bands
of Cossacks to keep watch on the smallest movement of
the nomads. But so skilfully did Obish Khan throw
dust in the eyes of the Russians that shortly before

the carrying out of the great enterprise the Empress's own chamberlain jeered at the Khan for his timid inactivity and called him " a bear on a chain ".

In order to divert the attention of the Russians from his plans the Khan sent thirty thousand men of his cavalry to their aid in the war against the Turks in the campaign of 1768-9. And in that campaign the Torguts distinguished themselves for their great gallantry, won independently many battles and brought home for their share rich booty of the firearms so urgently needed for the Khan's plans of revolt.

Clearly perceiving the power of religion over the souls of the nomads and in order at the decisive moment to win them completely for his plans, Obish Khan had sent a deputation to the Dalai Lama to solicit the counsel of the all-knowing. The oracular answer was that provided the revolt began in a " tiger year " or a " hare year " its issue would be favourable. 1770 was a " tiger year " and 1771 a " hare year " and the High Lama of the Torguts interpreted the Dalai Lama's words as meaning that if the exodus took place in the winter between the summers of these two years, the strength of the tiger and the swiftness of the hare would be conferred upon the fugitives. To make the flight possible for the part of the tribe settled to the west of the Volga the start must be made while the river was frozen over.

The secret preparations had long been in full swing, but still up to midwinter in 1770 the hundreds of thousands of nomads lived their tradition-bound life and pastured their flocks in profound unconsciousness of the terrible fate that so soon was to tear them from their peaceful home tents and cast them out into immeasurable sufferings.

This fabulous drama, directed by a strong man's will and affecting a whole people, began with the speed of a flash of lightning and developed with the violence of a thunderbolt.

One early winter morning a troop of couriers scattered at a fast gallop from the Khan's residence out among the tents of the steppe with the false alarm that their hereditary foes the Kirghiz and Bashkir had invaded their country, and within three days eighty thousand warriors were assembled at the secret meeting-place.

And then Obish Khan rose high in the saddle and spoke to his men. In words of flame he reminded them of the proud exploits of their fathers and quoted galling instances of the ruthless oppression of the Russians. Soon they would be transformed from free nomads into anxious tillers of the soil and no longer be able to answer their oppressors with the speech of their fathers which was that of the sharp steel.

The host was fired and shared the feelings of their Khan, and the morning air trembled with their thousand-fold cry of " *Yabonah.*"

On swift-footed horses the eighty thousand warriors now flew out over the Torgut steppes, and the urge to leave the country was communicated to every tent. The immense herds of cattle were driven together, the tents struck and packed on ox-wagons and the backs of camels. The lamas chanted round high-wheeled wagons on which the tent temples with their gods were stowed. The warriors gathered in " arrows ", and the " arrows " massed themselves round the *hoshun* banner.

Everything was done rapidly and in exemplary order, for decampment is the life of the nomads from birth.

De Quincey, who has so vividly described the flight of the nomad horde through Asia, characterizes it as an exploit without parallel in the history of the world.

On January 5th, 1771, the fateful hour of the departure struck, but, the night before, a violent storm had broken up the Volga's covering of ice, and the Mongols on the western bank were thus prevented from carrying out their Khan's order.

The great horde's migration occupied seven months and took them through two thousand five hundred miles of steppe and desert. The wretched fugitives were furiously pursued by Russian armies and ringed round by their hereditary foes, the Kirghiz and the Cossacks, with whom they had daily to fight bloody battles. The wells on their road were found to be poisoned. Men, women and children fell by the sword or succumbed to the pangs of hunger, thirst and exhaustion, but ever the horde pressed on through nameless terrors. Soon of the innumerable herds of cattle none remained. Dead and dying were left where they fell.

Four hundred thousand Torguts had left Russia. Less than a hundred and twenty thousand war-scarred men and tortured women reached the steppes that enjoyed the protection of the Chinese Emperor.

On arrival at the Ili river the fugitives were received by the Chinese governor, Shu Ho-te, whose frontier guard freed them from the pursuing scourge. The Emperor of China, who had been prepared by couriers for the arrival of the Torguts, assigned to the fugitives ten large districts on their forefathers' steppes in Dzungaria. Of these the four largest lay, one north of Khara Shar, one east of Tarbagatai, one between the Ili and Urumchi and one east of Kulja.

Father Amiot, one of the French Jesuits at that time resident in Peking, relates that on the arrival of the Torguts the Emperor wrote as follows :

> The Torguts came and on their arrival were given dwelling-places, victuals and all necessary things that could be procured.
> The principal chiefs were entertained and conducted with manifestations of honour to the place where I was. I received them, I talked with them and I perceived with pleasure that they shared with me in the enjoyment of the chase.
> Then they went in my suite even to the imperial palace at Jehol where I entertained them with banquets and gave them gifts with the same pomp and magnificence as when I receive other princes.

Of the Mongols left behind on the western bank of the Volga there were about fifteen thousand tents with seventy thousand inhabitants. It is their descendants who in our days live a nomadic life on the most barren salt steppes by the Volga, isolated among Turkish- and Russian-speaking peoples.

The word Kalmuck, which in the west has come to denote all West Mongols, is not of Mongolian origin, but is derived from the Turkish *kalmak*, " the remaining " or " the left behind ". With the passage of time it has been accepted as a designation by the remnant of a people beside the Volga, but among the West Mongols of Central Asia it is regarded as a term of abuse.

Observations among the surviving descendants of these people give a depressing idea of the fate which would have overtaken the whole of the proud Torgut people if Obish Khan with wise foresight had not ventured to flee with his nomads to the free steppes of Dzungaria.

The Danish physician and explorer, Hans S. Kaarsberg, who visited the Kalmuck steppes by the Volga in 1891, writes as follows :

> The race is looked down upon, but if the Kalmucks had not in past times helped the Russians the latter would hardly be what they now are in the Caucasus. The Kalmucks are Russian subjects, judged according to Russian law and are compelled to do military service in the Tsar's army. . . . The horse was once the Kalmucks' wealth, but that time is now past. . . . In past days a well-to-do Kalmuck owned a hundred horses, a rich one a thousand. One Kalmuck owned three thousand horses sixteen years ago ; now he has none at all. . . .

Kaarsberg saw in the Volga Kalmucks a dying people, by nature friendly, helpful and good humoured, but sodden with disease and vice. They have accepted civilization's evil gifts of alcohol and syphilis without having been able to make such use of its good ones as might have prevented a destructive degeneration. He estimated their number as ten thousand in all.

To his questions as to whence they derived and where people of their race were to be found the Kalmucks always returned the same answer.

They had come as a great and powerful people from the steppes far to the eastward and for many generations had pastured their flocks by the Volga. But at the end of the former century the horde had departed to return to their fathers' steppes. The fugitives had been overtaken by Russian soldiers, and only a small part of the participants in this migration had crossed the Volga— and had disappeared.

He heard the Kalmucks sing their forefathers' proud

songs of stout and warlike deeds, but what they sang of seemed as remote as the fabled steppes of Dzungaria.

Of the further fate of the Torgut horde after the great flight from Europe I never succeeded in tracing any satisfactory account.

In 1876 the Russian explorer, Prschevalski, on one of his many journeys through the Tien Shan mountains, passed the region where according to Chinese accounts the Torguts had been allotted grazing-grounds by the Chinese Emperor Chi'en Lung. On his arrival at Yuldus, north-west of Khara Shar, he received confirmation that he had reached one of the former territories of the Torguts. But the whole of that fertile highland lay empty of people and he encountered no Torguts anywhere. On enquiring among the neighbouring people he obtained the information that up to eleven years before his arrival Yuldus had been inhabited by ten thousand Torgut tent families who had been driven out or massacred by Yaqub Beg's Mohammedan Dungan hordes.

These negative reports, coupled with the romantic descriptions of a mighty Torgut Khan who ruled over a great people in the west, which had often captivated me during journeys among the Khalka Mongols, inspired in me a strong desire to seek out their country, and my longing to find a place in the intimate circle round their camp-fires had constantly increased.

I had not yet achieved any contact with Torguts. By Etsin-gol I had met with descendants of the Torgut group who long before the great revolt had separated from the Torgut horde during the reign of Ayuk for a pilgrimage to Lhasa under Arab Jur's leadership.

In the Däde Mongols in North-Eastern Tibet I had found descendants of the Khoshut Mongols who left the Dzungarian grazing-grounds three hundred years ago.

At Hami we had been taken captive by wild riders who called themselves Torguts and who brought us as prisoners to Urumchi, but these, who were far from their home steppes, had fallen silent as soon as we had tried to turn the conversation to their own race and its place of abode.

CHAPTER I

BEFORE THE GOAL

ONE early morning in September we set out from Urumchi.

There was an invigorating freshness in the air, and the sun poured its late summer glow over the mellow colours of the landscape.

Far off in the south-west the foothills of the Tien Shan range rose in a blue-violet ridge across the horizon line, and behind this were hidden the steppes of the Torguts.

I was wild with joy at the prospect of the long-sought goal, my two Mongolian-speaking Chinese sang at the tops of their voices and cracked their whips, and the six horses of the caravan trotted eagerly forward.

Sun-touched peaks began to appear behind the foot-hills, from the land that was the goal of my long journeys and my intense longing. They held out the promise of discovery and adventure, and I felt that one of the greatest events of my life was in front of me.

On the other side of the Dawan-Chen pass we came to the Turfan depression, some six hundred and fifty feet below sea level, and after that our way led us into the mountains. On the third day of the journey we reached Kumysh, " the silver village ", and there found two Torguts waiting to meet us. We first perceived the two sunburnt riders on dusty horses in front of the eastern edge of the little Sart village, but they had long seen us, and they knew where we had camped and what we had done ever since our start from Urumchi.

By their tall fur caps and brown Cossack uniforms I could see that they belonged to the same Torgut group that had taken us prisoners at Hami, and they at once addressed me by my name. Our conversation was extremely reserved, and much time was taken up in formal expressions of courtesy and silent tea-drinking before they came out with their errand.

The two Torguts had been sent by the leader of their people, the exalted and all-knowing Töin Lama, and their mission was, as a protective escort, to conduct me into the presence of their master.

Accounts of me and of my journey had come to the ears of the holy man through the Torguts who had met with the expedition's Mongols in Hami, and these, together with a message which he had received from Altai Gegen on the latter's return from pilgrimage, had induced in the ruler a desire to see me.

I discussed the route with my escort and soon understood that the one we were to follow to the ruler's abode had been chosen to keep the Chinese authorities in ignorance of the intended meeting.

Westward of Kumysh we left the highroad which goes on to Khara Shar and plunged instead into the low foothills of Tien Shan. We climbed between naked grey rock walls to a pass leading to the northern mountain slopes covered with autumn-tinted vegetation.

Later we came upon the tracks of cattle and at the end of the second day's march reached a delectable green alpine plateau. Colonies of Mongol tents were scattered over the steppe, and among the camps all was life and movement. Mounted youngsters were driving the cattle to the gathering-places, and the sound of shouting and laughter reached our ears. At the outer edge of the plain lay stone-paved ancient graves, and the pointed silhouettes of *obos* rose from the dominating heights in homage to the good spirits of these regions and as protection against the evil.

The grass was emerald green, the setting sun shone red and gold on the surrounding wooded mountain slopes, and the sky above seemed higher than in other places. The horses whinnied at the luxuriance and freedom around us, and the Torguts by my side rose in their saddles to strike up a lusty song of gladness at the sight of so much beauty.

Our gallop across the plain ended at its north-western

edge where four tents lay in shelter close to the hill-
side birch forest. Lissom Mongol women ran out of
the tents to catch up the barking dogs, and in front
of the principal tent a young Mongol whom I knew
stood smiling, Mongrolda Noyen, one of the chiefs of
the Khoshut Mongols and my former gaoler.

In the Khoshut camp round about there was a bustle
of preparation for departure, for it was the time when
the nomads move from the alpine summer pastures to
the more sheltered steppes along the banks of Bagrash-
Köl in the southern lowlands. But in Mongrolda
Noyen's tent the bustle gave way to hospitality, and we
ate and drank and let the time go by.

The young *Khatun* was a frank and fresh steppe
beauty who performed her duties as mistress of the
tent with youthful grace and practiced assurance.
Twenty-three summers stood behind her, and she was
in the full bloom of her beauty. Her carriage and
movements were those of the wild, modified by tradition,
her eyes were quick and limpid, and her teeth gleamed
with startling whiteness behind her bright red, smiling
lips.

She squatted in her tent-mistress's place south-east
of the fire and watched attentively over her husband's
comfort. The firelight played in her richly coloured
dress and in the dusky stones of her ornaments, and
her bracelets and earrings of heavy silver clashed when
she reached forward towards us in the exercise of her
duties as hostess.

Silently but alertly she followed the conversation of
the men and from time to time enhanced the gaiety
round the fire with her bubbling joyous laughter.

We spoke of how strange it was that the chief and I,
who had met before as gaoler and prisoner, should
now be sharing tent as host and guest, but we understood that now as then it was our roads of destiny
that met.

The young Mongol prince had changed the Cossack
uniform he had worn on our meeting at Hami for a
loose Mongol dress whose tightly drawn sash emphasized
his broad shoulders and slender youthful waist. Mon-

grolda Noyen was six years younger than I, and the same time had elapsed since his father had died and the chief's seal of the tribe had become his.

This and other things I came to know while the evening hours slipped quickly away. I told my story and he his, and it was a revelation to both of us.

The young hostess of the chief's tent was a daughter of the most powerful dynasty of the steppes and one of the oldest in the world. Her younger brother would one day inherit the Khanate of the Torguts which her father had held until his death, and the present holder, the renowned Töin Lama, was her father's brother.

Mongrolda's uncle, known and revered in the tribe under the name of Töin Geling, had secured to himself, his family and perhaps the whole Khoshut tribe the favour of the gods by renouncing the benefits of this life. Nine years before, he had withdrawn with two assistant lamas into a remote mountain tract where the three hermits now lived absorbed in holy writings and in the pure beauty of nature.

The three Khoshut tribes which now lead a nomadic life in the neighbourhood of the Torguts had shared much of the fate of the latter. Generations of Khoshut and Torgut tribes had together pastured their flocks by the banks of the distant Volga. It was one of Mongrolda Noyen's ancestors who had fled from the massacre in Dzungaria to seek refuge with the mighty Ayuk Khan and another who had listened to Obish Khan's cry of " *Yabonah* " and then with the Torguts had defied the sore distresses and fought out the bloody struggles of the long flight from west to east.

Thanks to his ability and the strength of his youth, Mongrolda Noyen had been appointed chief of the cavalry which the twelve Khoshut banners placed under the orders of the Torgut regent, and since his connection by marriage with the Torgut ruling family he had been made chief of one of the squadrons forming the regent's bodyguard.

Both Mongrolda Noyen and his Torgut-born *Khatun* were proudly conscious of the exploits of their respective forefathers and parent tribes. Both were of *tsaghan yasse* which in their own eyes and those of the people entitled them to profound respect. But their Mongolian pride was elemental and devoid of arrogance, and their own estimate of the loftiness of their persons was less than that of the people among whom they lived.

A couple of the prince's subjects had stepped into the tent. The one was old and grey, the other quite young ; two Khoshut generations who listened to the stories of their people's fate as generations had done before them. They were attentively ready to do their lord all imaginable services, but at the same time took part freely and smilingly in the conversation round the fire. It was clear that they had heard the same stories countless times, but equally clear that they could never tire of hearing them. And the young one would one day in his turn relate them to his listening descendants.

The fire burned down to embers, and darkness fell over the room. The two Mongols went out to close the smoke vent of the tent, and I heard them gallop off across the steppe to watch over their chief's herds of cattle.

The young hostess prepared my bed in the north-west corner of the tent and tucked the pelts in over me. The chief lighted the oil in the silver candelabra on the altar and threw himself on the raised sleeping-place to the east of it. His *Khatun* crept in to him between the skins after having performed nine *kow-tows* before the gods of the tent. I heard them yawn and stretch themselves, and soon they were breathing deeply and heavily in unison.

The gods twinkled dimly in the flickering light of the lamp flames, and the evening's stories passed in review under the tent roof.

I was tired from my journey and drowsy from the air, and it was good to be lying again in a Mongol tent for the first time for so long.

There, a bare yard away from me, were breathing the descendants of the great chiefs of the steppes who for so long had stirred my imagination—and I felt that the adventure had begun.

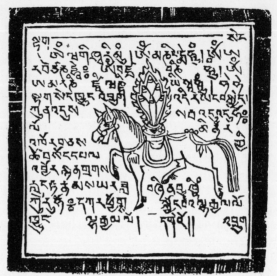

PRAYER-FLAG WITH SYMBOL OF HI-MORI AND SACRED TEXTS.

CHAPTER II

MY "AIR-HORSE" GALLOPS BEFORE THE WIND

High among the snow-clad peaks of the mountains stands a tent.

It is white as the sun-white peaks, and from its entrance Lobson Chanab gazes along the southern horizon.

His stallion is white and swifter than the arrow, and upon it he overtakes the wild deer.

The eagle on his strong wings hunts the wild swan, but Lobson Chanab is swifter than the strongest eagle.

Many have been envious of Lobson Chanab, but in battle they learned: Greatest of all is the black eagle Lobson Chanab.

•   •   •   •   •   •   •   •

I WAS awakened by the song of the Mongolian hero who fought and conquered the " turban-clad heads ".

The tent was empty, but the fire was crackling beside me, and the tea brewing in the big pot had begun to bubble. When the clear woman's voice had finished its song of Lobson Chanab I went out on to the steppe, out into the early morning.

Daylight was spreading over the eastward mountain crest, and life was resuming, having slept its fill. The women were milking to a singing measure, horses turned loose were galloping over the grass, and sheep hung like specks of light on the grey mountain-sides. Then the sun peeped over the hill, and a herdsman's pipe greeted it. Its notes came as a surprise in the clear air, so far away, so high above us.

Mongrolda came running with four horses, and his young *Khatun* at once hurried from the milking to her duties in the tent. My two Chinese began to saddle the horses for the day's journey. The chief intended himself to accompany me to the Torgut Regent's residence, and after a substantial meal of boiled mutton washed down with quantities of tea we set out.

My company, having first been increased by the two Torguts who had come to meet me at Kumysk and now further by Mongrolda Noyen and his four Khoshuts, formed a whole cavalcade. We climbed and galloped, kept a look out for game in the valleys and drank in the beauty of the wide spaces from the tops of the passes, and I had an almost religious longing to know and see all that appealed to these children of nature.

The approach of autumn was even more apparent on the heights. The birches on the northern slopes were yellowed by frost, and snow was lying on the higher fir trees. The horses climbed cleverly over the loose stones of the steep slopes ; the conversation of the men was subdued.

At times the Mongols and the horses checked and stood motionless as statues, and by following the direction of the men's glances I could discern the cause. On the most inaccessible rock ledges stood flocks of *argali* (Ovis ammon) in groups of twenty or thirty or only a few bucks whose imposing horns curved in fantastic silhouettes against the pale sky.

After a whispered consultation we rode on in a direction other than that of the shy game, but before we did so two marksmen had imperceptibly slipped from their horses to follow the game on foot. We all halted in the next valley, and the shots of the hunters were the signal which sent two of our Mongols back with their horses. Twice the hunters came back with white-breasted *argali*. The horns alone weighed anything up to forty-five pounds and, measured on the outer curve, had a length of nearly five feet. And yet the Mongols assured me that these sheep were only undeveloped youngsters.

We made camp before sundown in a high-lying mountain hollow, and I invited Mongrolda Noyen to be my guest for the night in my tent. The Mongols ate and were invited to lodge in the tent of the Chinese, but after the meal they soon wandered out into the open air where they lighted a big fire, and their saddles, laid out on the grass, showed where they preferred to take their rest.

In the course of the evening a small party of Torgut hunters arrived from the pass to the westward. They too chose our place for their night's rest, and by the fire exchanged news and told splendid stories which accorded marvellously with the wild atmosphere of the surroundings. The hunters were dressed in short sheepskin jackets which were tucked into their wide leather breeches. On their feet they wore light sandals of oxhide, and long knives and powder-horns hung from their belts. They had heard that multitudes of wild pig had appeared on the banks of the new river Kum Darya, and the credibility of the rumours was now eagerly discussed.

The leader of these hunters was a magnificent specimen of the man of the wilds, trained through a long life in the hard school of the powers of nature and familiar from childhood with that mysticism of the wilderness which a leader of nomads must be able to comprehend. His manner of speech was austere and individual, and he was splendid to look at.

Suddenly the old man's gaze shifted from the flames

Mongrolda Noyen

"Arselan Consul"

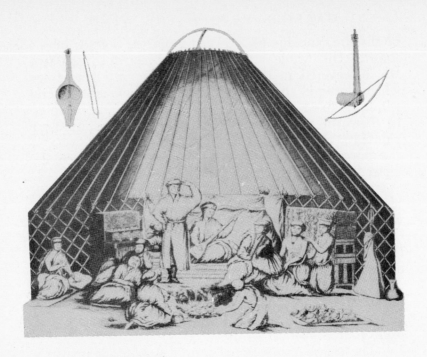

"The red Standard"

[face p. 225

of the fire, and his ears turned from the sounds of the forest. His whole attention was directed to my tent which wavered in the firelight, and to my prayer-flag which fluttered above its top in the capricious mountain wind. I fixed my eyes on the furrowed face, hoping to share the man's imaginative inspiration. The flag's painted " air-horse " leapt into a gallop before one of the hurrying winds of night, and its mystic formulæ glowed in the light from the fire.

It was the flag which Yolros Lama had given me with his promise of *Zayagan*, and my hope of an experience was so intense that I felt something must happen.

It had grown silent round the fire, and the glances of the Mongols wandered between the prayer-flag and the old man's face.

" Your air-horse endures and is strong," he murmured in a remote and impersonal voice.

" *Chindimani Erendi* sparkles with all his jewel radiance from your *hi-mori*.[1]

" The prayer-flag's sacred formulæ confer Manyusri's wisdom and Avalokita's protection against fear and an evil mind. They purify the soul from sin and guard against sickness and other earthly misfortunes.

" You shall accomplish a long and successful journey. A prosperous wind shall blow in your flag.

" We too, who sleep this night under its wind-blown prayers, shall acquire its blessings. It shall bring us hunting luck on our journey to the new river."

These were good words, and it was well that they were heard by many who could afterwards carry the rumour of my luck-bringing *hi-mori*. I told the old man from whom I had received the flag and with what promise, and he listened in tense excitement.

He willingly acceded to my request to explain the origin and meaning of the " air-horse ".

" The *hi-mori* flag is the strongest of all prayer-flags, but your life must be lived in accordance with its mystic formulæ in order that the wind may blow strength into your air-horse. If you defy the import of its symbol, its power is weakened, and you go towards misfortune.

[1] Mongolian *hi-mori*, Tibetan *lung-ta*.

" Once at the inception of the Religion the symbol of mankind was incarnated in the form of a horse ; it was at the time when the gods of Lamaism displayed their power before the gods of other religions.

" Very many years ago in Enet-khegien oron-etse (India) dissension arose between the lamas of Buddhism and those in the country holding different faiths. At that time a wise and mighty Khan ruled over India, and his command was that the strife should be decided not by weapons but by the power of the truth. And the Khan called together the country's wisest lamas and thinkers and made known that the doctrine which could give the strongest evidence of vigour in its faith that doctrine he and all his people would embrace.

" All the wise and holy men assembled outside the holy city of Buddh Gaya. The thinkers of Brahmanism sent assiduous prayers heavenward, and, behold, on a neighbouring height was born a supernatural horse. But the horse was powerless and remained lying down despite their most ardent prayers.

" After long hours spent in profound meditation the adherents of Lamaism let their prayers mount towards the sky. The eyes of all were turned upon the mystic horse, and behold, it rose up and became more and more vigorous as though in some miraculous way it had received nourishment from Buddha's words.

" This the Khan took as proof that the religion of the Lamaists was stronger than the philosophic doctrine of the others, and he determined that he and all his people should embrace the yellow faith.

" The *hi-mori* born of faith guards and helps the followers of the doctrine even to this day, if so be that they walk in the right way.

" It is a boon to have a strong air-horse, and when the prayer-flag is, like yours, marked with the strong formulæ of a holy man, its way is easy to follow."

I HAD become the focus of the lively interest of the Mongols, and I felt that the old man's pronouncement had raised me in their estimation.

Then they stretched themselves out on the saddle

blankets and discussed the promised abundance of game on the hunt until they slept. Nor could Mongrolda Noyen and I be induced to sleep in the secluded darkness of the tent, for the grass out there was soft as the muzzle of a horse and warmed by the fire and lighted by the stars.

All night long I galloped through the dream realm of the horse of fantasy.

NEXT morning our camp was early astir. The Torgut hunters had disappeared before sunrise in the direction of the indigo-etched mountain shapes in the south-east, and we encountered the first rays of the sun from the top of the pass, the last pass before the journey's end. Southward we looked out over a falling panorama of ravines and chaotic foothill crests until the prospect dissolved in the grey-black mists of the lowlands.

Hour after hour we scrambled downward. We followed a tumbling mountain stream which grew into a stately river and we passed shady groves of willow and elm in full leaf. Prickly berberis bushes hanging in the clefts made yellow patches, and steppe-hens and pheasants filled the air with sound.

The nearer we came to the lowlands the oftener we fell in with parties of Torguts on the move from their summer quarters in the mountains to their winter abodes upon the plains. There were large family parties of men, women and children with all their possessions of horses, cattle and sheep as well as their tent dwellings with their scanty appointments. The wandering nomad community filled the valleys with their joyous cries and the multitudinous sounds of the flocks and herds echoed among the hills.

CHAPTER III

I AM BROUGHT INTO THE PRESENCE OF "THE KHAN IN THE WEST"

" THE KHAN IN THE WEST." (Torgut Song.)

TÖIN LAMA'S winter residence was a snow-white
town which came as a complete surprise in its
wild surroundings.

Our little cavalcade rode in a wide curve round the
eastern outer wall of the town and halted before the
great central gate in the southern wall. The wall was
high, with crenellated top and solid watch-towers. The
Torguts in my company pointed with pride to its defiant
strength and asserted that the Torgut city of Öreget,
Töin Lama's work, was the noblest edifice in all Sinkiang.
Within this outer wall ran an inner wall, and the space
of about a hundred yards between the two formed a
quadrilateral of four straight fortress streets. Against
the inner side of the outer wall were low military barracks,
and the streets swarmed with soldiers and horses. The
soldiers wore brown Cossack uniforms, Russian riding
boots and tall black or white fur caps. Some of them

228

were busy cleaning rifles of relatively modern manufacture, and others were demonstrating cavalry sword play with barbarically antiquated but brightly polished Cossack sabres.

The horses were black, brown or grey, for the squadrons on guard that day over Töin Lama were of those colours. They were nobly built and spirited animals of the country's famous Khara Shar breed, which with the melons of Hami, the grapes of Turfan and the girls from Kucha form Sinkiang's four most celebrated products and once the country's principal tribute to the Emperors of China.

We wheeled into the western street, and wherever Mongrolda Noyen rode the soldiers stood stiffly to attention before their chief. In the middle of the inner wall of that street was a great gate, and from the wide watchtower above it our arrival was signalled by a fanfare of trumpets.

Within the inner wall lay a new system of straight streets bordered by the walled courtyards of flat-roofed whitewashed houses in the Tibetan style. These dwellings formed the winter residences of the Torgut chiefs and great lamas, and guest-houses for visiting dignitaries. Over the five largest houses floated different-coloured triangular banners each with a white disk in its centre, indicating that they were the quarters of the five *gusdä* [1] who lead the five " banners " of the Khara Shar Torguts.

A white cloister wall divided this section of the town from the strictly isolated inmost centre. Above the wall one caught a glimpse of the trees of a hidden garden and from the northern side of the wall could see the upper storey of a long white building. From the tree-grown region south of this emerged the hollow and peculiar sounds that characterize the lamaistic temple service.

Filled with amazement I followed my conductor through the streets so un-Asiatic in their cleanliness, wondering within myself where the tent-born nomad leader had obtained the impulse and the knowledge to erect these gleaming white brick buildings.

[1] *Gusdä*—commander of a " banner " (1,500–2,000 men).

Many of the houses were completely *funkis* in effect, and the architect had achieved a happy combination of Tibetan lines with occidental details.

The *yamen* of the Torguts, which we reached by way of the streets in the north and east, was the town's one building in the Chinese style. In the courtyard were a group of soldiers and a few Torgut malefactors who had been brought thither to receive sentence and undergo their punishment.

In a room with Chinese furniture we were received by the *tuslakchi* [1] of the Torguts and by two of the tribe's *gusdä* who with great courtesy bade us welcome to Öreget. The men wore silk robes of Chinese cut, but the colours and the dull patterns on their shining material were Mongolian of the steppes, and their headgear was the decorative cap of the time of the Emperors, from which nodded the peacock-feather symbol of chieftainship.

Then followed tea-drinking which was accompanied by the exchange of all the courteous phrases of Mongolian etiquette, but the high officials soon passed on to trying by discreet questions to ascertain the correctness of the fanciful accounts which, by indirect routes, the Regent had received of his guest.

It was incredible how much the Torguts knew beforehand about my personality, and the simple facts about me and my journey had acquired profound meaning and a significance incomprehensible to myself. But since I observed that their mystical interpretations forwarded my wishes I accepted them willingly.

Yolros Lama's prophecy had reached the Regent through the Torgut soldiers who had met our Chahar Mongols in Hami. He had also heard that a fair wind had blown for my strong " air-horse " on the journey through Black Gobi, and that our Mongols had observed many other signs propitious to me during the long journey. Altai Gegen had related that I was acquainted with mystic formulæ and that at Temerlik I had induced the hostile Däde Mongols to see a mystic sign pointed out by me.

With obvious satisfaction the *tuslakchi* ascertained that

[1] *Tuslakchi*—holder of the highest office of the tribe.

I had been born under the sign of " the sacred monkey ". The Regent had been born under the same sign, though his year, 1884, was that of the wooden monkey and mine, 1896, that of the Fire-monkey. And had I not borne from birth a sign over my left kneecap ? "Indeed I had." And I showed him my birthmark in the form of a rat, without understanding more than that in the eyes of the Mongols my disfigurement was a significant sign.

From their talk among themselves it appeared that they also counted in my favour the Tibetan prophecy which foretold that the spiritual leader now incarnate in the Regent's form would show sympathy towards a white man.

During our profound Mongolian conversation people had been coming and going, but I observed both that they listened and that they were the same listeners who came and went. They were young Torguts with intelligent faces, and two of them had their hair cut and parted in western fashion. Their dress consisted of long black silk cloaks over which they wore brown armless velvet waistcoats.

When the old official's interview with me was over, two of the black cloaks came smilingly up to me and begged leave to conduct me to the ruler's dwelling.

We followed the high inner wall and, through the gate on the south side, entered the guarded inmost portion of the town. An avenue of low trees led up to Töin Lama's residence which lay due north, stately and gleaming white. The upper storey of the palace had a large walled-in loggia, and beneath this was the wide, decorative main entrance on either side of which a file of Torgut Cossacks stood on guard. They saluted with their carbines in correct western fashion, and two of them followed us in, either in politeness or precaution.

We passed through a hall and a room in Chinese style, and in the smaller room beyond this I found my baggage unpacked, the toilet articles set out beside a basin filled with water and my sleeping-sack spread out upon the heated *Kang*.

My two conductors left me after having announced

231

that a meal would soon be served, and while I shaved and washed and put on my best clothes, my Chinese servants sang the praises of these Mongols, who were by no means so barbarous as Mongols were wont to be. They told me grinning that they were gloriously full and that the horses were standing in a comfortable stall, deep in hay.

My first meal in the Torguts' headquarters was an exquisite combination of Mongolian, Chinese and Russian dishes. The meal was shared by my two Torgut attendants, who proved to be Töin Lama's *chanse* (first secretaries), and the two visiting Tibetan Lamas who occupied the room leading into mine.

The Tibetans belonged to the staff of the prince of the church Panchen Bogdo, and had travelled the long way from Peking by boat to India whence they had crossed the Himalayas and the heights of their homeland to convey a message from Amitabha's reincarnation on earth to the ruler of the Torguts.

Weary with travelling and surfeited with surprises I crept early to bed.

I was now in the land of my dreams, but how differently I had conceived it !

I had hoped to discover the Torgut race, and I had imagined the remnant of a people living its nomadic life isolated among the mountains.

I found myself instead in the midst of a vigorous people, and its chieftain resided in an Asiatic model city.

NEXT morning tea and a kind of pancakes were served to me almost in my sleeping-sack, but fortunately for my Mongolian reputation I contrived to spring out of it and look lively before the Mongol servant with the tray came into the room.

Outside, the sun was shining on all the white walls, and the mysteriously monotonous sound of some temple service blended with the noise of barrack life. Signal horns blared, horses neighed and words of command tried to shout down the combined turmoil.

While I was taking my morning meal the Regent's two *chanse,* Lodong and Lyrup, came in and Doreche and Lobson, Panchen Bogdo's two envoys, all of whom seemed eager to meet me with kindness and understanding.

My first encounter with the Regent took place in the evening of that day. The reception-room was fitted with furniture imported from Russia, but the walls were hung with Chinese embroideries and red silk draperies with Mongolian mottoes.

The Regent of the Torguts was the same man who had come to meet us at Hami and had presented himself as a Chinese Marshal, and he at once enquired courteously after the health and future plans of my chief and other travelling companions. He was wearing Russian uniform with the insignia of a Chinese Marshal, and the orders on his breast were both of Chinese and ancient Russian origin. The Russian orders had been bestowed upon his ancestors, he said, but had come down by inheritance, and the chief had the right to wear them.

He asked my European name, and I observed that he entered it in Russian characters in a European notebook, and he offered me his open cigarette-case instead of handing me, according to the custom of the country, a cigarette on the upturned palm of his hand.

The European dress was unbecoming to him; he became small and insignificant, and his close-cropped head was absurdly like a full moon. But his eyes were arrestingly intelligent, and the longer one met his brilliant glance the more strongly one felt that ability lay at the root of his influence.

The audience-room was full of people, *chanse* in their dusky silk robes, servants in black cotton cloaks, self-important officials in gorgeously embroidered attire, and with the Regent's people were mingled envoys from other Central Asiatic dignitaries and refugees from territories invaded by the Soviet who had here found asylum. Among the latter were the princely families of two Torgut tribes in the Altai mountains who had been compelled to cede their territory to the Soviet.

The Regent so led the conversation that he might probe my political views, and I understood that much depended upon them. Feeling in the country was strongly influenced by the anti-Russian opinion which was disseminated with the immigrants from Soviet territory, and the high lamas warned the people against " the red doctrine " which accorded so ill with The Doctrine and the traditions.

The whole assembly of exalted and deposed Mongol dignitaries followed our conversation with attention.

It soon aroused a good deal of displeasure that I did not show any interest in the political questions of the day, but after I had made them aware of my honest interest in the past of the Torgut people and in all that was noble in their teaching and traditions, their mistrust disappeared and we passed from inflammable subjects to conversation which lay nearer to the tolerant habit of thought of the nomad.

Before the audience was over I took occasion to lay before the Regent my wishes concerning the work which I wanted to carry out among his people, and he promised me permission and all the help which it lay in his power to give. The two *chanse*, Lodong and Lyrup, were at once appointed as my assistants and with them the Tibetan lamas Doreche and Lobson soon associated themselves.

I could not have had more agreeable colleagues.

CHAPTER IV

THE MUSIC OF THE MONGOLS

I SPENT the first weeks in Öreget in carrying out anthropometric measurements among the Torguts and in recording some of that songful people's many folk-songs.

The first of these tasks met with much opposition from the populace, and it was difficult to explain its importance to the authorities. The Mongols have an inborn and virile abhorrence of letting themselves be touched, and when one opens one's case with its many nickel-plated measuring instruments, the proposed victim politely but decidedly retreats.

However, after a review by Töin Lama of his cavalry I succeeded in arousing his interest in the physique of the soldiers, and since he knew that these warriors were famed as the best and most stalwart in all Turkestan he had nothing against his widely travelled guest assuring himself of the fact.

Every morning he ordered a detachment of them into my room, and my young assistants soon became so efficient and interested that I was able to increase my material daily by twenty new measurements.

THE other part of my work was considerably easier, since both the Regent and his people from the first embraced it with enthusiastic interest.

Töin Lama sent out couriers to the various camps in his wide territories to summon the best male and female singers to the residency. They came in multitudes, bass-voiced hunters from the remotest forest tracts of the mountains and shyly smiling shepherdesses who sang of black alpine slopes, blue mountains and white peaks. For weeks the palace echoed with

235

the joyous notes of the singers, and life was one long festival.

So as to be able exactly to reproduce the peculiar melodies of the Mongols I had brought with me a small portable phonograph, but as my stock of wax plates was limited I was obliged sternly to weed out multitudes of songs in my search for the most interesting. During the first days singing competitions were arranged, after which the best performances were sung into the funnel of the phonograph. It was the task of Lodong and Lyrup to write down the words of the songs.

Unfortunately the Regent insisted on being present during the recordings, and this produced such nervousness in the singers that many of the results were less good than they might otherwise have been.

The delights of these days culminated in the evenings when I made the little machine give out the day's results. When they heard their own and their friends' voices well forth from the tin funnel they were wild with ecstasy. A Mongol laughs when he is happy, and that is his natural frame of mind, but when he is really amused his delight is exuberant, and the sound of it can be heard afar off. They rolled on the ground, slapped themselves on the thighs and one another on the back, and tears of joy streamed down their cheeks. The jubilation grew so violent that the horses tied up outside broke loose and rushed round the courtyard in panic.

And with the home-coming singers the stories spread abroad of their adventurous experiences at the court and of *Khilitai abder Kymin*, " the man with the box that can talk ".

If one would enter into the character and mental life of a people one must learn to know its art and its literature.

In these respects the steppes have few monuments to show. The hard and roving life of the sparse population does not create the conditions, the scanty space of the tent is a poor repository for any but the most necessary things, outside the tent door nature extends in holy beauty that does not permit itself to be copied, and imagination blooms far more freely in stories round the camp-fire than when fettered to sober paper.

But the life and the country shape the souls of artists, and cultivated China has found inspiration for some of its oldest and most vigorous creations in art and literature from the rude hordes of the steppes. The Chinese verse forms are built upon folk music which is in a large measure of Central Asiatic origin ; China's classical drama blossomed in the shelter of the Mongolian court ; her romances revolve on expanded popular versions of Buddhist texts.

China built her Great Wall as a defence against the barbarians, and the chain of the Himalayas was the barricade between the ancient civilization of India and the savagery of the Mongolian steppes. But the barbarians overstepped these obstacles and broke into the two civilized lands, and two of the works of man which have made by their beauty the deepest and most enduring impression upon me, the great Manchu emperor's Jehol and the great Mogul Shah Jahan's Taj Mahal, were both erected by descendants of the rude nomad hordes.

But it is music which affords the most immediate contact with a people's imaginative life, folk music which flowers through the centuries and lives on as the sons' heritage from the fathers, the heritage which most intimately binds the present to the past.

And in this respect the Mongols have an abundant treasure. Their folk music is far more than a cultured people's written but dusty store of memories ; it is a life-giving, freshly bubbling fountain, timeless as the eternal phenomena of nature.

The first time one hears a Mongolian melody one's thoughts may be led to Russian music. But the Mongolian music has not been subject to the influence of any foreign element ; it is directly derived from the inspiration of nature music. On the other hand Mongolian motifs have given birth to many of the features to be found in Russian melodies.

The Mongol sings by preference about nature, the endless steppes, the rolling rivers, the clouds in the sky. But he also sings the praises of the pilgrimages of the lamas, heroes and their exploits and love between man and woman.

The words are always elevated and cast in imaginative form, but the nomad is most moving when he sings of his animals and when he imparts to these his exuberant joy in life. Like the Icelander he delights in singing to his horse and in recounting to it all the wonderful things his eyes behold during the ride.

The words of the song are often bald in treatment, but they are always charged with feeling—the feeling which at the moment of singing so strongly possesses the singer that the words are born upon his tongue. There is *one* single emotion in the song which sings of blossoming apple-trees, wild and white, of playing children in the spring verdure of a sunlit valley and of the hungry younglings of the herds. There is *one* single emotion in the song which tells of the strength of the tent-poles, of the old father's young and vigorous sons and of the blessed stand-by of the nomad laws.

The rhythm is for the most part ♩♫♩♫ and the time two-four or four-four.

The melody has commonly two phrases which are repeated according to the number of the verses, or, if the music accompanies a dance, according to its phases. In the West-Mongolian dances impassioned variations in tempo occur, but they differ from the Russian dances in that the rhythm is unvarying.

The Mongolian music moves to a certain degree within our major and minor keys but the extent to which what we call the church mode, especially the Doric, is introduced, is strikingly great.

An accomplished singer should be able to take long intervals. The song is always unisonant, but when two or more Mongols sing together, the best singer likes to make a long fermata, as long as his lungs can manage. Then he goes on with the song as an echo of the others, and this gives the melody the semblance of being polyphonic.

The Mongolian songs can, without losing their charm, be sung without accompaniment, for they possess the feeling and all the most important characteristics of genuine melody. They are, however, often performed to the accompaniment of several 'cello or banjo-like instruments, and the tune is also sometimes played only on a single shepherd's pipe.

The ritual music of the Mongols is largely of Tibetan origin, and the chanting of the lamas is accompanied by a multitude of different wind instruments and drums. The queer harmonies of these exotic instruments sometimes affect western ears as an infernal din, but often musically beautiful motifs are introduced which seem to attune the mind to meditation.

DURING my stay among the Torguts I recorded sixty examples of their music, and since the guests assembled at the residency represented many of the nomad tribes of Central Asia I had extended opportunities of completing my musical material, the collection of which was one of my chief interests.

The music of the Mongols is my richest memory from those days, a fascinating link which chains me to the rugged and smiling beauty of the people and the country. For if one has heard a Mongol sing in the surroundings whose praises he is singing, one has felt the wonderful harmony between man and nature ; and if one has heard him relate his legends, full of mystic lore and decked with fantasy, in the light of the camp-fire, one carries away a memory of fairy-tales which were true to the children.

CHAPTER V

THE STRONG MAN OF THE TORGUTS

I WAS often summoned in the evening to the Regent's study, but it was always full of other guests and servants, and I never met Töin Lama in intimate colloquy. The relations between us long remained ceremonious and impersonal, but I longed to get into touch with him and obtain replies to the questions which only he could answer and which I must find opportunity to put to him without offending against Mongolian etiquette.

Everyone spoke of him as *Gegen* or *Töin Lama*. Neither was his name, but only denoted " the reincarnation " or " the princely lama ". About his real name and his lineage I could only interrogate himself, for a Mongol cannot utter the name of his father or his ruler, both of which are sacred to him.

Was he actually a descendant of Obish Khan or only the holder of his signet ?

And if he was the descendant of the ancient Torgut dynasty, how could he be the incarnation of a deity, when the laws lay down that such can only arise among the poor and humble ?

And what Asiatic deity was it that had been reincarnated in his body ?

My four young Asiatic friends willingly explained much that perplexed me ; only these problems we could never touch upon.

Töin Lama's brother had been Khan of the Torguts until his death in 1920, and since the present Regent as *hutuktu* was debarred from marriage, the power would pass at his death to the dead brother's son, now, in 1928, fifteen years old, whom the Torguts called Bichigen Khan, (the little Khan). Both Bichigen Khan and his sister,

Shiri, who " commanded the gliding, soaring and falling
of the notes like a proud eagle on the wing "

Torgut Married Women

The Torgut Regent's *bator* ready for battle. The horses are trained to throw themselves on the ground as cover for their riders

[*face p.* 241

the little seventeen-year-old princess Shiri Noyen, who was one of my best singers, lived in the princely palace. An elder niece of the Regent was the *Khatun* of the Khoshut chief Mongrolda Noyen of whom I have already spoken.

Töin Lama had spent his youth in theological study and his manhood in long journeys to the holy places of Buddhism. But on his brother's death the latter's son had been only an infant, and the leading Torgut chiefs had therefore sent couriers over half Asia to invite Töin Lama to become the leader of the people until the little Khan was grown up.

And Töin Lama had acceded to the wishes of the people, and from the day when he assumed the supreme power dated the many beneficial changes which were to bring the Torgut tribe to freedom and happiness.

My Torgut friends described with pride all the progress of recent years.

The herds of cattle had increased in size. The breed of horses had been further improved by the ruler's wisdom in buying magnificent thoroughbred stallions from the fleeing White Russians. He had tried with good results to produce the amblers so much in demand among the Chinese, and these now constituted the Torguts' most profitable export. He had bought arms and ammunition from fugitive Cossacks, so that it could now be said with justice that the Torgut army was not only the bravest but also the best armed in Central Asia.

But the greatest of the blessings which had followed upon Töin Lama's assumption of sovereignty was the clear fact that in recent years far more children had come into the world in the tents which before had been blessed with so few. The people ascribed this to their leader's divine qualities, but my enlightened friends understood that it depended more upon Töin Lama's human wisdom than upon his thaumaturgic powers.

Among the fugitives from Russia who had entered Torgut territory was a Tatar who had been educated as a surgeon, and Töin Lama had listened to his counsel.

The surgeon was now in charge of a building with twelve beds and a stock of medicines with which he was carrying on a vigorous campaign against syphilis and other sterilizing diseases.

Through the agent of a foreign firm in Urumchi Töin Lama had procured a number of objects of occidental origin among which was a camera. He was an enthusiastic photographer and did his own developing and printing. This interest of his in western inventions has aroused strong approval in his young Torgut entourage.

In front of the eastern gable of the residency a big racecourse had been laid out where Töin Lama's horses were trained daily. From a balcony the Regent and his principal guests and officers watched the performance of the horses and their riders. Töin Lama recognized every horse and knew to what herd it belonged and which stallion had sired it.

Races were often arranged between the best horses of the Regent and the Mongol nobles; and Töin Lama's people were constantly on the look out for new racing material among the colossal horse herds of the nomads. Besides galloping and trotting races there were exhibitions of circus-like cavalry acrobatics, and the nomad warriors' feats surpassed in daring and elegance all that I have seen any western cavalry perform.

One day I paid a visit to the barracks.

The nomad soldiers' western drill and equipment and their keen, smart appearance had struck me from the first.

The Torgut officers displayed the urbanity of occidentals, and one of them addressed me in Russian. In the course of conversation he told me that he was a descendant of the Torguts left behind on the Volga by the great flight of 1771. He had had a Russian education, had passed the officers' examination at St. Petersburg and had taken part in the great war on the Russian side in the Kalmuck divisions which had been raised in the Orenburg and Astrakhan districts. Later he had fought for Tsardom against " the red doctrine " and after the " White " collapse in Siberia had followed the stream of fugitives southward until he had encountered his own tribesmen whose ruler had accepted him and whose interests he now wished to serve.

The presence of this Russian-bred Torgut in the Regent's army explained many of the occidental phenomena in Öreget.

THE Torgut Regent's independent tendencies showed themselves also in his attitude to the outside world.

At his brother's court the Chinese interest had been all-prevailing, and the Mongolian national spirit which awoke after Töin Lama's assumption of sovereignty among the so long meekly obedient Torguts was observed by the Chinese authorities with a suspicion which soon passed into fear. The Regent was spoken of by the Chinese as " the Torguts' strong man ", and they made repeated attempts to put down the movement of which he was the origin and which in a few years transformed what had been a cowed population of herdsmen into a defiant and purposeful nomad nation.

When in 1924 the Chinese were to crush the leader of the Tungan revolt, Ma Ti-t'ai, the Governor-General, gave orders for the mobilization of Torgut cavalry and camel transport, but Töin Lama flatly refused the request of the Chinese for assistance. In the beginning of the year 1925 the Regent was asked to send his cavalry to Urumchi to check the " Christian " General Feng Yu-hsiang's threatening advance from Kansu, but again Töin Lama answered that his soldiers should not shed their blood in other's wars, but only for their own interests.

For generations the Torguts had been China's most reliable auxiliaries in Central Asia, and Governor-General Yang Tseng-hsiu perceived that if the nomads would no longer allow themselves to be compelled he must inveigle them with political craft and friendly complaisance.

Yang Tseng-hsiu represented himself as preferring for his bodyguard Torgut soldiers under a trustworthy nomad chief to Chinese riffraff under one of his intriguing and mutually jealous Generals. And his flattering request for a Torgut bodyguard resulted in Töin Lama sending him three of his squadrons.

Later on under the influence of his Chinese advisers, Yang invited Töin Lama to a friendly conference at Urumchi. The secret object of the meeting was to deprive the Regent of his power and transfer the signet of the Torgut Khanate to Bichigen Khan who was still a minor and who was then to govern the Torguts under the tutelage of a Chinese adviser. Töin Lama was to be persuaded to resume his former pilgrim life.

But to that meeting in Urumchi Töin Lama came surrounded by such a pomp and magnificence and with so numerous an escort of stern and purposeful nomad warriors that his arrival was like the triumphal entry of a conqueror. The political action designed by the Chinese was not so much as discussed, but Töin Lama was appointed a Chinese Marshal and supreme defender of the eastern front. It was in the latter capacity that in November, 1927, he marched to Hami to meet the new peril approaching from the east—the Sven Hedin Expedition !

Lodong and Lyrup told me that after the first reports of our expedition Töin Lama had perceived that the suspicion of the Chinese was unwarranted and that we were running errands neither for the Russians nor for the " Christian Chinese ". Töin Lama had saved the expedition's many rolls of unexposed film when the Chinese wanted to break open their wrappings in the belief that they were parts of a wireless transmission apparatus.

Taking it all together I perceived more and more that the expedition's successful surmounting of the many obstacles that it encountered on the frontier of Sinkiang was due more to " the Torguts' strong man " and the reports which he sent to the Governor-General of the province than to the many diplomatic phrases of protest from unacknowledged authorities and unknown ministers telegraphed in those days from the Far East to dim Central Asia.

In November I sent a courier to Urumchi for mail, and he was instructed to bring back a lot of illustrated papers from headquarters. I knew by experience what a highly

Baldan *gusdä*, the Regent, Lodong *chanse*, Lyrup *chanse*

Photo Hempel

Torgut Cavalry Acrobatics

[*face p. 245*

valued entertainment these were among the Mongols. I received a packet of old *Weekly Journals*, and their abundant photographic illustrations gave me a starting-point for many accounts of peoples and countries completely unknown to this isolated nomad tribe.

It was illustrated papers that were to open the way to the first intimacy between Töin Lama and me. He was the most eager of all my auditors, and every evening we went in detail through the pictures in a year-old weekly paper with all the matter for discussion to which each picture gave rise.

The number containing Charles Lindbergh's Atlantic flight lasted three evenings, and I wonder whether the exploit of that blond scion of Scandinavia with the monstrous *nisdeg telleg*, "ether-carriage", anywhere produced more astonishment and delight than among the Torguts of "the Mountains of Heaven".

The marvellous news of man's ability to follow the flight of the bird gave birth to a plan for the future in the primitive but progress-loving mind of Töin Lama. Of course it would be only a question of time before the Torguts would have their own "ether carriages", and with their aid one of the country's greatest riddles would be solved.

"Deep within the mountains rises a sky-piercing peak with steep sides and topped by an irregular plateau like a gigantic watch-tower. The bare grey precipices of the mountain are clothed at the top with pallid glaciers, and it needs courage to attempt to climb it. Yet the mountain has been climbed by two hunters of a former generation. They reached the top of the alpine tower and came back with an account of what they had seen. Those two hunters are dead long since, but the account of their wonderful experience survives and has tempted many a hunter of later times to the same climb, but none has been able to accomplish it. For terrifying sounds were heard from the sides of the mountain, and long before they reached the top they were seized with confusion of thought. Many have been entirely lost, but others have been found later at the foot of the mountain with no memory of what had happened after their minds were clouded and no knowledge of how they came down from the heights.

"But the sight that the two hunters saw was worth the hardships of the climb, for up there was a paradise for Mongols. High up, the mountain-sides ended in a mighty circular crater the slopes of which were covered with luxuriant vegetation. Through the green alpine meadows flowed foaming rivers, and on the slopes fat sheep and goats were grazing and multitudes of game. Deep down in the crater valley lay a blue lake on whose fertile banks and surrounding steppes cattle grazed in countless multitudes. White tents were scattered over the steppe and from their smoke-vents the heat of fires trembled in the pure air. But no human beings were to be seen. The tents stood uninhabited, the horses played in unsaddled freedom and nature smiled in secure blessedness."

In looking through the many newspapers we naturally came upon numerous pictures of the royalties of Sweden and other countries, and in the lives and governmental methods of these Töin Lama displayed the deep interest of a colleague. In particular I was required to tell him about the Asiatic ruler Amanullah who had introduced so much of the West into Afghanistan and who at that time was at the height of his power.

I had also to tell him about the monarch to whom the expedition owned allegiance. Since my knowledge of King Gustaf's life was strictly limited, the photographs in our newspapers were a great help, showing as they did His Majesty in uniform and in mufti, in his car, hunting, distributing prizes at athletic competitions and so on.

According to Mongolian ideas there were only four Great *Khans* in the world, and all other princes are tributaries to one or other of these.

These four Great *Khans* are incarnation of divinities: Srong-tsang-Gampo Khan who is the protector of lamaism, Jenghiz Khan whose rebirth the Mongols await with longing, Bogdo Khan who is the Emperor of the Chinese and incarnates the god of wisdom Manjusri (Jamyang) and Tsaghan Khan who is the ruler of the Russians and the incarnation of the goddess Dara äkhä.[1]

The Regent now learned to his surprise that in the wide world there were other independent sovereigns who stood in no tributary relation to any of the four Great *Khans*. And I succeeded in giving a convincing demonstration of King Gustaf's greatness by means of a picture of the day of the Swedish flag in which vast crowds of people and numerous deputations with a forest of flags are shown bringing their " tribute " to the chieftain of all the Swedes—" Sweduin Khan ", as I christened His Majesty.

[1] Dara äkhä is a lamaistic goddess of Mercy and the special patroness of women. She it is, too, who protects the traveller from falling rocks and from the obstacle of swift streams upon his way. Dara äkhä was formed of Bodhisattva Avalokites'vara's tears and reincarnated in two Buddhist princesses, one Chinese (Tsaghan dara äkhä) and one Nepalese (Nogon dara äkhä). These two princesses married the renowned ruler of Tibet, Srong-tsang-Gampo, who under the influence of his two consorts became in the eighth century a Buddhist and originator of the lamaistic form of Buddhism in Central Asia. These two *dara äkhä* are among the host of *dolma* who are also called among the Mongols " The mothers guiding to Nirvana ". *Dara äkhä* is the Mongols' popular name for these exalted beings who possess besides a large number of titles which are contained in a manuscript, " The divine and venerable *dolma's* eight hundred and eight names ". The number eight hundred and eight is sacred and is found again in the eight hundred and eight beads of the lamaistic rosary.

That the Tsars of Russia have, since the Empresses Elizabeth and Catherine, been reckoned by the lamaists as incarnations of *Dara äkhä* is the result of political cunning on the part of the Russians. When the West-Mongol and Buryat delegates were received at the end of the eighteenth century in ceremonial audience at the court, they saw the Empress " in divine splendour and celestial surroundings ", and it was easy for the Russians to convince the simple nomads that their ruler was a divine being.

CHAPTER VI

"THE PRIMORDIAL SPARK"

THE nationalist political agitation which originated with the Regent was very noticeable in his entourage.

Couriers came and went daily between the residency in Öreget and the tents of the subordinate Torgut princes. Galloping riders carried despatches to far-dwelling Mongol leaders who were interested in the aspirations for freedom. In the halls of the palace *hutuktus* expelled from Khalka, high lamas and chieftains discussed the modern spirit which threatened the steppes, and envoys from far-off princes of the lamaistic church sought out Töin Lama to confer as to the measures to be taken to defend "the yellow doctrine" against the anti-religious propaganda from the north.

Sometimes I was afraid for the ultimate consequences of this rapidly growing independence movement among the nomads, and I once hinted to the Regent at the responsibility he was assuming. He did not take my outspokenness amiss, but was at the pains to detail the convictions which dictated his actions.

"We nomads have no need of the self-interested guardianship of alien powers. We have tolerated it for generations, and the consequence has been the decimation of our people and the corruption of our traditions and our way of life.

"Just as a man safeguards the tradition of his tent so must a people watch over its way of life, if it would preserve the vigour conferred upon it by the gods.

"Our greatest danger lies in the transplantation to the steppes of the ways of life of neighbouring nations, for these effeminize our people. A good horse and a free steppe under God's heaven is the Mongol's

Seng Chen Gegen, Lodong and Lyrup

[face p. 248

Photo : Ambolt

Young Torguts

[face p. 249

only need, and the nomad life of his forefathers is his happiness.

"But so soon as we confine ourselves to the peaceful pastoral life our restless neighbours seek to change our freedom to slavish subordination.

"The past has taught us that only by the rattle of arms and savagery can we prevent the ploughman from violating the freedom of the steppe and the trader from contaminating our manners.

"Once we were powerful upon the earth, and the neighbouring peoples trembled when they heard the thunder of our horses' hooves. But now by cunning they have put our strength in chains, and our fierceness is powerless against their machines. We have been tossed to and fro between east and west, and we have sought help and sympathy from the one against the other.

"You wonder that I should seek after western knowledge. I do so because I must needs strengthen my people for self-defence with the West's own weapons, and I desire knowledge of the development of the white races so that I may avail myself of such of the results as are fitted for us and reject the others.

"Once China's overlordship was our protection, and from China our religion once received its renewal, but at that time descendants of the nomads sat upon the Dragon Throne. China's overlordship does not threaten our traditions, but brings with it the extermination of the nomads.

"The 'red doctrine' from the North may give to the nomads material prosperity, and its spread may bring about the increase and physical improvement of our people, but the 'red doctrine' has *Sansara* (the Material) for its god, and its spirit strangles the truest instincts of the nomads.

"And with the nomads dies the spark of the primordial.

"For we represent the primordial itself, and in the genuine nomad burns the flame of the primordial which all peoples have possessed and which alone confers true human happiness.

"Our neighbours the Russians and the Chinese do

not perceive this truth, for they wander in a dense fog of the greed of gain and the desire for earthly benefits.

" In our lamaistic world I am the reincarnation of a deity, but my body was born to a mission that concerns the world. My mission is to gather together the people of the steppes and to uphold our forefathers' way of life which is the salvation of the nomads.

" Beyond the most distant borders of our neighbours live other peoples who also languish in the pursuit of vain earthly profit, but they will perceive the need of deliverance long before our neighbours. They will return to seek the primordial spark ; they will seek it in nature and they will find it among our flocks.

" From us shall come the salvation of mankind.

" The primordial spark shall be derived from us, but its light shall be spread from the West.

" But still for many years, until the end of the present *kalpa* (era), shall humanity be urged towards its false goal, and our era shall end in a war between the nations which only the seekers after truth shall survive.

" Thereafter shall arise a very great and good Khan to whom all the peoples of the world shall pay allegiance, and that Khan shall be of your race.

" When the Khan has grown old his only son shall fall sick, and the most skilful medicine men of the white race shall be powerless before his sickness. But then shall a Buddhist lama go up to the Khan's son's sick-bed, and the miracle shall happen that he who has been given up for dead shall become strong.

" That Mongolian lama is Maidari the Saviour of mankind in a new era.

" After this his first miracle Maidari shall go to the sacred mountain, and it shall open for him, and there he shall receive Gautama Buddha's celestial reflection.

" In a new era the light of Amitabha shall spread from the region in which you were born, for I foresee that a coming Panchen Bogdo shall be reincarnated in a man of your race who shall be born in the North.

" All divine wisdom is to be found set down in our sacred books, and the capacity to take hold of the several truths of this Omniscience has been apportioned among people of different races.

"The Chinese have acquired the knowledge which combats the diseases and weaknesses of the body. The westerners have the capacity to create the machines which produce the toys they delight in.

"But to us nomads Buddha gave insight into life's profoundest truths. He bade us live in nature and, in the silent loneliness of the great spaces, devote ourselves to the exalted peace of meditation in which alone the voice of truth can be heard.

"My body will not live to see my people's day of liberation, but I shall blow life into the dying spark of the primordial which the nomads shall preserve for the world. And in a coming *kalpa* a new reincarnation of my divinity shall see humanity regain its lost felicity.

"After my body's annihilation a new leader will stand ready to carry on the nomads' independence movement."

TÖIN LAMA never named to me the coming leader, but I understood that the nomads' independence movement included beings no less exalted than Dhyanibuddha Amitabha's earthly incarnation, Panchen erdeni Bogdo, and Hsuan Tung, China's exiled Emperor and the last descendant of the Manchu dynasty to sit upon the Dragon Throne.

Two years later I was in Tientsin.

In the hotel where I was staying I repeatedly noticed a couple of men in Chinese dress but of Mongolian appearance, and sometimes I felt that I was being shadowed by them. One day they spoke to me in the street. Their speech was Mongolian and they knew my Mongolian name. They asked me to dine with them at a Chinese restaurant so that we might, as they said, talk about Mongolia, and at that dinner they asked to be allowed on the following day to conduct me to their master who also wished to talk about Mongolia.

The next day I was fetched in a closed car which drove to the Japanese concession of Tientsin, and the man in whose presence I was soon standing was Hsuan Tung, the last Emperor of China, who had sought refuge there under the name of P'u Yi.

The twenty-four-year-old ex-Emperor urged me to join the nomads' independence movement and go in his name to Töin Lama on a weighty mission. As a protection against the dangers of the long journey he gave me a talisman which made its bearer invulnerable by "fire and cold steel".

On many grounds I declined this suggestion, but I kept the talisman and afterwards showed it to a couple of trustworthy friends as an illustration to my account of the adventure. But both my amulet and my accompanying political observations were received with hearty laughter.

YET now P'u Yi once more holds an imperial title, and Hsuan Tung has become K'ang Te and is to-day Emperor of Manchukuo and the chosen leader of many of Mongolia's nomad tribes.

Inhabitants of Temerlik

Torgut camp

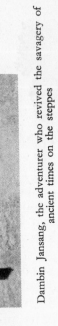

林 剌 音 諾

丐 大 有 日 福 王

Dambin Jansang, the adventurer who revived the savagery of ancient times on the steppes

Torgut Chiefs (*merin* and *gudä*)

[*face p.* 253

CHAPTER VII

THE RULER'S BODILY AND SPIRITUAL BIRTHS

FROM the evening when Töin Lama confided in me his views and object in life our intercourse entered upon a more intimate phase, and it often happened that he asked me to come to his room to discuss the most varied subjects. In these meetings the two delegates of Panchen Bogdo regularly took part, but otherwise the room was emptied of guards and guests.

Töin Lama's was a fascinating personality. He was deeply versed in lamaistic metaphysics and other Buddhist learning, and he had an astonishing knowledge of parts of the world with which he had never been in contact. His information upon the republican mode of government and life in Paris appeared to be derived from a Torgut princess who had received a western education in Peking and was now completing her studies in France. He had not seen this princess since she left the steppes as a child, but he often received communications from her and endeavoured to bring the contents of these into agreement with the learning he himself had acquired at Lhasa.

This princess's brother was the present chief of the Torgut tribe at Khara Ossun (*taburn notog*), who in his youth had served as a page at the Russian court. That these young Torguts had found their way to a world so remote from their steppes was explained by the fact that their father had served in the Peking government during the first year of the Republic when everything western was the fashion in China.

One evening when the two Tibetans and I were again with Töin Lama the conversation turned to the holy city of Lhasa, and our host showed many interesting photographs and gave us much information in connection with them.

Töin Lama had been in Lhasa at the time when the English military expedition under Younghusband arrived there in 1904, and he expressed his abhorrence of the depredations of the fugitive Chinese garrison and his admiration for the exemplary and dignified behaviour of the Anglo-Indian force.

It was on this occasion in Lhasa that the Dalai Lama displayed human fear, and the conversation now turned on his personality and the policy he represented. I observed that in the eyes of my three lamaistic friends Panchen Bogdo stood far closer to their ideal of a divinity than the Lhasa pontiff.

This conversation about persons and places sacred to them served as introduction to Töin Lama's account of his own person and the divinity reincarnated in it. What he related was not new to the two Tibetans, but they listened with profound devotion as recipients of a divine message.

And my interest was not less than theirs, for what Töin Lama now related supplied the solution of some of the riddles which had so long disturbed my peace.

Töin Lama's fleshly descent contains in itself a complete explanation of his dominating power over his Torgut subjects, for he was seventh in direct succession from the great Obish Khan and could thus trace his descent back to the Torgut chief Boro Örölok who in 1618 migrated with his horde from Central Asia to take possession of the steppes by the Volga. But the deep reverence in which he was held by the whole lamaistic world depended not upon his exalted origin but upon the divine power which Fate had reincarnated in his body.

He told us later of his spiritual fathers and his own divine birth.

" ONE of the hidden valleys of the ' Mountains of Heaven ', called *Olon Chogorso Hagochin Toredolok*, is a frequent resort of pilgrims, for there are to be found clear traces of the miracles which occurred there in 'the year of the Tree Monkey' (1884).

" In that year the Torgut Khan's white tent stood pitched in the luxuriant beauty of the valley, and there was joy among the nomads, for in the tribe's chief-tent an heir was expected.

" On the same night when the little prince came into the world hunters in the surrounding mountains met with proud deer of more than earthly beauty, and when at sunrise they explored the steep mountain-sides where the supernatural animals had appeared, they found their hoof-prints clearly marked in the hard rock.

" The lamas of the princely tent cast a brilliant horoscope for the little prince, and they named him after the qualities which should most strongly distinguish him, Tobn Tserend-yömbil (he who possesses unlimited faith and ever unfolding righteousness, whose life's work shall not cease with his death).

" The little prince's bodily perfection was blemished by a deformity in one of his knee-caps, but his first steps in life were so firm that they imprinted deep tracks in the hard rock from which he first saw the sun rise over the eastward mountain rim. These footmarks in the rock, as well as the hoofmarks of the celestial deer which appeared on the night before his birth, are to be seen even to this day.

" In ' the year of the Fire Pig ' (1887) an event occurred in far-off Tibet whose wide-stretched consequences were soon to reach the Torgut prince, then three years old, and wholly to determine his life.

" The holy monastery of Dongtse lies between Lama-ism's two most sacred places of pilgrimage, Lhasa and Tashi-Lhumpo, nearer to the latter but farther south than both. The Dongtse monastery looks out not towards the holy splendour of Lhasa, but towards the snowy peaks of the Himalayas, towards the sun at its highest and towards the land that saw the birth of Buddha and the first unfolding of his teaching.

" Dongtse is dedicated to Seng Chen Doryechan, the Tiger divinity, and in the uppermost of its temples is the room where four of the reincarnations of the divinity passed their lives in meditation. The earthly remains of the three first of these holy men are venerated as relics, and three white pagodas, gleaming with gold, at the foot of the monastery are their last resting-place.

" The lama who was the fourth reincarnation of the Seng Chen divinity possessed great learning and noble qualities and the crowds of truth-seeking pilgrims to Dongtse increased greatly during the years when he was the monastery's inspiration. And so widely spread the fame of the holy man that Buddhist pilgrims came to him even from Manchuria and Japan. The monastery grew rich in goods and gold and honour, and the high lamas of Lhasa became deeply jealous.

" Seng Chen's fourth reincarnation defied Lhasa's decree that the holy places of Tibet should be wholly restricted to the devotees of the lamaistic faith and contested their assertion that alien peoples wished to steal Buddhism from them. His aim was to raise the religion above the pettiness of sectarian strife, and he sent out his disciples as missionaries to India with his message of love to mankind.

" Rumours of this influential lama reached the government of India, and the eminent Indian explorer of Tibet, Rai Sarat Chandra Das, was sent with rich gifts to Dongtse. Despite the Dalai Lama's threats Seng Chen lodged the Indian mission in his monastery and replied to the warnings of his friends that he foresaw the martyrdom of his body without fear. Until this came about he must continue in his heaven-inspired vocation of disseminating the truth of Buddhism not only among his compatriots but among all mankind.

" Rai Sarat's stay in the Dongtse monastery brought about the destruction of the Tiger god's fourth reincarnation on earth. In 1887 Seng Chen was condemned by Lhasa's hierarchic government as having ' given refuge to foreigners in his monastery and betrayed the secrets of lamaism to the envoy of a foreign power '.

" Calmly he received the tidings of his doom and went of his own accord to the Kongbu river, by the bank of which he took up a position on a rock jutting out high over the water. A countless host of sorrowing

The Dongtse Monastery in Tibet, Seng Chen's spiritual home

[face p. 256

Photo Hummel

[*face p.* 257

Tibetan High Lama

Painting of Obish Khan

disciples lay at the foot of the rock listening to his last pronouncements from the holy books. Even the executioners despatched from Lhasa were so seized by the power of his words that they fell to weeping, incapable of performing their commission.

"Then Seng Chen ceased his reading and said to his executioners : 'Weight my body with stones and sink me swiftly in the river. My time is come, and by the destruction of my body my soul shall be delivered from the faults which this my body has committed. My impending death shall give birth to a new and stronger reincarnation of Seng Chen Doryechan who shall be born in a felt tent in a land in the North.'

" Three times his stone-weighted body appeared above the waters of the river, and each time the drowning saint murmured blessings upon those who had brought about the fulfilment of his destiny. In the end the stones broke loose, and his body was carried away by the rushing waters of Kongbu which, far away in the south, joins the sacred Bramaputra.

" The Dalai Lama, who has power over souls as well as bodies, forbade thereafter the reincarnation on earth of Seng Chen Doryechan. Many of the inmates of Dongtse were cast into prison and tortured, and the monastery soon fell into decay.

" Three years later, rumours of the miracles occurring at the birth of the little Torgut prince were spread by Torgut pilgrims, and since they were further able to testify that their prince bore the bodily defect which characterized Seng Chen's earthly incarnations, a deformity of one kneecap, the faithful remembered the prophecy of the martyr saint of Dongtse of rebirth in a land of felt tents, and Panchen Bogdo himself in his omniscience proclaimed that the three year old Torgut prince was Seng Chen Doryechan's fifth reincarnation on earth.

" This exalted recognition deprived the little prince of his baptismal name, and he exchanged it for Seng Chen Doryechan, 'Powerful Tiger-Jewel-Treasure', and since this name was altogether too precious to be uttered by any, he was simply called *Gegen*, ' the reincarnate ', or *Töin Lama*, ' the princely lama '.

" Soon the little *gegen* had to leave his parents and the tent where he was born. He was taken to Tibet where he spent his youth in the comprehensive studies which should prepare him for his vocation.

" He was obliged always to live far from the Dalai Lama, for the latter had never recognized him as the reincarnation of the divinity which he had wished to destroy. But the prince of the church at Tashi Lhumpo had in his divine wisdom recognized the incontestible truth and had become his protector and guide during his youth."

SENG CHEN'S account of his bodily and spiritual birth had made me forget both time and space.

The light in the two candelabra in front of the altar had almost burnt down. Seng Chen's yellow silk robe came and went in gleams of gold in their fluttering light. At times his face appeared out of the darkness, and I could read in the grave features and far away eyes that all he told was for him great and pregnant truth.

I had seen tears in the eyes of both the Tibetans when Seng Chen was describing the martyrdom of his spiritual father, and I had seen the hundred and eight beads of the rosary pass between their swift fingers marking time to the fortunate fulfilment of their faith.

For a while we sat silent. The luminous dial of my wrist watch was like an eye of fire. It was long past midnight.

Töin Lama had risen.

" My life is a continuation of my spiritual father's path, and like him I am willing to give the clear message of the Doctrine to all those who seek the truth of life, even if they be of alien race and faith. Every truth is a ray of the divine, and each one who lives by truth reincarnates the intention of a divinity upon earth."

He clapped his hands, and two servants hurried in with lighted lamps. Slowly and heavily he followed them out of the room, heavily and wearily and limping slightly. When I heard his steps grow distant in the adjoining hall I copied the rhythm of his walk in order to find out which of his knees was deformed. It must have been the left.

Could that have been the reason for the Torguts' interest in the birthmark above my left knee ?

CHAPTER VIII

THE LAWS OF THE STEPPE

" Borotala Ola." (Chahar Song.)

AS my relations with the ruler of the Torguts grew
more friendly so did the confidence of the
inhabitants of the town in their guest from afar
increase. I could stroll unhindered through the streets
and lanes of the Mongolian metropolis to study their
way of living.

South of the Mongolian town and at a distance of
three " hails " from it lay a Sart village of about a
hundred houses, called by the Mongols Khoten Sumon.[1]
These Sarts were the Torgut Regent's subjects and
looked after the cultivated land necessary for his horses
and performed other duties beneath the dignity of the
nomads.

This peculiar circumstance of a whole Mohammedan
community being subject to a Mongolian Regent was
said to be due to the fact that the inhabitants of Khoten
Sumon were descendants of a part of the rebel army of
the Mohammedan leader Yaqub Beg who, after their

[1] *Khoten* is the Torguts' name for the Mohammedan Sarts, and the
word has the same derogatory implication as the Turkish word *Kalmak*,
which is the Mohammedan's name for a Mongol.

SFENE TORGUT

Altai Beise   Altai Ulji Wang

Etsini Beile

KHOCHEN TORGUT

EAST WING
RIGHT EAST WING   Dorji Wang
Taburn

CENTRE   LEFT EAST   Djingin Beile

SOUTH WING
RIGHT SOUTH CENTRE   Khobok Sairi Taiji

NORTH WING
RIGHT NORTH   Khobok Sairi Taiji

NORTH CENTRE   Khobok Sairi Chinwang

Torgut Khan

SOUTH CENTRE   Taburn Notog Beise

LEFT NORTH WING   Döoner Kung

LEFT WING   Döoner Beile

LEFT SOUTH WING   Döoner Taiji

THE THIRTEEN SIGNET-BEARING PRINCES.

(Outline sketch of the formation of the Torgut Horde's Thirteen Tribes.)

defeat by the Chinese sixty years earlier, had sought refuge with the Torgut Khan of that time.

In the quarter surrounding the *yamen* the long-distance post riders and couriers assembled during their brief stay in Öreget, and by talking to these eternally travelling men and the officials to whom they were immediately attached I was able to keep myself informed about conditions among the nomad tribes and to picture to myself their organization and location.

Many couriers assured me that all the Mongol princes of Central Asia looked up to the Regent as the man who should gather the nomads and regenerate the great Mongolian nation—Seng Chen, "the Tiger god", the only Mongol chief who still had his Khanate in possession.

The aggregate numbers of the Torgut tribes were stated at figures so divergent as eighty and a hundred and twenty thousand. Of the organization of the tribes I learned as follows :

Each of the thirteen Torgut principalities is ruled by its *Jassak* (hereditary chief), but the chief of the Khara Shar tribe is the Khan of all the Torguts, and the other twelve are subordinate to him for military and other important purposes.

Of the twelve subordinate chiefs two bear the title of *chin wang* (prince of the first rank), two of *chün wang* (prince of the second rank), three of *beile* (prince of the third rank), one of *beitse* (prince of the fourth rank), one of *kung* (duke of the first rank), and three of *taiji* (noble of the first rank). Each *hoshun* (principality) has a *tuslakchi* who is its civil administrator and is appointed by the chief.

For military purposes each *hoshun* is divided into *sumon* (arrows) of which five constitute a "banner" under the command of a *gusdä*. The military strength of a *sumon* is recruited from one to two hundred tents and is under the leadership of a *meiren*. The total Torgut force under the Regent's command amounts to a hundred and fifty-four *sumon* of which fifty-four are furnished by the Khara Shar tribe alone.

In addition the Regent has a personal bodyguard of

fourteen hundred picked and well-equipped warriors who bear the name of honour *bator* (heroes).

The various tribes live a nomad life each in an allotted territory, and nine of these are so situated as to form a barrier round the Khara Shar tribe. The ten Torgut tribes who thus dwell near to one another are named in common Khochin Torgut (the old Torguts), and to these also belong, theoretically, the distant Etsin-gol Torguts.

The two tribes in the Altai are called Shene Torgut (the new Torguts), because they returned from the Volga later than the ten tribes settled in Sinkiang. The chiefs of the twelve tribes constitute, with the chief of the Etsin-gol Torguts, *araben-gurben tamag-tai noyen* (the thirteen signet-bearing princes).

The most important grazing-grounds of the Khara Shar Torguts lie by the Tsoltus whose watering places they share with three Khoshut tribes.

Other large Torgut settlements lie by the rivers Jirgalan, Chingho, Hobog Sairi, Bulugon, Tekes and Khunges and beside the Eren Habirga mountains.[1]

The military forces of the three Khoshut tribes by the Tsoltus were, under the command of Mongrolda Noyen, incorporated in those of the Torguts.

Seng Chen had besides entered into an agreement for mutual help in war with the group of Chahar Mongols in the Borotola valley, whose forefathers had come to their present grazing-grounds with the Manchu Emperor's armies in the middle of the eighteenth century, and also with the scattered, leaderless Ölet bands whose tents, poor and few in number, lay scattered along the rivers Tekes and Kash and on the steppes round Tarbagatai.

Among the couriers, dripping with sweat, who came and went at a gallop between the Torguts' *yamen* and the distant dwelling-places in the endless wastes of Central Asia I paid special attention to a type of horse-

---

[1] All these names except the first two appear on the map brought home by Renat from Dzungaria to Sweden in 1734. They must thus have been taken over by the Torguts on their arrival in 1771 at the grazing grounds formerly in possession of the West Mongols exterminated by the Manchus.

man with strikingly shabby clothing and equipment but of distinguished bearing. They were slender, well-built men of Mongolian appearance, but the melancholy expression of their faces was seldom lighted by a smile.

Their clothes were of Chinese cut, but from the sashes round their waists hung the whole customary equipment of the nomads. They spoke a language that was new to me, but between them knew enough Mongolian to allow of conversation between us.

These men called themselves Manchu-solon and belonged to the district of Ili. They knew themselves to be descendants of Khara Kitad, the people from whom the Ta K'i-tan dynasty derived which a thousand years ago ruled the whole of Northern China. In 1736 four *aimak* of their forefathers had been transferred from their native district by the Amur to guard the western frontier of the great empire, and to-day these four *aimak* still dwell by the Khorgos river in the Ili district. Out of sight and forgotten and deprived of their leader, they have sunk into poverty. When their herds of cattle died out they had been obliged to abandon tent life and build their huts of grey mud, and their existence now depends upon such ploughing as they can do of the grass steppe. They plough no more than hunger compels them to, and in years when game is plentiful they do not plough at all. They have preserved their nomad instincts, and their seat on a horse has not been spoilt by their ploughing. Their language and their view of life they have retained unaltered, which is not the case with their kinsfolk who remained in the homeland.

In the *yamen* building the Torguts pay their taxes, and here are settled the disputes that are of so grave a nature that they cannot be adjusted by the subordinate local chiefs. At the head of the various offices of the *yamen* is the first Tuslakchi of the Torguts who also, in the Regent's absence from Öreget, holds the signet of the Khanate and the power which it symbolizes. The Tuslakchi, however, can never carry out a death sentence without having first obtained the Regent's approval. The last sentence of death was carried out in 1925 when a Torgut accused of murder was hanged.

The administration of justice in the Torgut court is based upon ancient traditions and agrees in essentials with their forefathers' conception of justice which was codified in 1640, when forty-four Mongol princes and lamas assembled in conference to draw up the *Tsächin Bichik* of the Öret Mongols.

This collection of laws is the result of the introduction of Buddhism on the Mongolian steppes and signifies an attempt to introduce a more humane spirit among the nomads whose savage code had earlier received its imprint from the stern *Yassa* of Jenghiz Khan.

The sentences in the Buddhistically influenced *Tsächin Bichik* are considerably more lenient than in the statutes of the Shamanistic era, but on the other hand the law of the Mongols lost, when the lamas obtained a place at the council table, a part of the democratic spirit which the greatest warrior figure of Mongolia had bestowed upon them.

Jenghiz Khan exalted a man according to the measure of his services, and everyone had the chance of attaining the highest positions. On the other hand he dismissed and punished anyone who failed to fulfil a duty entrusted to him. According to *Yassa* the same crime received different punishments in that a rich and enlightened man might have to expiate with his life a fault which a less exalted person could redeem with a fine of cattle according to the size of his herd, while a poor man escaped with a beating.

Tsächin Bichik on the other hand especially protects the clergy, the princes and the rich by punishing crimes committed against them more severely than the same crimes committed against men of the people. In many cases the rich man can atone by a fine that which the poor man must pay for with his life.

But many of Jenghiz Khan's maxims hold good upon the steppes to this day.

Jenghiz Khan said : " None shall ever defile water or fire, but neither shall any ever make distinction between clean and unclean, but shall learn that all things are clean."

He ordained : " All religions are to be respected and none

preferred before the others, for thereby one pleases The Great God."

He said : " When a traveller passes people who are eating he shall have the right to unsaddle and eat with them without asking leave, and none shall hinder him."

He bade them show respect to the old and to beggars.

He decreed : " Children born without wedlock shall be regarded as true children and receive their share of the inheritance with their father's other children."

He said : " The man who can govern his tent can also govern many tents ; he who can lead ten men well can be entrusted with a great army, and he will lead them well also."

He said also : " As a guest among friendly people a man shall be as a calf, little and tractable, but in time of war he must be like a hungry falcon on the hunt ; he must go into battle shouting savagely."

He said also : " If a man cannot possibly abstain from drinking, let him get drunk three times in a month ; if he gets drunk more than three times in thirty days he does wrongly ; if he gets drunk twice in a month it is better, and if he only gets drunk once in a month it is better still ; and if a man never gets drunk it is best of all. But where is such a man to be found ? "

WHEREAS *Yassa* ordains tolerance towards those of other faiths as pleasing to the one Almighty God, the code of 1640 proclaims Lamaism as the only true doctrine and renders the adherents of Shamanism punishable.

Yassa punishes adultery within the tribe ; *Tsächin Bichik* protects the married woman only if she be a mother, and the paucity of children in the tents is the reason of the rule that the childless married woman may not deny a traveller a place in bed by her side. At the same time " the man who lays hold of the breast of a girl more than ten years old " is punished.

The law of 1640 exchanges many of the death sentences ordained in *Yassa* for fines in the form of cattle. *Yassa* condemns a man who has overeaten himself to be dragged through a hole under the tent and killed outside it, while the later law stipulates a fine of five head of cattle for the same offence, with the further proviso that if any overeats himself in the tent of another it is no sin to kill him.

Yassa imposes the death penalty on the person who urinates on the fire or steps over the flames ; *Tsächin Bichik* ordains high fines for him who defiles the fire or throws incombustible objects upon it.

The Mongolian woman has long been under the protection of the law, and even before the code of 1640 it was a punishable offence to "tear the hair from a woman's head or the tassel from her cap." *Tsächin Bichik* shows great respect for the woman ; as mistress of the tent she is inviolable and he who insults her brings the vengeance of the law upon his head.

> When the mistress of the tent takes up the place proper to her alone, to the right of the entrance, between the hearth and her lord's sleeping place, no one may touch her, but she may unhindered revile the stranger, yes, even throw wood and other objects at him. But if the woman's wrath should drive her from her place in the tent or should she step outside her tent, she loses her privileged position and may be punished for her outrages.

Another clause in the law of 1640 says :

> If a woman go to her chief to beg grace for offences committed by herself or any member of her family, her request shall be granted and the punishment mitigated in consideration of her sex.

The fines laid down in *Tsächin Bichik* for certain kinds of theft give an idea of the war equipment of the West Mongols at that time.

> for the theft of cuirass, armour or a good bow with ten arrows in the quiver shall be fined thrice nine head of cattle.
> for the theft of helm, cap, a good sword or a middling bow with quiver shall be fined nine head of cattle.
> for theft of a good lance shall be fined three head of cattle, for a poor one, one horse, for a good crossbow with quiver and ten arrows twenty seven head of cattle.

WHEN the Manchu Emperor Ch'ien Lung conquered the Dzungars he promulgated new laws for the population of the conquered territory, "the first ordinance of the Chinese Colonial Ministry", which came into force probably in 1789. These ordinances were to a large extent based upon the nomads' own laws enlarged by a number of paragraphs which were necessary to bring the judicial systems of the two peoples into agreement.

In 1815 these laws were revised and enlarged with a view to further bringing the primitively conservative nomads under Chinese influence. The efforts of the Chinese were directed to breaking up the military organization of the Mongols, and the Manchu Emperors erected numerous temples on the steppes and in all ways fostered Lamaism as a means of taming the savagery of the nomads.

So long as the descendants of the Manchus sat upon the Dragon Throne and so long as their governors and garrisons kept guard over the steppes the ordinances of the Chinese Colonial Ministry of 1789 and 1815 constituted the laws of the nomads. But the principles of justice introduced by the Chinese never struck deep roots among the people of the tents in the wilderness. With Buddhistic submissiveness the nomads accommodated themselves to the Chinese judicial system, but they continued to judge the worth of their fellows according to the ancient moral conceptions of their forefathers.

When the Chinese overthrew their Emperor they also abolished the power which had upheld law and justice in the Middle Kingdom, and that great country has since passed through the chaos of lawlessness. But for the nomads the only consequence of the impotence of the new provincial governors was that the moral conceptions and the rules of justice which are in harmony with their inmost character and nomadic upbringing came once more into prominence.

SENG CHEN's far-sightedness and his method of ascertaining by experiment the relative merits of the old and the new came also into play in regard to the judicial system. One case in particular gave him much to ponder over.

A soldier of bad reputation, one Nimgher, had long been wanted for horse stealing, on account of which his life was forfeit. The Regent's people traced the deserter to Urumchi where he was in the service of the eminent English medical missionary, now deceased, Mr. P. Mather. Mr. Mather had devoted many years to the study of the Mongols, spoke their language and understood their temper, and had won the deep affection of the nomads who had sought his aid as a doctor.

When the Torgut patrol came to arrest Nimgher, Mr. Mather begged for his life and promised that, if Seng Chen would pardon him, he would himself answer for it that Nimgher should live honestly for the future.

The Regent acceded to Mr. Mather's request, but continued to keep himself informed as to Nimgher's conduct. When I was in Öreget, Nimgher, after two years stay at the English Mission station, had become a Christian, and Seng Chen had been able to satisfy himself that he was leading an exemplary life both as Christian and nomad.

We had many talks about this case and discussed the problem whether it was Mather's personality or the power of his doctrine that had prevailed within one life-time in transforming this condemned criminal into a righteous man.

For according to " the yellow doctrine " many torments and rebirths would be necessary to bring about such a result.

CHAPTER IX

IN THE OPEN

ONE evening I was sitting in the guest-room occupied by the two Tibetans talking with my four Asiatic friends. They were narrating nomad legends, and I was telling Northern fairy tales, and we were all enjoying ourselves.

Lodong Geling was just going to begin a new story when the legendary atmosphere was rudely dispersed by blaring trumpet blasts from the town's watch-towers. The hour was late for the announcement of a visitor to the Regent, and we wondered who it could be. Lodong went away to find out, and it was long before he came back with news.

A mission had arrived that evening in Öreget from the Chinese *tao-t'ai* [1] with orders to demand information as to my place of abode and intentions. The Chinese authorities, who followed the doings and movements of the members of the expedition with constant attention, had lost track of me at Toksun and now suspected that I was being secretly harboured by the Torguts. They demanded my surrender that I might be taken to Khara Shar to give an account of myself to their *tao-t'ai*.

Lodong had been commissioned by the Regent to warn me, since if I were found in Öreget it might occasion me grave inconvenience on my return to Urumchi. Seng Chen had himself answered the messengers that I was presumably hunting in the mountains, and the place he named was inaccessible enough to damp the zeal of the Chinese for continuing the search.

I was to leave Öreget at once. My horse stood ready

[1] *Tao-t'ai* was in the time of the Empire the designation of a district governor, and the title continued to be used in Sinkiang.

270

saddled and laden with provisions outside the outer
wall, and I was to ride to the monastery of Shara Sume
whither Lyrup Geling would follow me with further
instructions.

It was only a short day's ride to the monastery, and
I knew the valley in which it lay.

Clad in furs and ready for the journey I followed
Lodong through the darkest alleys of the sleeping town.
He gave me a letter to the prior of the monastery and
pointed out the stars by which I was to shape my course.

My horse was fresh and in fine fettle after weeks of
lazy living in the stable. "*Tsa Yabonah*," I shouted,
and "*Sain Yabonah*," answered Lodong. After that I
heard nothing but the hoof-beats and saw nothing but
the stars.

The night was full of infinite freedom, and my thoughts
toyed with the fascination of the unknown. It was
wonderful to be outside the limits of the town walls,
once more to be without a roof over my head. I let
go the reins and left it to my horse to choose our direction
and our resting-place for the night. We galloped across
the steppe, scrambled over low foothills, groped our
way up through pine covered slopes, saw the wide
starry horizon from the summit of the pass and came
down again into the valleys.

We made a halt under the lee of a steep mountain-
side. There was dry wood in plenty for the fire, and
the moss made a soft sleeping-place for the night.
Buran rubbed his sweating flanks against a tree-trunk.
High up stood a single windblown pine whose naked
trunk and swaying crown stood out like a dark palm
tree against the pallid starlit sky.

An owl hooted, and the cry was answered by the
mysterious spirits of the mountain.

" EREN HABIRGRAN OLE'N." (Torgut Song.)

271

I awoke to the notes of a distant song.

It was before sunrise, but above the tallest tree-tops rested already the dawn's faint veil of light. The flames from the fire still contrived, though it had soon burned down, to cast mysterious reflections on the night-black stems of the surrounding trees.

It sounded as if the song were coming nearer. But then it died away and left a sense of oppressive loneliness in the silent forest.

Buran had come up to the fire and was now standing with his head held high and his ears twitching, listening and peering into the darkness to westward. In the horse too the unexpected notes had aroused a longing for company.

Suddenly the sound was resumed on the mountain side to the northward. The singer was yodelling and playing with the echo which joined with his own clear voice in a symphony of bright morning greeting. Slowly he moved along the steeps above our heads.

It sounded as if he were testing the acoustics of the forest valley, and when he had found the place from which his song rang fullest he struck up *Ili'en shara Ködä*, the song of the golden meadows of the Ili river.

It was very evident that the notes were the natural expression of the singer's mood and that the words were directly improvised out of the nomad's harmony with nature and joy in the beauty of existence. I had to lie on my back to let the eye of fancy lure forth against the enchanting background of the dawn the images of which the unseen voice was singing.

The melody was known and dear to me, but the words were the singer's and the moment's. They described his happy memories of autumn in the luxuriant Ili valley where sturdy cattle and muscular horses stood right up to their bellies in succulent yellowing grass. They told of the herdsman's love for the herd and his delight in the gambols of defenceless lambs and frisky foals among the meadow flowers. And the singer cautioned the little ones and promised them his protection against beasts of prey and other perils.

He sang and sang, and at last it was impossible for me to withstand the poetry of the moment. I had to join in the tune.

At first I was afraid that my first notes would discordantly disturb his mood. But after a brief hesitation the singer again took up his melody on the mountain side, and not until the sun's rays were gilding the tree tops and together we had sung in a new day did our song fall silent. And when the last echo had rolled away we heard the soft cooing of the wood pigeons.

The sound of hooves announced the approach of a horseman, and the singer came into view.

"*Amorkhan sain, mendo sain*, peace be in your soul, health in your body," was his greeting, and he dismounted to lay down in front of him the unfriendly rifle.

He was dressed in a cloak of the gayest blue, and round his head and waist he had tied gaudy cotton handkerchiefs, the blood-red and flame-yellow ends of which fluttered freely in the wind. On his feet he had lashed pieces of untanned cowhide with the hairy side outward. After the fashion of laymen he wore a long shining black pigtail down his back. His face was sunburnt and tanned with the wind, and his eyes were surrounded by a fine network of young wrinkles carved by intensive peering against wind and weather and by many a happy smile.

Our pipes passed between us and all the courteous questions and answers of Mongolian etiquette. But after we had enquired after the health of our respective horses and cattle, assured one another that water and

273

pasturage were plentiful and asked one another whence we came and whither we were bound, the singer was able to express his more personal curiosity.

" You sing our songs—is it that you are *Khilitai abder kymin* (the man with the box that can talk) ? "

And when I confirmed this he knew all about me, all that I knew myself and much besides. Baying Surong was his own name, and he was a herdsman and hunter.

I was now to accompany him to his camp on the other side of the pass to the east, for there dwelt Shiri, the pride of the camp, a young girl who commanded the gliding, soaring and falling of the notes like a proud eagle on the wing.

After half an hour's climb through the dim pine woods on the western slope of the mountain we reached the pass and the sunlight, and down below in the next valley, still asleep in the grey dawn, lay Baying Surong's familiar world, the four nomad tents which constituted his home.

All was dead silent and still, while the sun's rays glided slowly deeper and deeper into the valley. Now their reflection in the blue-gleaming ribbon which showed the river's winding course twinkled at the four closed tents.

As chequered specks in the green meadows we could see the cows on their way to the milking-place. White flocks of sheep were moving out into the sunlight from the dark woods on the opposite mountain side, and where the deep blue of the river stood out against the bright green meadows the horses of the camp were rejoicing in the morning.

White smoke rose as a sign of life from one of the smoke-vents, and before long four slight pillars of smoke were soaring skyward as a first announcement of the awakening of the camp.

We had thrown ourselves down on the grass, and now watched across the pearly dewdrops the little nomad community's meeting with a new day. The tent openings were pushed aside to let out a swarm of tender calves and lambs which ran instinctively towards their lowing and bleating mothers. The brightly coloured, slender figures of the young daughters and daughters-in-law of the camp came into view as with laughter and happy cries they took up their multifarious morning tasks.

The sound of the clearest girl's voice rose towards us. " That is Shiri singing," Baying Surong informed me.

" Soon there will be five tents in our camp, and to the new one I shall carry ' the delight of the camp '."

The young nomad's expression, which hitherto had been so undemonstrative, now shone with the feelings which informed him, heartfelt love and exultant gladness.

For Baying Surong was rich, the possessor of the best in life.

The notes from the valley floated like light and graceful birds' wings when Shiri with her pure girl's voice sang of all that her eyes beheld and her hands accomplished. And after every verse the other girls joined in the chorus :

" Our labour is not hard but light
because our work is our delight."

It sounded like a hymn to industry and the joy of work.

CHAPTER X

UNDER THE SMOKE-HOOD

DOWN in the camp we were received with joyous greetings and curious questions, and the young people shouted with joy when they heard that the white guest was "the man with the box that can talk". Great indignation was aroused by the fact that I had not brought my wonderful "box" with me, but a part of the phonograph's popularity nevertheless attached to its owner.

In the principal tent of the camp I was welcomed by two fine old nomads. One of them was the headman of the camp, and the other had been guest for the night on his journey from the Khobok Saïri tribe far in the north to Öreget. Both had been great hunters and entertained one another so well with tales of hunts and adventures on the northern and southern slopes of the "Mountains of Heaven" that the host was loath to let his guest depart, and the guest to break the circle round the fire.

The old Khobok Saïri hunter wore a plain silver ring in his left ear. It swung to and fro in the firelight with the man's lively movements of the head and aroused my violent curiosity.

It was not the first time I had seen a man wearing such an ornament, but it was not a common sight. The first Mongol I had seen with earrings was the wild nomad in Puntsuk's tent among the Etsina Torguts, and I had since heard that he had been a scout sent out by Seng Chen to enquire into the truth of the rumours which Chinese caravan folk had carried to Sinkiang of our expedition's powerful armament and hostile intentions.

I had later observed similar earrings on some of the

Torgut soldiers who had carried us captive to Hami
and on certain of the couriers who visited Öreget. But
I had not encountered any of these men in circumstances
which allowed me to win their confidence and inveigle
them to talk. Seng Chen's smart young secretary had
told me that the earrings were nothing but an absurd
decoration which some isolated mountain tribes had
adopted in imitation of the Tibetans or the Chinese or
perhaps the women.

In China one sometimes sees small boys wearing rings
in their ears like girls but this is an attempt by the
anxious parents to make the boy look like a girl, so as
to mislead the evil spirits which seek out boys far more
than girls. And so soon as the boy has passed the
perilous age of childhood he is relieved of his feminine
ornaments.

It was not until towards evening that the mood of the
tent became such that I could venture on a question, and
Purup, who by his own account was eighty-four years
old, recounted the legend of the origin of the earring.

" Very many years ago my tribe was ruled by a wise
and mighty Khan whose *tsagan yasse* traced its origin
from the tent of Jenghiz Khan himself.

" This Khan possessed cattle, tents and women in
abundance, but rich as he was he was nevertheless poor,
since even in the autumn of his age he had no son in
his tent.

" At that time my forefathers pastured their flocks by
the Ili river, and every morning the Khan's men went
down to the water to fish, for in his old age the chief
had acquired a taste for fish. One morning the fisher-
men saw a remarkable object drifting with the stream,
and they threw a line to draw the object ashore so that
they might investigate its nature.

" It was found to be a little man-child, still alive,
and the Mongols brought this strange catch home to
their master with the day's catch of fish. The lonely
old man was delighted with the well-made little boy
and determined to adopt him as his son. He taught
him to ride in his own saddle and educated him to
occupy the chief's seat in the tent with dignity.

"But the fishhook which had been cast for the boy when he was floating with the stream had fastened in his left ear, and it proved impossible to take it out. So that the boy should not become an object of derision among the people of the tribe, the Khan in his loving wisdom had the fishhook overlaid with silver, and ordained that all the male members of the tribe should wear a silver ring in the left ear.

"The boy became the ancestor of a long line of chiefs, and the hunters who to this day wear a ring in the left ear are faithful to the tradition born of the good old Khan's wise ordinance very many years ago."

FOR three days I stayed in that secluded Mongol camp, and for so long did old Purup put off his departure for Öreget. I smoked pipes and drank tea with the two ancients, and roving hunters and herdsmen from neighbouring camps came to hear new things and to relate old. In three days we devoured the sheep slaughtered on the first, and life in the camp was blissful.

Two of the visiting hunters greeted me as an old acquaintance and turned out to have belonged to the group of Torguts who had slept one night under my "air-horse" on their journey to the hunting-grounds by "the new river". Their leader's prophecy of good hunting luck had been abundantly fulfilled, since the eight hunters had in three days brought down forty-three wild pig and could now look forward with equanimity to the winter.

On the morning of the third day a report came into the camp that horse-thieves had been active in the next valley. This communication immediately transformed the smiling and hospitable nomads into raging wild beasts. The Kirghiz who had their tents on the northern side of the mountain got the blame, and soon every man capable of bearing arms was riding at a wild gallop towards their camp.

The women at once took up the work of the men as guardians of the herds of cattle, and their happy femininity acquired a touch of masculine decision. My old host, the eighty-four-year-old Purup and I were left sitting alone by the fire. Round about us the children shrieked and yelled like small wild beasts, for they were playing horse-thieves and herdsmen. None of them wanted to be Kirghiz, for the Kirghiz were going to be thrashed.

IN travelling through Mongolia and Central Asia from east to west one finds the first Kirghiz settlements between the Kobdo and the Altai mountains. If one continues westward as far as the Torgut territory in the Tien Shan mountains one meets as often Kirghiz as Torgut hunters. But their camping-places always lie in different valleys, and one soon perceives that these two nomad peoples live constantly at daggers drawn.

Both peoples support themselves by cattle raising and hunting, and the tents of both have the same construction and almost the same form. But the Kirghiz are Mohammedans and, as such, circumcised, and their dress differs considerably from that of the Mongols. For instance the Kirghiz wear boots with two and a half inch heels, while the footgear of the Mongols is heelless.

I had often noticed that when the Mongol and Kirghiz hunters meet in No-man's-land out in the wilderness it is usually the Kirghiz who retreat and the Mongols who keep on after the game. Still farther to the westward there are wholly Kirghiz districts which I do not know and have never visited, but wherever Kirghiz and Mongols live together the Kirghiz are poorer and have much smaller herds of cattle than their neighbours.

In the eyes of the Mongols all Kirghiz are horse-thieves. The Kirghiz often grow obese when still young and then prefer to sit at home by the fire, leaving hunting expeditions and other manly occupations to their younger brothers. This immeasurably degrades the Kirghiz men in the eyes of the Mongols, and I have heard them revile those of their fellows of whom they disapproved for being " fat-bellied as Kirghiz " no matter how slim the man in question might be.

The Mongols laugh scornfully when they see the Kirghiz, as he mutters his prayers, passing his hand over the place where according to the prophet's precept he should have a long and dignified beard, for the Kirghiz is almost as beardless as the Mongol.

I ventured to suggest to my host and Purup that perhaps the Mongols were sometimes a little too hard in their judgment of the Kirghiz. But they were struck with amazement. Did I not know what scum the Kirghiz were ? Did I not know they were under the curse of the gods ?

And since I seemed not to know this, I was soon informed of the reason for their contempt.

"The great Jenghiz Bogdo Khan had many women, for it was his manly inclination and pleasure to " imbibe youth and womanly charm ". But to one of these women he devoted his deepest feelings, and when scarcely more than a child she bore him a son.

"When this son became a man he violated his own mother who by these base means brought forth a child. This crime enraged the great Jenghiz Khan who in his righteous indignation banished the two malefactors and their godforgotten progeny to the country far away in the west. But first he ordered that the heels of the outcasts should be cut off and his own son and his son's son be circumcised so that they might be distinguished from all honourable people.

"The exiles adopted an alien faith and, to conceal their mutilation, wore boots with high heels. Their descendants are the Kirghiz who to this day have to circumcise their male offspring and to this day wear boots with high heels. It is the duty of all to abhor them for the children of sin that they are."

In the evening of the third day Lyrup Geling arrived at the camp in the valley with two Torgut soldiers. After seeking me in vain at the monastery he had traced me hither. When we met Lyrup was a little hurt, and I was a little ashamed of myself, but in Mongolia such feelings do not last long, and when we rode away together towards the sunset we were singing the same tune.

Lyrup had orders from the Regent that we were to keep out of the way in the mountains until the Chinese

Fresco in the Dongtse Monastery representing Seng Chen's spiritual father, the Tiger god's fourth reincarnation

Torgut Temple Tent
From Pallas' "Sammlungen historischer Nachrichten über die mongolischen
Völkerschaften", St. Petersburg, 1776

[*face p.* 281

had returned to Khara Shar, after which he would send for us.

All the magnificent landscape lay silent and apparently lifeless, for most of the Torgut camps had followed their herds of cattle to seek shelter from the winter in the lee of the mountain's southern slopes.

Then the first snow fell. Everything acquired a new beauty, and the ground was covered with the tracks of hunters and of game. On the lower slopes we kept a lookout for the wild mountain sheep, but we had a long and difficult climb before we reached the haunts of the rock goats. We spent the nights in the simple tents of the hunters and sat through the evenings by the fire talking of the summer and of Tsoltus which is the chief gathering-place of the Khara Shar Torguts at that season.

The Torguts love Tsoltus and are convinced that their land is the most beautiful on earth.

The name of the place implies that its fertile valleys lie higher than many of the mountain crests. The Torguts say with pride that from the high steppes where they spend the summer they can let their glance rove over a hundred peaks that lie lower than the valleys of Tsoltus.

From June to August "the river valleys that rest upon the hundred mountain crests" are a Mongolian land of Cockaigne. Millions of fat-tailed sheep, horses in hundreds of thousands and an innumerable multitude of cattle wallow in a sea of succulent grass, and on the mountain slopes the herdsmen sit amid a blaze of flowers revelling in the loveliness of nature which gives birth to beauty in the notes of their pipes.

By the evening camp fire the hunters sang of the dancing flight of the rock-goats towards dizzy peaks and of life and death struggles between man and savage beast in the lonely gloom of the pine forests.

There was always room for the guest in their small tents, and with the inborn tact and cordiality of the child of nature they were ready to share fraternally all that the tent could provide.

To know the child of nature in his natural surroundings is a wonderful experience.

CHAPTER XI

THE TENT TEMPLES OF THE TORGUTS

BY the beginning of December we were back in Öreget.

On journeys out into the wilds and when staying among people of alien race nothing so arouses the longing for home or homelike surroundings as the approach of Christmas. I got ready for departure and intended to return to the circle of my friends at the expedition's headquarters in Urumchi.

But before I could leave the Torgut capital with an easy mind and a clear conscience one matter remained to be investigated.

In the park to the southward of the Regent's palace stood seven magnificently appointed temple tents before whose altars the highest and most learned lamas in the land performed their unending temple service. At every hour of the twenty-four their chanting voices could be heard, and at dead of night the mysterious sounds of bassoons, conchs and hollow drums arose from the inner sanctuaries.

This the most holy precinct of the Torgut nomads bore the name of *Dolor burkhani ordo kharchi*, and the altars of the seven (*dolor*) temples are sacred to lamaism's supreme gods (*burkhan*) and to the branches of " the yellow doctrine " which these gods represent. One temple was devoted to astrology (*tsurkha*), another to medicine (*manba*), and a third to occultism (*yute*), and these temples were called *tsurka-yin-ordo, emchi-yin-ordo* and *yute-yin-ordo*.

The last-named temple was occupied by two aged lamas who were skilful astrologers and enjoyed a great reputation for their knowledge of the mystical *tantra* doctrine.[1] Every morning these lamas were informed of Seng Chen's dreams of the night before and received orders as to the problems to which they were to devote their attention during the coming twenty-four hours. The Regent never began upon a new undertaking or entered into relations with a new person without having first obtained the opinion of the astrologers.

Another of the temple tents was called *gegen-ni-ordo* and this, with the lamas who tended the flame upon its altar, always accompanied Seng Chen upon his journeys.

Chief among the gods of this temple was Maidari the coming saviour, the deity whom the ruler of the Torguts most highly honoured.

To the left of the altar stood the canopied throne from which, in his capacity of reincarnation of the Seng Chen deity, the Regent dispensed blessings to the assembled pilgrims. In front of the throne stood a richly carved and cunningly painted table spread with all the sacred attributes proper to a *hutuktu*. Along the eastern side of the tent stood the red lacquered and gilded bed which Seng Chen used on his travels.

The interior of the tent was draped with blue and red silk, and from the roof hung temple banners with representations of *dokshit* of terrifying aspect for the protection of the gentler gods upon the altar. Cult objects of massive silver glittered in the fluttering light of the oil-lamps, and the strong and strident colours in the dim interior of the tent produced a concentrated effect of Asiatic splendour and hallowed mystery.

The temple tent is the nomads' original form of shrine, and it was under Chinese and Tibetan influence that they later took to building permanent temples of timber and masonry.

The " Yellow Hats ", the sect founded by the Tibetan reformer Tsong Kapa (1356–1418) who preached " the yellow doctrine " as the only true form of lamaism, spread from Tibet into Dzungaria and thence to the Tusheto Khanate in Khalka Mongolia. But up to the end of the sixteenth century lamaism in Mongolia was

[1] *Tantra* doctrine—the study of mystical and magical formulæ, among other things for the attainment of communion with the gods.

solely represented by the orthodox " Red Hats ", and the great mass of the nomads long remained in bondage to the shamanistic cosmogony.

According to the Mongolian chronicle it was Tümeng-khen, a son of the Khalka prince Unugu, who first went over to " the yellow doctrine ". Abatai, a brother of Tümengkhen's, visited the Dalai Lama, the pontiff of " the yellow doctrine ", and was deeply impressed by the splendour and mystery surrounding its divine service. The Dalai Lama succeeded in convincing the two princes of the power of his creed and in order to make of them influential missionaries of " the yellow doctrine " among their people he bestowed on Tümengkhen the name of *Sain noyen* (the good prince) and Abatai was proclaimed a *hutuktu* and allotted a relic of Buddha.

After his return from Lhasa, Abatai in 1586 erected the first Mongolian monastery by the river Orkhon. The new monastery which was given the name of Erdeni Dzu, " The Jewel Wreath ", became the first centre from which Tibetan and afterwards Mongolian lamas preached " the yellow doctrine ".

In 1640 the Mongols acquired their own " yellow " pontiff, in that the fifteen-year-old son of Tusheto Khan was, under the name of Lobsang Damba Dshamdsan, proclaimed *gegen*, " enlightened ", and it is his rebirths who down to 1925 have been the Mongols' spiritual leader Bogdo Gegen, " the living Buddha " in Urga.

Several Mongolian monasteries derive from the latter half of the seventeenth century or are even more recent, for the new Manchu dynasty had numerous temples built on the wide expanses of the grasslands in order to transform the warlike nomads into peaceful herdsmen, and pious monks. Herein lies the explanation of the fact that most of the monastic buildings of Mongolia are built in the Manchu-Chinese style and not in the Tibetan, although " the yellow doctrine " originated in Tibet.

The Mongols have an innate aversion from fixed buildings, and in many places in Mongolia—in the principality of Dondurgun for example—it is still forbidden to all, including the Chinese traders, to erect permanent masonry. The free steppe is not to be "bound" by heavy buildings, and the nomads are never to forget their first duty, that of following the herds of cattle on their eternal wanderings to new grazing-grounds and new watering-places.

But to monastery and temple these rules do not apply, for these form the dwellings of gods and their servants the lamas, and for such human considerations do not come into question.

Until 1920 no lay buildings existed among the Torguts, and the first to be erected was Seng Chen's summer residence in the Tsoltus mountains. In his capacity of *hutuktu* he was able to override human ordinances, and since the Torguts had learnt that the Regent's actions brought blessing in their train, it aroused neither opposition nor apprehension when he founded the town of Öreget and ordained that his officials and attendants should in the winter inhabit those buildings of wood, stone and brick.

The Torguts point with pride to Seng Chen's work Öreget with its towers and walls and imposing buildings, but none the less the inhabitants of the town dream all winter long of the summer when all the people, chiefs and herdsmen alike, dwell in tents. During the warm season Öreget is a deserted and barred-up town, for then the Torguts follow their herds up to the highland steppes, and the garrison of the fortress walls alone remain, dreaming of Tsoltus and with their longing gaze upon the distant snow peaks.

On my earlier travels in Central Asia I had visited innumerable Mongolian monasteries, but only on a single occasion came upon one small and insignificant tent temple, and it may seem strange that it is in Öreget with all its solid buildings that tent temples are still in use.

That the old nomad tradition that even the gods should be lodged in tents as mobile and free as the wanderings of the herds is still alive among the Torguts may be due to the fact that between 1618 and 1771, the period when their kin on the home steppes were receiving their most vigorous religious impulse from

Tibet, the tribe was living beyond the frontier of distant Russia.

On one of my last evenings in Öreget I followed Seng Chen into *gegen-ni-ordo*, and he did not hinder me. We had just finished the usual discussion of the actual problems of a sinful world, but when he changed his European costume for the long yellow lama's robe it was as though the man before me changed his nature. The quick intelligent glance grew introverted and unseeing, the lively play of feature subsided into tranquil receptivity.

I saw him sink down in prayer before Maidari and the other gilded images of gods which to him symbolized lofty ideals and profound truths. The sacred colours of the silken hangings and temple banners, white, yellow, red, green and blue, shifted in the dim light from the altar, and the mist of incense floated about the kneeling being in the flame-yellow silk robe.

The *hutuktu's* orientally slender hands carried out plastic movements, tracing sacred symbols in the air.

Then he aspersed *darpana*, the dull bronze mirror of the Omniscient with drops of holy water—and I left him, for alone with his gods must the Holy one decipher *darpana's* all-knowing answer.

For long I walked about in the neighbourhood of the tent, for its atmosphere held me. I drank in the steppe wind and counted the stars. I hummed the nomad's lovely songs and thought their happy thoughts.

And then was born my dream of bearing such a sanctuary to the remote West, for this—far more than books, pictures and disconnected museum objects—would convey the spirit of Mongolia.

CHAPTER XII

ACROSS THE MOUNTAINS

A WEEK before Christmas I started from Öreget with my two Chinese servants. Pack-horses were laden with the collections resulting from our stay with this interesting Mongolian tribe. The leave-taking of my Torgut friends was cordial, and Seng Chen's farewell words to me were that I must come back soon, so that I might learn to know the Torguts still better and that he himself might hear more about my people.

On our rested horses the ride to Urumchi went swiftly. We avoided all inhabited districts and on the fifth day of our journey turned up unexpectedly at the headquarters of the expedition. Quantities of Christmas letters and parcels from home had already arrived, and the accumulated mail of the past months was awaiting me.

The idea which had come into my head during my visit to the Torguts' temple tent, that I should try to procure such a sanctuary for the expedition's collections I now confided to Sven Hedin, and to my delight he received the proposal with the enthusiastic understanding characteristic of him. I obtained his sanction for my return to Öreget after the holiday, and a substantial sum was put at my disposal in the event of my being able to secure Seng Chen's permission for his craftsmen to produce an exact copy of one of the temples with all its appurtenances.

A letter to the Torgut Regent was composed in English and Mongolian, signed by Dr. Hedin and garnished with as many imposing stamps and seals as we could procure.

287

His Holiness Seng Chen Doryechan,
He who holds the Signet of the Torgut Khanate,
Öreget, Khara Shar.

Arselan Noyen, subject of Christian, Khan of Denmark who is a brother to Gustaf, Khan over the Swedes, has made me aware of all the kindness and help that has fallen to his lot from Your Holiness during his sojourn in Your palace.

On behalf of my Khan and my people I desire to express my deeply felt gratitude to You and my hope that the friendly relations which have been established may continue and be improved in the future.

I desire also to thank Your Holiness for the invitation to Arselan Noyen again to visit your city.

With us in Sweden a Mongolian tribe, the Lapps, has settled. Many years ago they left their original home in Mongolia and now live in friendly understanding with our people, under the protection of our Khan.

Just as six hundred years ago when the two great Mongol Khans, Jenghiz and Kublai, sent their ambassadors to distant foreign lands and invited people from those lands to their court to see and study foreign manners and customs, so have I and my expedition come here by desire of my Khan and my countrymen.

In Sweden many different religions are represented, but hitherto no lamaistic temple has been erected there. There is a strong desire in my Khan and my countrymen to see and learn how the Mongols worship Burkhan Bash and the other gods whom Your Holiness represents.

I send Arselan Noyen to Your Holiness with my cordial greetings and pray Your Holiness to support him with counsel and help in this his task so important to my expedition.

I can assure Your Holiness that all religious objects and symbols that are carried to our country will be regarded as such and treated with the greatest respect and reverence.

I hope that we may soon meet so that I may be able personally to thank Your Holiness for Your friendship and hospitality shown to Arselan Noyen.

I take this occasion to assure Your Holiness of my deepest respect and esteem.

Sven Hedin,
Seal.

In the baggage for my new expedition to Öreget I was further to take a photograph of Sven Hedin's meeting with Panchen Bogdo in Peking, taken before the expedition's start from that city, as well as two sets of telephone apparatus with their accessories which had been given to the expedition by the L. M. Ericsson Telephone Company.

My departure was fixed for the end of January, but one morning in the middle of the month two horsemen arrived at headquarters on horses white with frost, couriers bearing Seng Chen's invitation to me to return to Öreget and charged to conduct me thither. So my preparations were hastened.

The very next day one courier started with my little caravan in charge of two Chinese caravan men, and on the following night I once more left headquarters in the company of the other Torgut.

At our first camping-place a Torgut officer was waiting for us with a small escort of soldiers, and with them was the hermit Töin Geling, the uncle of my friend Mongrolda Noyen, who now for the first time for nine years had quitted his solitary cave in the mountains. The Torguts had powerful horses with them for my baggage, so my own animals, with the exception of Buran, were taken back by a Torgut to the expedition's headquarters.

The leader of the Torgut escort ascertained with satisfaction that our departure from Urumchi had escaped the attention of the ever-suspicious Chinese. And now we were already deep in among the foothills of Tien Shan, far from highroads, and would soon be upon the Torguts' secret mountain-paths.

The farther we penetrated into the mountains the deeper lay the snow, and on the fourth day of the march the last vestige of a path disappeared beneath three-foot drifts. The passes on our way were so ice-covered that the small ponies could not find any foothold, and on several occasions we had to return to the last camping-place in order to seek a new line of advance along another canyon.

On the tenth day of our journey we had strayed to the foot of a pass which had before us only been climbed by mountain sheep, rock goats and the intrepid hunters who follow their trail. Here a snowstorm came upon us, and to save the last powers of the already exhausted horses for the climb in better weather we were compelled to camp.

Töin Geling sat all day long in his corner of the tent and let the beads of his rosary slip through his stiffened fingers. The leader, Shageder, of whom it was said that he knew " the Mountains of Heaven " like his own tent and who had his ruler's commission to conduct the foreign guest to Öreget, went out into the storm to find his bearings.

And after a day and a night the snowstorm ceased as suddenly as it had begun. The sunrise spread its beauty over a glistening white fairy landscape, and the sun brought warmth and cheer to both man and beast. The horses, lately so dispirited, shook the frost off their coats and began to paw the snow, seeking for fodder. Töin Geling pointed happily to the southward where behind sharp ridges a saddle-shaped pass broke the line of lustrous mountain wall against the blue January sky. The pass was Tekhe'en Dawan itself, the Rock-goat's Pass, which is the entrance to the Torgut country. And Shageder came back happy and hopeful, for he had found fresh human tracks leading in the direction of the pass.

We set out with renewed courage and began the difficult ascent. The foot tracks in the snow encouraged us, and we were full of gratitude to our unseen guide and of admiration of the hard struggle he had fought out alone against the raging elements. His tracks were deeply imprinted in the new fallen snow, but half filled up again, which showed that he had performed this severe climb during the actual storm.

Ever upward trudged the mountain-trained ponies. We followed them on foot, step by step, sweating and out of breath. The shouts of the Mongols urging on the ponies rolled about the mountain walls, and the echoes hung long in the thin frosty air. An eagle with shining topaz eyes hovered above us poised in luminous space.

The nearer we came to the summit of the pass the more eager became our efforts. The Torguts were impatient to see once more the known features of their own country, and I was animated by the feeling which drives one on towards each new pass, the longing to reach the point from which one looks out over a new and unknown world.

As the winter sun went down in flaming splendour we reached the top of the pass.

For the last hour we had had no track to follow. At the point where it ceased sat the half snowed-under body of a man. When we passed it the Torguts had said prayers to appease Yama the great god of death, but Töin Geling had tarried with the dead man. Muttering prayers for the dead he had bared the breast and belly of the corpse to attract the roving wolves of the mountain, and to summon the birds of prey had turned the dead man's eyes skywards.

For not until the dead has fulfilled his last earthly mission of maintaining and merging in other lives is the soul liberated and gains the right to pass on into a new life born at the moment of his death.

If one looks out on a clear day from the summit of Tekhe'en Dawan one sees on the northern horizon three shimmering clouds. By day they are white as sea foam ; at sunset they take on the tender tints of flowers. The clouds never move ; eternally they interrupt the blue of the horizon in the same place. They are the three snow-clad peaks of Bogdo Ula.

The sight of the sacred mountain made us forget all our perils and hardships.

Bogdo Ula no longer lies in Mongolian territory, for the Chinese have for long been in possession of the surrounding country, and the Governor-General of Sinkiang has built a temple of his own upon its slopes. Yet the Mongols still regard the sacred mountain as their property ; it has retained its ancient Mongolian name, and many nomads still make pilgrimage to its heights.

Bogdo Ula plays a prominent part in the historical legends of the West Mongols.

" At the time when the West Mongols were fighting their desperate struggle against the Chinese it often happened that an aged lama appeared among the Mongolian leaders. Always the old man brought good counsel, and always he could give information of the position of the enemy.

" The old lama who came to the aid of the Mongols was the human reincarnation of the spirit of the sacred mountain. The lama could bestride the mountain's highest peaks with ease and he would spread out his yellow lama's robe as a bird its wings and soar through space like a proud eagle. Thus he could survey the enemy's position from the air and then communicate the result of his observations to the West Mongols."

In silent adoration the Torguts turned their gaze towards the south where, behind boundless deserts and high plateaux beyond the range of vision, their religion had its source. Their thoughts went on pilgrimage to the castle of Potala, the seat of the Dalai Lama, and they saw the hallowed incense rising from the sacred mountain Budul Ola. The incense took the shape of three mountain sheep of celestial beauty that ran through space to meet their pilgrim fancy ; the golden bird of imagination (*altan khan-grän gruregroldä*) soared heavenward, and the miraculous stag of inspiration (*minjä khan-grän boro*) bounded on nimble feet across the mountains.

" Minjä Khan-grän Boro." (Torgut Song.)

The sun sank down and darkness rose up out of the depths. The " Rock-goat's summit " retained the last lingering gleams of day. We stood there and watched the darkness climbing up to meet us. During the descent star after star was lighted and grew in brilliance. The stillness of the frosty night was broken only by Töin Geling's prayers for the dead and the long-drawn howl of the wolves gathered on the northern side of the pass.

At moonrise we pitched camp on a snow-covered plateau. There was not a scrap of fuel to be found, and we had to freeze till daybreak, when Mongrolda Noyen arrived with a detachment of soldiers. These brought with them a fresh horse for me and fuel and fodder for the horses.

Mongrolda Noyen eagerly assured me that the worst

of the journey now lay behind us and that I might without anxiety leave the caravan and ride on in advance with him. The same evening we reached his camp, and some hours later Töin Geling also turned up. We sat late into the night round the open fire in the tent, stretched ourselves out on bearskins, passed round the pipes, sipped steaming tea and revelled in once more living in luxury and extravagance.

Out in the night sounded a snow-owl's strident shriek. It sounded like the cry of a frightened child.

" The unhappiness of children was the cause of one of the greatest migrations of our people," said Töin Geling and then told the legend :

" Very many years ago we Torguts and Khoshuts came from a country far beyond the great Kirghiz steppes. We came from the steppes by the great river Ejil-Tsar (Volga), and there a great part of our people still remain in thraldom.

" For long we lived there happily, for the water of the river was good and abundant, the steppes were wide and fertile and the neighbours feared our strength.

" But the holy places which are our religion's inspiration lay far from us, and with the years the happiness we had brought with us from the home steppes faded away. Our free steppes in that foreign land were hemmed in by alien peoples, and temples arose in our neighbourhood over whose white lamas our religion had no power.

" In time we were forced into subjection to *tsaghan* Kharr, the white Tsar of the Russians, and the tribute we must yearly pay was five hundred fifteen-year-old boys and girls. And we submitted to this, for the Russians said that our children should live happily and have a good upbringing with the white Tsar—and we believed them.

" But in the ' Tiger's year ' one of the surrendered youths came fleeing back to his people, and when he told of the fate of our sons and daughters we understood that the Russians had deceived us.

" The boys and girls who, with the one who had returned, had been sent to the Tsar had been taken by his soldiers to a distant camp. There they had lived in freedom but could never leave the camp, which was guarded by the Tsar's soldiers. In time each boy chose the girl who pleased him, and they were happy. But so soon as a girl became pregnant she was, to her lover's despair, carried away from the camp and never returned.

" One day the girl of the youth who came back was carried away, but his love for her was so great that he escaped by night to follow up her trail.

" After searching for days he came to a great fire by which sat a magician. He was just in time to see the magician cast his beloved to a gigantic serpent which swallowed her and their unborn child. When the serpent had devoured its hapless victims it was thrown into a great cauldron that was boiling over the fire. The white magician ceaselessly muttered secret spells, and from time to time he stirred the cauldron with a staff.

" Towards night the magician fell asleep and the terror-stricken youth ventured forward to the fire. An oily brew was bubbling in the cauldron, and the boy made bold to seek with the staff for a fragment of his beloved, whose skull might serve him as a talisman. Suddenly he stumbled and dropped the staff, which fell so that it struck the sleeping magician's hand. In a moment the man was writhing in his death agony.

" The contents of the cauldron were a deadly magic poison for the preparation of which was required a serpent that had swallowed a young girl bearing her first child in her womb.

" The Torguts now understood that all the young people whom they had trustfully delivered to the Tsar had become the victims of his evil desire to possess this dreadful poison.

" This was the occasion of Obish Khan's decision to get away from Ejil-Tsar where the Torguts lived surrounded by white magicians, and to make his way back to the free steppes of his forefathers in Central Asia where they could live under the protection of holy Potala."

At daybreak Töin Geling left us to seek once more his solitary refuge in the mountains, and a little later I went on with Mongrolda Noyen and his escort.

The same evening we arrived at the gates of Öreget.

CHAPTER XIII

THE YEAR OF THE "IRON SNAKE"
COMES IN

M Y four Asiatic friends visited me early the next morning, and I spent the whole forenoon in audience with the Regent. The letter I had brought duly impressed him by its size and its foreign seals and gave occasion for the bestowal upon me that same evening of another Mongolian name.

The Regent gave a gala dinner and at it ceremoniously announced that Arselan Noyen was to be known in future as Arselan Consul. The Regent had met the Russian Consul in Urumchi, and had become aware that a Consul was a free nation's representative with another free nation. I was Consul, the first Consul accredited to the free Torgut nation.

I myself greatly preferred my old name, but a hint to that effect produced a slightly irritated enquiry as to whether I did not regard the Torguts as a nation. And as I was unwilling to deprive the Torguts of that coveted appellation, I was obliged to submit to being called " Consul ".

The next day a new ordinance was issued that the title " Consul " should correspond with the Mongolian title *taiji* of the first rank, and the Regent presented me with the festival dress of my new dignity.

The main point of the letter, our request for permission to have one of the Torgut temples reproduced, had evidently escaped the Regent's attention, but when I later raised the question he promised to put no obstacles in my way. And soon skilful craftsmen were set to work upon the copy of *gegen-ni-ordo* which I so ardently desired.

I myself began the installation of the telephones I had

brought from Urumchi, a task which Seng Chen followed with immense curiosity and eager expectation. With three intervening poles I connected the Regent's study with the room in the *yamen* occupied by the *tuslakchi*. The Regent was enraptured, grateful and proud about his new acquisition, but the conservative official on the other hand was less enthusiastic over coming into such close contact with his energetic ruler.

When the Khan had guests, his marvellous new possession had to be demonstrated in the most effective way. Accordingly he announced to his amazed audience that at a time fixed by himself the *tuslakchi* would come into the room without anyone having been sent to fetch him. A ring of the bell ; a few orders on the wire, and there stood the venerable official breathless in the doorway !

The *tuslakchi* had seven children who, after the manner of children, loved forbidden pleasures. The shining telephone with its bell and other mysteries tempted them irresistibly, and the moment they had a chance they threw themselves upon it. The bell rang often in the Regent's room, and when he took up the receiver to listen to his minister's subservient voice he heard only the laughing prattle of children. This happened over and over again, there was a scandal, and the whole pack of children got a whipping. The *tuslakchi* came to me and asked my advice in his trouble, and our conference led to the telephone being moved to a place high up under the ceiling. Then a ladder was made by which the telephone could be reached, and after use the ladder was laid down again on the ground, and its weight was beyond the united forces of the children.

After a few days the *tuslakchi* was a declared opponent of western invention, and one day when the telephone had been ringing unusually often he declared, groaning miserably, that machines and suchlike novelties might be all very well for the westerners but were by no means suited to the nomads.

THERE was a great commotion in Öreget. The women sewed, the soldiers polished their weapons, houses and walls were hung with banners and prayer-flags, and in the temple tents chanting and beating of drums went on more persistently than ever. We were approaching the Mongolian New Year.

And so "the Earth Dragon's year" went out, and "the Iron Snake's year" came in.

Shene Jil, the Mongolian New Year, is ushered in by *tsaghan sar*, the white month, and the year's greatest festivities are celebrated during the first half of that month, when the nomads, chiefs and herdsmen, acclaim the return of light and spring.

On the first day of the New Year a new tent was set up in front of the palace. It was of imposing dimensions, about forty-five feet in diameter, and gleaming white, for the felt which covered its surface was prepared from the wool of young lambs.

Internally the tent was a riot of colour, and through the smoke-vent the New Year sun fell upon glittering gold and silver brocades. Its vast roof was upheld by four red-lacquered pillars. In the background were three canopied thrones, whose antique silken hangings, embroidered with dull gold and silver, were of radiant beauty.

On the largest throne in the centre stood a great silver coffer whose richly ornamented front was fretted with nine openings through which the jewelled golden images of the gods kept inside the coffer were dimly visible. Of the two lesser thrones that on the right was the larger and the more ornate.

The floor of the tent was covered with thick rugs whose colours showed them to be of old Khotan make. Round the inner circuit of the tent stood leather-covered chests. worn and damaged by many and long journeys. Along its walls hung paintings of stern warriors and men in sacred robes. In its middle stood a silver-mounted box guarded by two tall Torguts clad in the ancient dress of the tribe. They held bows and arrows in their hands, and ancient swords were thrust into their girdles.

Nothing in the tent was of recent manufacture ; every object was a treasure inherited from their fathers, and the erection of the tent was an annually recurrent ceremony symbolizing the tribe's adherence to the time-honoured traditions of its fathers.

This was the Khan's tent of the Torguts, and the silver chest on the ground contained the ancient signet of the Khanate.

The place in front of the tent was swarming with Mongols dressed in their gaily coloured holiday attire. The air was full of the hum of voices, and the Torguts leaped about like great children, fell on one another's breasts, bent the knee reverently to their elders and betters only the next moment to slap them heartily on the back. "*Sain shini-lu,*" (a blessed New Year), they shouted at one another, and all were convinced that the New Year would be rich in blessing.

In various places soldiers and secretaries stood to receive the people's New Year's gifts to the Regent. Herdsmen were leading mettlesome horses, mighty oxen and fat sheep, all festally adorned with silken ribbons ; hunters brought precious furs or live *maral* [1] fawns, and the poor brought whatever their tents could afford ; all were gifts to the country's ruler.

A blast on a horn hushed the turmoil and reduced it to a devout silence. Through a thousand-headed crowd of kneeling men Seng Chen stepped slowly out from his palace towards the Khan's tent of the Torguts. He was robed in the sacred garments of a *hutuktu*, and his yellow mantle shone in the sun like hammered gold.

Before him walked two old hunters in simple deerskin dresses. Both carried silver-mounted muzzle-loaders over their shoulders, and costly hunting-gear hung from their belts. These hunters were descendants of two warriors of Obish Khan's bodyguard, and the ancient guns with their appurtenances were a part of Obish Khan's personal war booty from the campaign against the Turks in 1768.

After the Regent came the procession of chiefs and nobles from the various Torgut tribes, *hutuktus*, great lamas and chiefs taking part in his liberation movement, who had come all the way from Tibet and Khalka Mongolia—and " the Consul " from the far north.

---

[1] *Maral*—the Asiatic equivalent of our red deer.

Slowly the festal procession passed through the silent multitude. The sumptuous colours of the dresses shone and burned in the dazzling winter sunlight, the wind played in the peacock-feather plumes of the chiefs and in the fringes of the lamas' gladiatorial helmets.

One by one the lordly men followed Seng Chen into the tent, one after another they made obeisance before the three thrones, first before the gods, next before the ruler of the Torguts and reincarnation of the Seng Chen divinity and last before the young Bichigen Khan, the Torguts' future chief.

And when this ceremony was ended a new bond had been forged between the primitive nomad traditions and the spirit of a new time, between the nomads and their progressive leader.

The ancient tradition is kept up among the Torguts that the first fifteen days of the year are set apart for feasting with the fifteen personages of highest standing, only selected guests being invited to these feasts. And since I now enjoyed the privilege of being invited to these fifteen banquets I was brought by the Regent into touch with all the influential people in that part of the world.

The series of feasts was begun at Seng Chen's on the first day of the new year and ended with the youngest of the tribe's five *gusdä*.

At the appointed time the whole of those invited met in front of the palace, clad in the traditional festival dress of their tribe and rank, and conducted the Regent in festal procession to the house of him who was host for the day. The way was lined with soldiers of the guard.

The host received his guests in the courtyard by the outer gate, and all, according to their spiritual or temporal rank, were brought to their places at the table. No empty bowings of politeness or attempts to depreciate his rank, such as are common in Chinese society, were made by any. Each was tranquilly aware of his own and his neighbour's worth.

The second day's feast was given by Bichigen Khan. The first part of the dinner consisted of Chinese

299

delicacies served on porcelain plates, and with these Chinese or Mongolian spirits were drunk out of jade cups. There were clumsy attempts at Chinese table etiquette, but none of the Mongols was very skilful in manipulating the slender chopsticks. When therefore Seng Chen ordained that every one who lost his grip of his unaccustomed implements should empty his beaker to the bottom it was not long before the mood of the party grew fraternal.

Töin Lama himself and the other lamas present drank only tea, but for all that they were by no means displeased to see their worldly brethren sinking further and further under the table. On the contrary Seng Chen declared with pride that those of the guests who were really thirsty were the true Mongols.

And no doubt he was right.

At last all the Chinese kickshaws were removed, and a mood of expectation spread along the circle of men sitting on their hunkers round the long low table. Some unfastened their fine silk dresses at the neck, others turned back their cloaks from the upper part of their bodies ; the peacock-feathered caps were tossed to the servants, the Chinese chopsticks flung contemptuously aside. Silver-mounted knives were drawn from their belts, and one thought illumined the faces of all, that now there would be something to eat.

The loud conversation sank into a profound silence, and for a while the jade goblets stood untouched. The eyes of all were turned upon the entrance door of the hall. And then came the longed-for moment when the doors were opened wide, and in came servants carrying a vast wooden trough in which lay a sheep boiled whole. The woolly head grinned horribly at us, and the unflayed legs dangled over the edges of the trough. A soldier cut up the reeking mutton into large pieces which were handed round on heavy silver dishes.

And now the real feast began and grew into an orgy of half-raw meat, succeeded by the obligatory belchings. They chewed and they gnawed and enjoyed themselves. The highly salted meat stimulated thirst ; goblets were drained to the bottom ; and the servants ran to fill them again to the brim. Laughter and song alternated with merry tales ; faces shone with mutton fat, wine and happiness.

Sometimes a Torgut would disappear to throw himself whooping and yelling on his horse. Like a wild man he galloped round between the town walls, dreaming that he was out on the wide steppe, that he was riding to victory with the great Jenghiz Khan.

Seng Chen sat upon his yellow cushion and watched his people, and upon his face was an expression of great contentment. Despite the lively mood, which towards the end grew quite uproarious, respect and veneration for the Regent and the other exalted personages were still observed, and I witnessed nothing which even a sober man could not excuse. And to me, the stranger, of another race and creed, they displayed always the greatest cordiality.

AFTER five days' feasting I could bear no more.

I had heard that, at the same time at which the New Year was brought in with feasting by Torgut " society " in Öreget, the victory of Buddha over " the six heresies ", of the true doctrine over the false, was being celebrated at the monastery of Shara Sume a day's journey north of the town.

I rode with Lyrup Geling to the monastery, where we lodged with the prior.

CHAPTER XIV

THE ORIGIN OF THE TORGUTS

S HARA SUME was a stately and well-preserved pile of buildings built upon the southern slopes of a wide valley. The monastery consisted of nine temples surrounded by a jumble of low dwelling-houses in which the lamas had their cells. Their number was estimated at fifteen hundred, but Seng Chen when he took over the government had reduced the number by more than two thirds. He had sent all unlearned and therefore unworthy lamas back to their family tents to resume the nomad life, marry and beget offspring.

Those who remained were all well instructed in one or more of the departments of learning which constitute " the yellow doctrine ", or were masters in some art or craft. Such work had earlier been mainly performed by Chinese, but when Seng Chen came into power he expelled these with the exception of a few who were regarded as particularly skilful, and these he compelled to replace their Chinese pupils with Mongols.

By 1929 there were no Chinese left in the monastery, but the Torgut painters, sculptors and silversmiths who had replaced them were doing more beautiful and more individual work than I had seen anywhere else in Mongolia.

The prior of the monastery was an intelligent and learned high lama who maintained strict monastic discipline, and the idleness usually characteristic of Mongolian monasteries was here replaced by industry and joy in work. Besides the usual theological schools whose written language and text-books are Tibetan, instruction was also given at the monastery in reading and writing in Mongolian, for those of its lamas who possessed these accomplishments, unusual in Mongolia, had each been allotted five boys from among the laity for whose instruction they were responsible.

In the neighbourhood of the monastery the lamas had fenced in a large tract of forest, and it was Seng Chen's intention there to establish a *maral* farm. The hunters had received orders to make their New Year's gifts as far as possible in the form of *maral* fawns, and the stock on the farm now amounted to about fifty animals. The antlers of the *maral* fetch an enormous price from the Chinese who use them in the preparation of medicine for preserving youthful vitality, and it was Seng Chen's idea that the farm would become a valuable source of income to the tribe, without the capital represented by the animals, which were scarce and hard to come by, being diminished by their slaughter. Each spring, when the antlers were new and full of blood, they were to be cut off, and each animal would thus bring in an annual income of upwards of a hundred and twenty *taels*, fifteen to twenty pounds.

DURING our visit to Shara Sume we attended the last of the fifteen sacred readings which introduce the monastic New Year.

At the earliest streak of dawn the hortatory call of the conchs summoned the inmates of the monastery to assemble on the space in front of the chief temple, where they squatted in long rows facing towards the temple. Soon after, the prior arrived followed by the high lamas in gorgeous robes and little novices swinging thuribles.

The prior was assisted to his high seat on the holy chair upon the temple porch, and the novices ranged themselves on either side of it, while the high lamas took their places on yellow cushions laid on the ground in front of the prior.

Dead silence fell upon the great assembly as the prior resumed in a clear and melodious voice the previous day's reading of the lamaistic scriptures. With devout faces the great crowd of lamas listened to his expository comments. There was a complete absence of mystic atmosphere, for the sunlight flooded the hill-sides, and the birds of day were clearly visible in the blue of the winter sky.

The old prior's voice penetrated to the farthest corners of the valley and his speech was in harmony with surrounding nature and with all that is good in humanity. And, sitting there in that gathering of seekers after truth, I was sensible of their mood, and it was one of intense solemnity.

In the afternoon I accompanied the prior on a round of the monastery. The gods of the temples stood in dreaming quietude, and in the cells of the lamas a meditative peace prevailed.

The western quarter of the monastery was occupied by the lamas whose lives were devoted to handicraft. After visiting these craftsmen I began to understand the source of the peculiar beauty and the individual style that characterizes every line of their work. To them the work was an act of religion, the result of their absorption into the spirit of the divinity whose symbol or image they create.

In one cell I found to my amazement a woman, still young, who was busily engaged in embroidering a large silken cloth in wonderfully lovely colours. On my appearance in her solitary cell, an occurrence which must have been highly surprising to her, she raised her head only for a moment, whispered a greeting and at once began with feverish zeal to thread her needle.

All the while she muttered prayers, and the prayer-mill beside her was never allowed to stop. The work she was executing was an image of Tsaghan Dara äkhä, the Goddess of Compassion, and to that divinity she devoted all her thoughts and prayers.

She was of noble family and mistress of one of the tribe's greatest tents. But she was childless, for on the four occasions when she had been with child the powers had slain the living embryo before it was ripe for this world's life.

Now she prayed to the great Mother of Compassion for grace and protection against the affliction that pursued her. All her thoughts and prayers, all her time and strength she offered to the goddess that she might protect

[face p. 304

The Author with Lamaistic Philosophers

the new life which she felt beneath her heart. And her work became a work of art, lovely and individual as a mother's love.

The monastery possessed an ample library which was kept in various temple buildings. The number of the books was immense, and my time was limited, so I had to confine myself to questioning the most widely read lamas as to the titles and contents of the various books, preparatory to trying to discover possible new and interesting manuscripts. But the library seemed to consist of the Tibetan transcripts of sacred books commonly met with in lamaistic monasteries, until a conversation with the prior revealed the existence of an ancient work compiled through the ages by Torgut historians and entitled *Toregut rarelro* (the origin of the Torguts). This work like many other ancient Torgut manuscripts was held by the tribe in an almost religious veneration, and only a chosen few had access to the pavilion in which it was kept.

The origin of the Torguts !

Never had I heard or read of the existence of this manuscript, and I determined to try to obtain permission to study its contents.

That same afternoon Lyrup set out for Öreget to obtain the Regent's sanction for my admission to the repository of the manuscript. Two days later he returned with my permit and brought with him Lodong who was specially skilled in deciphering manuscripts.

TOREGUT RARELRO consisted of a collection of loose leaves of a kind of shantung which lay packed between two richly carved and painted slabs of wood, which in their turn were wrapped in several layers of leather and brocade. The leaves, six by fifteen and three-quarters inches in size, were written in Torgut script in black and red, and the chronicle had evidently been recorded by various persons and at different times. The writing of the introductory leaves was faded and hard to read, but one could nevertheless form the conclusion, from the tone of the introductory words, that the writer had been a lama.

For days on end we now sat bent over these records of legend and historic fact set down by industrious monks through the ages and, like a Torgut Edda, bringing to posterity tidings of a dim and distant past.

We read of the remote ancestor of the Torgut Khan dynasty who had migrated northward from India before the birth of Christ, of the roving and chequered life of his descendants and of the source of the tribe's name: Torgut, (the stately ones).

The introduction in *Toregut rarelro* to the account of the reigning dynasty from Geril Däre Khan to the sons of Shykyr Daichin, between whom the Torgut horde was apportioned in the still existing tribal divisions, reads as follows :

TOREGUT RARELRO

Om, sain amorolan boltora (O that fortune may continue)

Inspired by the life of the three worlds and Lama nome'en Khan Bogdo Tson Khapa I insignificantly meditate and acquire strength to write this book which contains the family tree of the *khochin* (old) and *shene* (new) Torguts' Khan noyen.

In Enet-keghien oron-etse (India) was born Geril Däre Khan (Khan of supreme radiance). He later travelled to Sinanfu [1] where Khara kitad lived.

There " he captured " the golden signet and became Khan. Before that happened Khara kitad had had no Khan or *noyen*. For many many years after Khara kitad was ruled by his descendants and one of these bore the name of Naren Khan (The Sun Khan).

Naren Khan had thirty sons, and the eldest became Tangman Khan who also had many sons, and one of these was On-Tas.

On-Tas had contentions at home and left his homeland with nine followers. After long journeying On-Tas came with his following to his mother's elder brother Gramin Khan who ruled in Mörindäva.

Gramin Khan gave On-Tas many people to rule.

On-Tas dwelt there for many years, after which he determined to travel out among the Mongols and came to Jenghiz Khan.

Jenghiz Khan gave On-Tas his daughter and many people to rule, and On-Tas took up his abode in Böge Mörin.

[1] Sinanfu—probably means Sianfu.

Three generations of On-Tas ruled there, and the fourth descendant was Kibving Noyen.

Kibving Noyen sent Tushure with five others of his men to the Öret Khanate to see whether it was good land.

When Toro Taiji Khan of Öret saw Kibving Noyen's six messengers he burst out : " *Önge, biye sahan tanar yun iche turelluk biyetai sahan olos bie* " (What tall and stately men you are).

From the word *turelluk* (tall, stately) came later the word *toregut*.

Toro Taiji gave his daughter to Kibving and two hundred and fifty tents for him to rule over.

The two hundred and fifty later became many, and Durebet Öret (the four Öret) later became one.

The family tree of the Khans from Geril Däre is not written here but is among the archives of Khara kitad.

Geril Däre Khan was very mighty and pious, and his descendants reign to this day.

Kibving Noyen became Wang Khan.

His eldest son was Boro Örölok Khan, and his son was Shykyr Daichin who had many sons.

The eldest was Toregut Khan, and the rest were

Khobok Saïri Chin Wang,

Taburn Notog (Khara Ossun) Jy Wang.

Dööner Beile

Taburn Notog Beise.

Dööner Gyn.

Khobok Saïri Taiji, two.

Dööner Taiji.

Etsini Beile.

Wang Khan's fifth son Losang became Jingin Beile and his son Oskhon Chabchin became Altai Jy Wang.

One of Oskhon Chabchin's sons became Altai Beise.

AMONG the ancient manuscripts in the locked pavilion there was also a short bamboo tube in the hollow of which was a rolled-up document in Chinese and Mongolian text. It contains the Manchu Emperor's invitation to the Torguts by the Volga to return to their ancestral steppes in Dzungaria. It was the actual secret document which was sent by the Emperor K'ang Hsi in 1714 with a mission from Peking to the steppes by the Volga, the mission which the Caroline J. Chr. Schnitscher accompanied from Tomsk to Ayuk Khan's camp at Saratov.

To read through only the most interesting of the manuscripts at Shara Sume would be the labour of years, and I had but eight days at my disposal. It was hard to tear myself away, but was made possible by my determination to return later to the monastery and resume the fascinating study.

WHEN we got back to Öreget the magnificent Khan's tent had disappeared from the place in front of the Regent's palace.

I had not been able closely to examine the treasures of the tent during the New Year's feast days, but when I now asked permission to photograph the interesting objects, I was taken to their repository, a large room on the upper floor of the palace of whose existence I had hitherto been unaware.

The room was fitted up as a museum of objects to which tradition ascribed a connection with the departed Khans of the Torgut ruling dynasty. On the walls hung paintings of the chiefs of former times, beginning with Obish Khan himself, the leader whose memory the nomads still extol. Written accounts exist, both Asiatic and European, of Obish Khan's person and life-story, but, so far as I know, the picture which I photographed at Öreget is the only extant portrait of the great nomad leader.

Underneath this painting were displayed in miniature on the one side the portrait painter and on the other the Khan's biographer, both engaged on their respective tasks.

After six paintings of Seng Chen's forefathers comes the first photograph in the gallery, representing Seng Chen's father Tu-yen Meng-ku who in his youth performed a pilgrimage to a Buryat monastery. The photograph was taken by a Russian Buryat and shows the Khan in the holy robe of a penitent. Tu-yen Meng-ku, who assumed the Khanate in 1891, was succeeded by his son, who in turn was succeeded by his brother, the present Regent, in 1920.

In the museum there was also the silver-mounted box in which the signet of the Torgut Khanate was preserved. The signet was presented to Obish Khan in

1776 by the Manchu Emperor Chi'en Lung in exchange for an earlier one received from the Ming dynasty. Seng Chen himself unpacked the symbol of his authority from its many wrappings of silk and brocade. The handle of the heavy seal, which was all of pure silver, represented a lion, and the face of it, six and three-quarters inches square, was engraved with Chinese and Mongolian inscriptions.

One whole wall on the farther side of the room was occupied by bows, arrows, knives, muzzle-loaders and heavy swords, and the place of honour among these ancestral weapons was given to two silver-mounted muskets which had been booty taken by Obish Khan from the Turks.

Assisted by both the *chanse* and the two helpful Tibetans I resumed the labours which had been interrupted by the New Year celebrations. Lyrup and Lodong made neat fair copies of the scribbled transcriptions of manuscripts which we had brought from Shara Sume, while I, under the direction of Doreche and Lobson, recorded the appellations and the symbolic significance of all the sacred objects in *gegen-ni-ordo*.

During the course of the three seasons which I spent as the guest of the Torguts I was constantly in the company of these four young Asiatics, and the relationship between us deepened and ripened into sincere friendship. All four were irresistible in the intensity of their convictions. Lodong and Lyrup wished by means of the currents of the new era to find a path which might lead their people towards a brilliant future, and Doreche and Lobson had all the true believer's devotion for their exalted master and his teaching.

I found in them all an uncorrupted simplicity—the widest of all human horizons—and I venture to assert that I won a friendship beautiful and true as a memory of childhood.

I regularly spent the evening hours with the Regent. The photograph I had brought of Sven Hedin fraternally pressing the hand of Panchen Bogdo himself interested Seng Chen enormously and led us to a new evening entertainment. I translated into Mongolian the chapter in

Sven Hedin's book which describes his visit to the pontiff at Tashi-Lhumpo twenty years earlier. And the circumstance that his divine brother and my chief were united in the bonds of old friendship was, in Seng Chen's eyes, sufficient evidence of the lofty purpose of our whole expedition.

The Regent now began to devote more and more of his time to superintending the work upon the temple tent. We worked with feverish zeal, for my stay among the Torguts might at any moment come to the knowledge of the Chinese authorities, and this would certainly lead to my recall to Urumchi.

But the weeks went by without interruption, and the work was nearing its completion. The women combined smooth silk and glittering brocades in symbolic patterns, accomplished lamas painted temple banners and prayer-flags, and the Regent's personal *darkhan*[1] hammered copper and silver into pots and sacrificial vessels. Every detail was carefully carried out, and the industry and achievement of the craftsmen were worthy of the promised payment.

Nevertheless the new *gegen-ni-ordo* was a disappointment to me. The copy had none of the atmosphere of its prototype, and this was not to be bought for money. The sharp brush strokes of the symbolic paintings lacked the warm patina of time, the hammer marks on the metal objects had not been worn by the hands of the faithful, the fragrance of incense, the flames of the lamps and the fervent prayers of mankind had not breathed life into the altar's images of gods. The temple was an article admirably executed for export, cold and stripped of the profound significance of its original.

It was then that I conceived the bold idea of trying to acquire the ancient sanctuary in exchange for the copy, and I cautiously sounded my friends Lodong and Lyrup. But they assured me that this was impossible, since an unconsecrated person may not take charge of a consecrated temple, far less carry it away to a country outside the lamaistic world.

But the gods of Asia were once more to smile upon me.

[1] *Darkhan*—craftsman, originally smith.

CHAPTER XV

OCCULTISM IN A TEMPLE TENT

IN the course of a night ride across the ice-covered
surface of Lake Bagrash-Köl I had lost my companion and for his guidance had set fire to a reed
bed which stuck up through the ice. Worn out with
weariness and cold I went to sleep close by the burnt-
out but still glowing remains of the fire and awoke to
find that the heat had scorched and charred a third
part of my big wolfskin coat.

On my return to Öreget my burnt coat aroused far
more remark than I was able to explain, and to my
amazement my Tibetan friends carried the coat away
after having closely examined its damaged part.

The hardships of the preceding twenty-four hours
sent me early to bed, but in the depth of the night I
awoke to see Lobson Geling by my side. He was sitting
crouched over the glow of the brazier, and its feeble
light picked out his face as an amber yellow mask against
the formless gloom of the surroundings.

Dazed with sleep I sat up in my sleeping-sack, a
confused question on my lips.

"Dress yourself in Asiatic clothing," whispered the
yellow mask, "for you will soon be summoned. Gegen
and his mystical adepts are at this moment divining
your destiny in accordance with the will of the gods.
Listen!"

The hollow thud of drums sounded from somewhere,
the strident note of some instrument was born and
died away like the howl of the night storm across the
steppe. I dressed hurriedly and sat down beside the
Tibetan, but all his senses were lost in listening to the
sounds of the night, and he left my wondering questions
unanswered.

The moment the pulsation of the drums ceased out there Lobson bade me follow him. In silence we walked towards the enclosure of the seven tents. The night was pitch dark ; only here and there a pale star peeped through the storm-torn clouds. We passed six sleeping tents, but strange sounds came from *yude-yin-ordo*, and a cone of light rose from the roof-opening of the sanctuary.

Then I followed my guide in through the tent door and set foot in the dim temple of the *tantra* cult. The air was thick with incense, and the dark mysticism of Central Asia closed in about me. In the restless light from the fire and the oil lamps I caught glimpses, through misty veils of smoke and incense, of the room's astounding colours.

In the middle of the tent, behind the crackling fire, sat Seng Chen between the two lama astrologers, and I was conducted to the place opposite to him, so that the circle was completed. On the floor between us lay my burnt wolfskin coat.

Yellow-clad lamas sat round the inner circuit of the tent. Their chanting voices rose and fell in monotonous cadences whose dreary rhythm was drowned time after time by the rumble of the drums. The temple banners swayed slowly with the movement of waves of hot air, and their awe-inspiring images of gods glared malignantly through billowing clouds of smoke.

The three holy men sat long, intent upon the holes and wrinkles in my scorched wolfskin, and, muttering prayers, they passed their fingers softly over the burnt fur. Time after time they exchanged glances of common understanding.

Incense was thrown on the fire, which sent up clouds, soot-black, silver-white and rust-red.

Gegen and the astrologers straightened themselves up from their crouching position, the lamas fell silent and the orchestra's infernal discord ceased. For a while the three holy men gazed at me, but impersonally and absently as though they saw me not. Then their strained and sweating faces lighted up with friendly smiles and their kind glances met my astonished eyes.

312

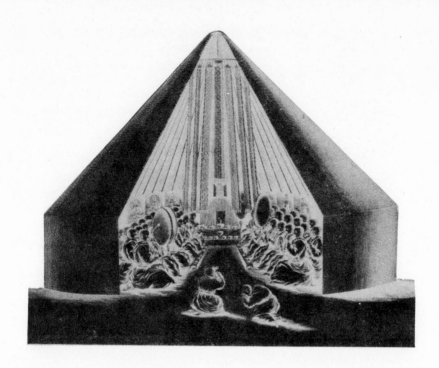

"Baredo soldep" (Tibetan prayer)

[face p. 312

And then the elder lama astrologer spoke :

" This night we have interpreted the writing of the fire upon your wolfskin. We have found many propitious signs which confirm what we have long surmised.

" It is not by chance that our *gegen's* Tibetan name Seng Chen and your Mongolian name Arselan both signify ' The Tiger '.

" It is not by chance that our time's incarnation of Seng Chen and your body were both born under the sign of ' the sacred monkey '.

" And it is a sign from the higher powers that the deformity which from birth distinguishes the earthly reincarnations of Seng Chen the Tiger god, has been laid as a shadow over your left knee.

" That which we have now divined provides the confirmation of what the Allknowing Yolros Lama long ago foresaw, for the meeting between Seng Chen and Arselan is a link in Yolros Lama's prophecy of Zayagan.[1]

" Seng Chen and Arselan are foreordained by the gods as *akha-due*,[2] and Destiny has brought your earthly paths together here that the will of the gods may have an earthly ratification."

A lama glided forward to our circle, carrying a smoking incense dish which he placed on the wolfskin round which we were standing. The bottom of the flat dish was covered with embers from which an ash-grey column of smoke and a heavy, stupefying odour arose. Two long incense sticks lay on the wide rim of the

---

[1] This is the only instance of divination by the effect of fire and heat upon skin that I know of in Mongolia. A method of solving the riddles of the future much practised among the Mongols is to study the lines and fissures produced by the heat upon an animal's shoulder-blade laid in the embers of a fire, and in Northern Mongolia I once saw a lama practise divination from the burnt remains of a Russian settler's house. Probably these forms of divination are relics surviving from the nomads' ancient fire cult.

[2] *Akha* is the Mongolian word for an elder brother ; *due* denotes a younger brother. *Akha-due* is a bond of friendship entered into between two men and may be compared with the Nordic *fostbrödralag* (sworn brotherhood).

dish, and Seng Chen thrust the ends of these into the embers.

The circle of yellow lamas had resumed their chanting, but they now crooned their ritual quite softly, and the drums were silent.

Then the old lama on my right grasped my left wrist and rolled back my wide Mongolian sleeve to the elbow. At the same time the lama on my left took up one of the lighted incense sticks and lightly placed its tip upon the inner side of my bared forearm.

The procedure was inexplicable to me, but I saw from the friendly faces of the lamas that they wished me no ill. At first I felt nothing, but after a nerve-racking eternity, which perhaps was a matter of seconds, I became aware of a slight tingling sensation where the glowing point touched my bare skin. The irritation gave way to acute pain, and there was a smell of burnt flesh. I contracted my muscles and began to count, and when I reached nine I wrenched my arm away.

The wound burned, smarted and throbbed while the lamas narrowly examined its character, but they gravely shook their heads, and I must needs again go through the same procedure. This time the incense stick was placed more firmly and against a more fleshy spot two inches above the first, and I had to contract my muscles harder and count louder, for this time my arm was held steadily in the grip of strong hands.

My second burn turned out to the satisfaction of the lamas. They nodded amiably, anointed my arm with oil and wrapped it in wadding and linen.

A gleam of dawn stole in through the roof opening, and the mystery of the tent evaporated before the blue-green reality of daybreak.

Stupefied and bewildered I followed Lobson out into the early morning. Like a sleep-walker I reached my room. From the temple of the mysteries still sounded the braying of bassoons, the clash of cymbals and the hollow thud of drums.

" Now you are an initiate," I heard the Tibetan say. " You are one of us."

My last visual impression before I fell asleep was of

Lobson. Again he was sitting by the brazier, but now his smiling face and the whole room lay in the clear light of the morning sun.

WHEN the ringing bugle-call from the guard on the town wall announced the setting of the sun I awoke out of my trance. Insane dreams stuck to my brain, but the bandage round my arm and the pain I felt at every movement convinced me that the nightmares had a substratum of reality.

Ravenous as a desert wolf I bellowed for food, and to my surprise my summons was obeyed not only by the friendly Torgut attendants but also by my two Chinese, whom I had not seen for a long time. Lao Chang and Suidör were in ecstacies over the prospect of departure, for the Regent had given them orders to get ready for our start. In their eyes the Torguts were not bad as Mongols went, but the Chinese quarter of Urumchi beckoned to them with all that is dear to a Chinaman's heart.

The report of the Chinese was confirmed later in the evening by my four Asiatic friends. Yes, I was to go. I was to return to the west, and the two astrologers had said that I must hasten both my departure and my return.

Lobson conducted me to Seng Chen who on our entrance ordered his guard and his servants to leave the room, and Lobson too withdrew. It was the first time during the whole of my stay in Öreget that I had been alone with the holy man. He was attired in the garb of a Living Buddha, the sumptuous folds and blazing colours of which looked incongruous among the sober European appointments of the room.

That night Seng Chen gave me his confidence and threw open to me the storehouse of his mind. His dreams, hopes and view of life seemed to me to throw light upon two sides of the *hutuktu's* complex personality, sides as dissimilar as spring and autumn and both authentic as the alternations of nature.

Profoundly conscious of his divine calling, Seng Chen spoke of the sublimity of life and of the world-embracing mission for which he had been reincarnated. But he spoke also with the joy in life of a man still young of his longing for new experiences, and the degree to which his heart was set on satisfying his curiosity about the great world beyond the steppes seemed a little pathetic in his Central Asiatic isolation.

He explained to me in detail the happenings of the previous night and laid stress on their importance to us both. Our life paths had crossed each other here because it was the will of the gods that we should stand by one another. He knew my wishes, and through him they should be fulfilled, for my wishes accorded with his mission.

" It is not the new copy of our temple that you shall take to the West, for the worth of this is only the worth of metals and stuffs and their fashioning. No, it is the consecrated sanctuary itself, whose gods inspire mankind's highest and noblest thoughts, that you shall carry with you, and its worth cannot be sold or bought with earthly money.

" You shall carry *gegen-ni-ordo* to the Khan of the Swedes as a gift from Seng Chen Doryechan, with messages from a divinity of Buddhism and from the nomads of the steppes to the people in whose midst Panchen Bogdo shall one day be reborn.

" There is need of haste for your departure and there is need of haste for your return, for other tasks await us which require our co-operation—and my days are numbered."

Eagerly he planned in detail the transport of the temple and its erection in that distant land. So that the sanctuary might remain as long as possible under the blessing of his influence and protection, his lamas and soldiers should carry it to our expedition's headquarters, and Lyrup Geling should accompany it until we were out of Chinese territory. To avoid the attention of the Chinese *amban* in Khara Shar the temple and my caravan were to travel to Urumchi by different routes.

Seng Chen foresaw with stoical resignation the violent end of his existence, for the astrologers had foretold that he would meet the same fate as his spiritual pre-

316

decessor. But before this he wished to see the world that lay outside the steppes. When I returned I was to take him out into the wide world, so that, like the Khan of the Afghans, he might be able to possess himself of the western learning which might give strength to his people.

After that he would place at my disposal men and camels for expeditions which should bring to the West new knowledge of the nomads and therewith understanding of the truths which alone bring blessing. He would unveil for me the profoundest learning of the Torguts.

We talked long of East and West, and it was wonderful how well they met.

I WENT blissfully to bed, for now I had reached the goal of my dreams.

This was Zayagan.

CHAPTER XVI

FAREWELL

THEN came the day for my departure from Öreget and farewell to the people whose life I had shared through autumn and winter.

And now it was spring.

The birds of passage had begun their yearly flight to the north, and the rustle of their wings was the song of the roving instinct that goads us towards new goals. The sun smiled, and with the spring the people of the steppe awoke to song of verdant steppe and thriving cattle and love between man and woman.

I WENT to Seng Chen to say farewell and try to express the gratitude I felt. When I left his room he followed me over the threshold, and, contrary to the etiquette of his rank, the ruler accompanied me right up to the caravan's starting-point by the southern gate in the outer wall of the town.

Our ten pack-horses were heavily laden with boxes and saddle-bags containing the results of the winter's work, and Buran my saddle-horse was carrying an empty packsaddle in place of my usual riding-saddle. Round our group thronged friends and well wishers. Servants brought parting gifts, which were presented with great ceremony and loaded on Buran, and when the gifts became so many as to exceed the horse's capacity, Seng Chen at once presented me with a new pack-horse.

Among the gifts were objects which I had long coveted but which I had scrupled to try to acquire. The old *tuslakchi* brought his family prayer-mill. It was heavy with silver and richly fashioned, and the texts in its interior meant blessing and protection to him and his descendants. Lobson Geling put a silver-mounted brace-

318

let on my arm. It was formed of a coarse grass from one of the most sacred mountains of Tibet, and it protected its wearer from dangers and the infirmities of old age.

And then came the Regent's personal parting gifts. A soldier stepped forward with an ancient weapon, and Seng Chen handed it to me. It was one of the two muskets which his ancestor Obish Khan had taken as war booty from the Turks. A new wolfskin coat was hanging on the soldier's other arm, and this too was loaded on Buran. Then came soldiers leading a magnificent horse, and the animal was carrying my saddle. It was one of the Torguts' most famous horses, *Erekenchi bichigen sharara* [1] (the little dun with lively ears).

The caravan set out in the direction of Bagrash-köl, and the circle of leave-takers closed up round me and Lyrup. Just as I put my foot into the stirrup to mount my new horse the Torguts struck up their farewell song. The *tuslakchi* improvised about the steppes and their wildness, about splendid horses and about storm-blown clouds, and at the end of every verse the rest joined in in a tribute to my horse who was the incarnation of all whose praises had been sung.

" EREKENCHI BICHIGEN SHARARA."

Erekenchi bichigen sharara snorted and pawed the ground, while the *tuslakchi* continued the song with

[1] The name is a Mongolian expression denoting that the horse possesses strength and spirit.

wishes for good fortune on the journey to new goals. It was no longer possible to hold in "the little dun", and we rode at full gallop after the receding caravan.

A veil of sprouting verdure lay over the drab carpet of the steppe, and chalk-white glacier water from the mountains was bubbling in the brooks. The flocks, dingy and emaciated after the winter, had a white sprink-ling of playful lambs, the cows were heavy uddered, and one could count the mares in foal.

Over the western shores of Bagrash-köl screaming lapwings and mandarin ducks were circling in search of breeding-places, and the lark rose towards milk-white clouds to drop like a stone again to guard its nest.

Buran was too restive for his lifeless load, so Lyrup took him in exchange for his own gentle pacer. In the course of the day's march we often parted company with the slow-moving caravan to visit the scattered camps on steppe and mountain. Everywhere they were preparing to break camp. The hunters had exchanged rifles for lassos, and in the tents the women were stitch-ing boots for a new batch of Torgut youngsters now ready for their first ride.

Then we came to the pass from whose summit one hails and bids farewell to the land of the Torguts. Lyrup pointed out the loved mountain peaks of his own country, and I imprinted on my mind a last memory picture of the world in which I had enjoyed so much happiness.

The expedition's headquarters at Urumchi lay almost deserted. Sven Hedin and Hummel were in the United States to arouse new interest in our researches and so make possible the continued existence of the expedition ; some of our friends were still out in their respective fields of labour, but most of the members of the great expedition had gone home. At headquarters there were only the convalescent Ambolt, whose Scanian humour had completely survived his long illness, and the mechanic A. Carlson, who was watching by his sick-bed.

On arriving at Urumchi I at once telegraphed to Stockholm for instructions concerning the temple and

Corner of *Gegen-ni-ordo* after its erection in Stockholm

Photo Sv. D.

[*face p* 320

Interior of *gegen-ni-ordo* o

The three Thrones in the Khan's Tent of the Torguts

its erection in Urumchi

" Tsagachin Beile often appeared in an ill-fitting Russian costume "

Baldan *Gusdä*

[*face p.* 321

presently received orders to convey it as soon as possible to its destination.

And then came the day when the caravan with the temple filed in to the expedition's courtyard. The leader of the caravan was the stern Baldan *gusdä*, and the twenty camels were conducted by six Torgut soldiers. Behind the caravan rode four red-clad lamas whose task it was to attend the temple's gods with prayers until the moment when they were delivered into my charge.

Seng Chen had given orders that the tent temple was to be erected in our quarters under my superintendence, so that the four lamas might make certain that, on its coming installation in a foreign land, all the gods and sacred objects would be put in their right places.

For five days and nights the lamas performed divine service in the sanctuary, and during those days our headquarters were a goal of pilgrimage for Tsagechin Beile and his people as well as for many other Mongols in the neighbourhood who, in their flight from their home steppes, when these were occupied by the Soviet, had lost both their temples and the means to replace them.

As soon as I had obtained the Governor's permission to leave Sinkiang with my collections I equipped myself for a fresh start.

The first stages of our twelve days' journey were the slowest, for at every sixth mile Baldan *gusdä* turned up with his six soldiers to say good-bye and welcome again to Öreget. The thirsty nomad had, with the best intentions, brought with him from Urumchi a supply of Caucasian wine and capacious goblets which we had to empty in token of friendship at each farewell. After three days the last of the many bottles was empty, and Baldan *gusdä* was able with a clear conscience to gallop back to distant Tsoltus to inform his ruler that the guest of the Torguts had been given both a cordial and a happy send off.

We were now in old Dzungaria, on the steppes which had produced Tsewang Raptan and his wild following and had once known the West Mongols' period of greatness. Hither it was that Brigitta and the Caroline Renat were brought as slaves of the Mongols; here they had endured seventeen years of hardship among savage barbarians, but had also gained the nomads easily won affection for what is in their charge.

We marched through an infinity of featureless steppes. The tents had disappeared with the extinct Dzungars. The lush May grass waved before the steppe wind, but the abundant herds had vanished. The marmots sat by their burrows and squeaked with surprise at seeing human beings, and flying herds of antelope sent our thoughts straying far afield.

The heavy caravan worked its way slowly to the north. May passed into June, and the steppe decked itself with blue iris.

One day we were overtaken by twenty galloping Torguts. They were lusty youths on spirited horses wild with the delight of speed across limitless steppes. They checked their course for a while to exchange gay greetings and inquisitive questions, and though we had never seen one another before we were soon like old acquaintances.

They muttered hasty prayers before the sacred burden of my caravan, extolled the goodness and wisdom of Seng Chen and smiled at me. They were Torguts from Khara Ossun on their way to meet their princess. And their princess was almost akin to me, for she had lived many years among my people and was now in possession of all the wonderful knowledge of the white race. Now at last she was coming back to the grazing-grounds and the people she had left as a child, and they had been sent to welcome her. The horses curveted, and the twenty riders resumed their gallop, riding to meet their princess.

What was all this about a princess, I asked Lyrup. Did I not know? Nirgitma of the Torguts was expected back on the steppes from the land of the Franks.

Nirgitma of the Torguts, that was of course her whom Seng Chen had so often quoted and of whom I had heard in the tents so many unbelievable things that I had come to regard her as a figment of the imagination, the Mongolian girl who spoke the language of the West and whose qualities had made her a legendary figure on the steppes.

The same evening we came, dripping with sweat and dusty, to the frontier town of Chugochak where I was to experience a marvellous encounter. She, Nirgitma of the Torguts, was a slender young woman whose exquisite Parisian clothes looked exotic against her dark Mongolian beauty.

It was only two days since she had left the wagon-lit that she had boarded in Brussels, and her speech and bearing had been formed by seven years of university study and life in European capitals.

As many years of nomadic life lay behind me.

And so it came about that we sat there giving one another widely separated impressions from East and West—but it was she who brought news from my world in the West and I who told of the unchanging steppes from which she sprang.

Our environment was the sun-drenched courtyard of an Asiatic *sarai* with horses, asses, camels and caravan people coming and going.

She had a complete and elegant command of the speech of western culture and to all my questions she had apt answers. For fourteen hours we talked, and, as the hours went by, her speech slipped more and more into Mongolian lines of thought. When we separated to go to the starting-places of our respective caravans we had long been in Mongolia, and our farewell words were spoken in Mongolian.

LYRUP blessed my caravan's holy burden, and at parting his eyes were full of tears.

And I too must part from my horses, for the galloping steppe days were over, and motor-cars, trains and steamboats awaited me. As I was fondling Buran, who had carried me so many hundreds of miles through the wide spaces of Mongolia, I was seized with a desire to assure him a safe future. I knew what fate continued life with the expedition might bring, and I felt how happy a horse-existence would be his if he became one of a rich Mongol's herd of thousands.

So Buran was my parting gift to the Torgut princess, and I entrusted "The little dun" to Lyrup's keeping until I should return to the steppes.

Chinese soldiers conducted me across the half-mile strip of no-man's-land which constitutes the boundary, to the Russian outposts, and two days before midsummer I was in my native country which I had not seen for seven years.

In August *gegen-ni-ordo* had been set up in Stockholm, and on the eighth of September the ceremony took place at which Sven Hedin delivered Seng Chen's gift to His Majesty King Gustaf V.[1]   The King in acknowledgment created the Regent of the Torguts a Commander of the Royal Vasa Order.

The commission entrusted to me by Seng Chen was accomplished.

[1] The tent temple was later handed over by the King to the Ethnographical Museum.

THE same autumn I was again on my way to the steppes. But I was never to reach the land of the Torguts. This time I started from India, but one of the black panthers of the Himalayas stood as an obstacle in my path.

Again I started from Kashmir, despite the warnings of my lamaistic companion, and on the thirteenth of January, 1931, came the avalanche which forced me to go back to Europe.

Zayagan had left me, "for," said my caravan men, "we had tried to go to the eastward although Yolros Lama had foretold that the path of the sun was the way of my fortune."

THEN came the years on a sick-bed during which I often received news and greetings from Seng Chen and his men.

In the beginning of 1932 the good news ceased, and then came the information through Princess Nirgitma that the Torguts' proud dreams of the future had been crushed.

A movement of revolt against the Chinese provincial government had arisen among the Mohammedan population of Sinkiang. The Governor invited Seng Chen to Urumchi in order, as he pretended, to discuss with him the suppression of the revolt. Seng Chen arrived surrounded by his most powerful chiefs, but no discussion ever took place. For after the first day's banquet, as the Torguts sat drinking tea in the Governor's *yamen*, he had the whole of the guests shot from behind by his servants.

IN consequence of the shortsightedness of an incompetent administration many able and innocent persons

325

were lost to the world, and a noble and humane aspiration was changed into meaningless chaos.

The leader of the Torguts, Seng Chen, Mongrolda Noyen, Baldan Gusdä, Lodong and Lyrup—all are gone now. The people, formerly so well disciplined, whose influence and firm organization had hitherto so strongly contributed to the maintenance of the balance between the many different races of Central Asia has been transformed into a ravaging horde, thirsting for vengeance. After having driven out the murderers, who were obliged to flee the country disguised as coolies, the Torguts withdrew to the mountains and are now completely indifferent to Central Asia's political future.

SINCE that time I have only received intelligence from Sinkiang through such members of the expedition as have returned later, and what they have to tell of conditions there is disheartening.

My friends also relate that the Torguts have proclaimed my Buran the reincarnation of an Exalted One and that he now belongs to the sacred horse herd of the monastery of Shara Sume.

AND I rejoice when I think of Buran galloping unsaddled over the luxuriant high steppes of Tsoltus.

AUTHORITIES

Baddeley, *Russia, Mongolia, China.* 1919.
Buddhist Catechism, ed. by H. S. Olcott. Madras, 1915.
Buxton, L. H. Dudley, *The Peoples of Asia.* London, 1925.
Consten, Hermann, *Weideplatze der Mongolen im Reiche der Chalcha.* I–II. Berlin, 1919.
de Quincey, Th., *Revolt of the Tartars,* ed. by Ch. S. Baldwin. New York, 1898.
Filchner, Wilhelm, *Kumbum Dschambaling.* Leipzig, 1933.
Grünwedel, Albert, *Mythologie des Buddhismus in Tibet und der Mongolei.* Leipzig, 1900.
Kaarsberg, Hans S., *Gjennem Stepperne.* Köpenhamn, 1892.
Kawaguchi, Ekai, *Three Years in Tibet.* Madras, 1909.
Korostovetz, I. J. *Von Cinggis Khan zur Sowjetrepublik.* Berlin and Leipzig, 1926.
Kozlow, P. K., *Zur Toten Stadt Chara-Choto.* Berlin, 1925.
Lattimore, Owen, *The Desert Road to Turkestan.* London, 1928.
Leder, Hans, *Das geheimnisvolle Tibet.* Leipzig, 1909.
Orientalische Reisebeschreibung, von Jürgen Andersen. Hrsg. von Adam Olearius. Schleswig, 1669.
Parker, E. H., *A Thousand Years of the Tartars.* London, 1924.
Polo, Marco, *Travels.* London, 1925.
Prschevalski, N. M., *Explorations in Central Asia.* Edited by Sven Hedin. Stockholm, 1891.
Riasanovsky, V. A., *Customary Law of the Mongol Tribes.* I–III. Harbin, 1929.
Schnitscher, J. Chr., *Berättelse om Ajuckiniska Calmuckiet.* Stockholm, 1744.
Toregut Rarelro. Mongolian manuscript.
Waddell, L. A., *The Buddhism of Tibet.* Cambridge, 1934.
— *Lhasa and its Mysteries.* London, 1905.

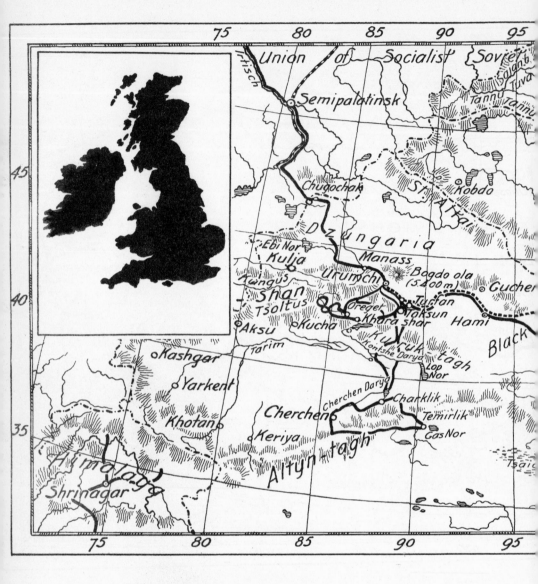

Scale : 1 _ 12,000,000.

Inset Great Britain on the same scale.

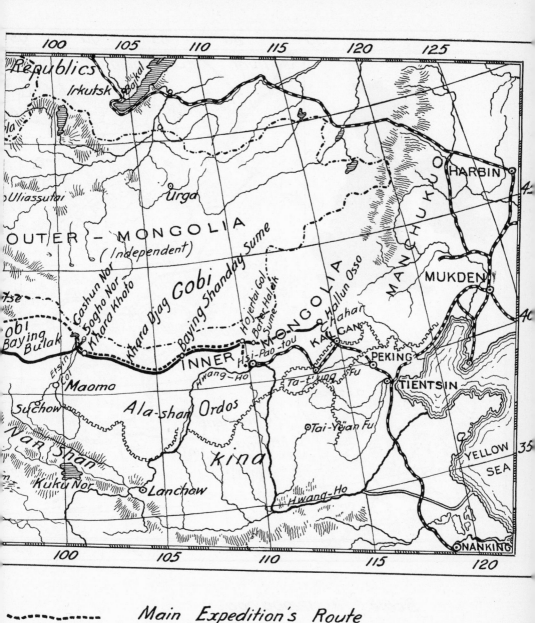

Main Expedition's Route
Route of the Author's Journeys 1927-1930

INDEX

Abatai, first Mongolian monastery erected by, 284

Abdal, oasis of, 184

Adultery, law regarding, in *Yassa* and *Tsächin Bichik* contrasted, 266

Afghanistan, ruler of, 246

Aimak, 120 ; division into *hoshun* (banners) (footnote), 120 ; Mongolian denomination for chief's territory (footnote), 120 ; four, transference and present residence of, 264

Air-horse painted on prayer-flag, 223, 225

Akha-due, meaning of (footnote), 313

Alcohol, modern Kalmucks victims of, 215

Alkaline water, thirst accentuated by drinking, 75

Altai Gegen, 218

— (*hutuktu*), meeting with, 199 ; sheep given in compensation by Yetum presented to, 199 ; caravan of, overtaken, 201 ; confessions made to, by Yetum, 202

— Mountains, 167, 279 ; descendants of original Dzungarian Khoshut tribe living among, 200

Altan Khan-grän gruregroldä (golden bird of imagination), 292

Altyn-tagh mountains, 182, 185

Amanullah, ruler of Afghanistan, 246

Amblers, exported by Torguts, 241

Ambolt, convalescence of, 320

Amitabha, 250 ; reincarnation of, 232

— Buddha, 4

Amu Khatun (Queen), wife of Galdan, 206 ; slain in battle while fighting, 206

Amulets, dug up from desert, 110

Amursana, Dambin Jansang descendant of, 154 ; Dambin Jansang, incarnation on earth of, 165 ; Ölet chieftain, 207 ; exploits of, still extolled, 207 ; war of liberation of West Mongols against Chinese conducted by, 207

Amyot, Father (French Jesuit), on Chinese Emperor's account of his reception of returned Torguts, 214

Andersson, Professor J. G., 12

Anglo-Indian Force at Lhasa (1904), Töin Lama's admiration at conduct of, 254

Antelope herd, superstitious belief regarding, 22, 23

— herds, ravages among, from wild animals at calving-time, 22

Antelopes, herds of, on steppe, 20

— yellow, of steppes, calving-time of, 22

Anthropometric measurements : of Mongols, attempts at, 33 ; success in obtaining, 61 ; of band of ex-robbers, 64, 65 ; of Etsina Torguts, 121 ; carried out among Däde Mongols, 199 ; of Torguts, 235

INDEX

Chinese (*continued*)—
  among the nomads by, 268 ;
  immense price obtained from,
  for *maral* antlers, 303
— army, Khara Khoto besieged
  by, 107, 108
— authorities, search for Haslund, 270
— Colonial Ministry, Ordinances
  of (1789, 1815), 267, 268
— drama, Mongolian court pat-
  ronage of, 237
— Empire threatened by West
  Mongols, 204
— forces, hopeless struggle of
  West Mongols with, 207
— Foreign Office, Penal code
  for Mongolia compiled by
  (1789) : punishment for
  camel stealing (footnote), 91
— manuscripts, knowledge of
  West Mongols obtained from,
  203
— Marshal, Töin Lama ap-
  pointed, 244
— name for Bater Halak Sume
  monastery, 29
— officials and colonists, oppression and interference with
  Etsina Torguts, 120
— Provincial Governor, Sinkiang, base and treacherous
  conduct of, 325
— Republic, foundation of, 29
— territory, Bogdo Ula now in,
  291
— verse forms, origin of, 237
— and Mongolian territory, stone
  marking boundary between
  (1750), at Maomo (footnote),
  119
Ching-Chang Railway, course of,
  9 ; terminus of, 9, 17
Chingho, River, 263
Christian, King of Denmark, 288
Chün wang, prince of the second
  rank, 262
Cleanliness, Jenghiz Khan's
  maxim regarding, 265

Coins collected by former consul
  of Sinkiang, 164
Consul of Torgut nation, Has-
  lund created, 295
Cossack uniform, wearing of, by
  Mongols, 217, 219 ; Torgut
  soldiers wearing, 228
Cossacks : bands of, spying upon
  Torguts, 211 ; hereditary
  foes of Torguts, 213
Craftsman, *darkhan*, Mongolian
  word for, 30

Däde (dwellers in high altitudes),
  199
— Mongols : aggressive character of, 193 ; characteristics
  of, 193 ; arrogance of chief
  of, 194 ; anthropometric
  measurements carried out
  among, 199 ; origin of, 199,
  200 ; by Gas-nor, constitu-
  ting one " banner " of Teyiner *notog*, 200 ; locality at
  present inhabited by, 205 ;
  in North-Eastern Tibet, descendants of Khoshut Mongols among, 216
Dageling Gompo, monastery of,
  126
Dalai Lama : counsel of regarding exodus of Torguts sought
  by Obish Khan, 212 ; first
  expression of human fear,
  254 ; jealousy of, aroused
  by popularity of Seng Chen,
  256
Daler, Swedish coin, used as
  amulet, 164
Dambin Jansang : false lama,
  90 ; robber chief of Black
  Gobi, 147 ; fortress of, in
  Gobi desert, 152 ; force of
  will and hypnotic power of,
  153 ; extent of travels of,
  154 ; adventurous career of,
  154-8 ; cruelty of, 155 ;
  Mongols' national struggle
  for freedom inspired by,

334

349